THE BROADCAST INDUSTRY:

An Examination of Major Issues

The
BROADCAST INDUSTRY

An Examination of Major Issues

Edited by

ROBERT H. STANLEY

Hunter College, City University of New York

for

The International Radio and Television Society

Introduction by

JOEL CHASEMAN

President, Post/Newsweek Stations, Washington

COMMUNICATION ARTS BOOKS

HASTINGS HOUSE, PUBLISHERS
New York 10016

To Charles S. Steinberg—

Mentor, Colleague, and Friend

Library of Congress Cataloging in Publication Data

Main entry under title:

The Broadcast industry.

    (Communication arts books)
    "Based on the proceedings of the fourth annual faculty/industry seminar of the International Radio and Television Society, Inc., held at the Tarrytown House Conference Center, February 11–15, 1974."
    Includes index.

    1. Broadcasting—United States—Congresses. I. Stanley, Robert H. II. International Radio and Television Society.

HE8689.8.B76   384.54′0973   75–6674
ISBN 0–8038–0768–6
ISBN 0–8038–0769–4 pbk.

Published simultaneously in Canada by
Saunders of Toronto, Ltd., Don Mills, Ontario

Printed in the United States of America

Contents

Preface

THE BROADCAST MEDIA, radio and television, are an extraordinarily pervasive and influential force in American society. As communications philosopher Marshall McLuhan has noted: "Everything is changing—you, your family, your neighborhood, your education, your job, your government, your relation to 'the others.' And they're changing dramatically."

Some 98.6% of all U.S. homes have at least one working radio. There are over 353.5 million working radios in the United States. In the last 25 years (the period of television's tremendous growth) Americans have purchased 767 million radios.

Television has a 97% saturation. According to the A.C. Nielsen Company, in the average TV household the set is in use more than 45 hours a week. All the books published in the western world in a year reach only a fraction of the people reached by broadcasting in the United States during a single day.

Despite the pervasiveness of the broadcast media and the tremendous impact they have on American life, the general public knows very little about the major issues confronting the American system of broadcasting in the 1970s. This book presents the views of prominent broadcasting practitioners and teachers on the problems facing broadcasters. Several major issues are examined, including: license renewal, short- and long-term economic questions, the impact of new technology, political broadcasting, fairness, and news management.

The information presented in this volume is based on the proceedings of the Fourth Annual Faculty/Industry Seminar of the International Radio and Television Society, Inc. held at the Tarrytown House Conference Center February 11-15, 1974.

The International Radio and Television Society (IRTS) has been in existence, under one name or another, since 1939. Robert H. Boulware, the Executive Director of IRTS notes that the organization began rather informally: "A number of radio advertising executives who enjoyed each other's company met at regular intervals for beer, sandwiches and shop talk." These early meetings were known as the "Broadcasters' Bull Session."

As the meetings became larger and more formalized, the group became the Radio Executives Club and, with the advent of television, the Radio and Television Executives Society. In 1962 "international" was added to the title to include the Society's worldwide membership. Today, IRTS has over 1,200 members. Membership is on a personal rather than a corporate basis.

As the Society's programs grew more ambitious, the income from dues could not support its projects. The dues are deliberately kept low in order to encourage membership from all levels of the broadcast industry. Accordingly, the IRT Foundation was incorporated to raise funds for the Society's projects. In 1973 the Foundation obtained financial support from 83 corporations as well as a number of personal donations from IRTS members.

Each month IRTS holds a "Newsmaker Luncheon" to provide a forum for topics of importance to the broadcasting industry. The principal activities of the Society, however, are in the field of professional education. In the early 1960s the IRTS initiated an "Annual College Conference" designed to bring college students from across the country into New York for a direct learning experience with practitioners of broadcast/advertising. During these conferences the student participants expressed the need for more practical and less theoretical instruction in their schools and textbooks. It was in response to this student-expressed need that the concept of the Faculty/Industry Seminar was developed.

For the past four years the International Radio and Television Society and the IRT Foundation have held annual seminars in an effort to facilitate better understanding and cooperation among members of the academic community and the broadcast industry. The Faculty/Industry Seminars focus on critical problems in virtually all aspects of the broadcast media. Both the faculty and the industry participants have found these seminars most valuable.

The continued success of the Faculty/Industry Seminars is due primarily to the efforts of the Seminar co-Chairmen, Gene Accas, Vice President, Leo Burnett USA, and Aaron Cohen, Vice President, NBC Television Network. Several months before each seminar they work indefatigably formulating and researching problem areas, recruiting faculty and industry participants, contacting possible guest speakers, and attending to the innumerable details that make a seminar successful.

The tone for the 1974 Seminar was set by Gene Accas when he paraphrased W. Somerset Maugham: "A seminar is what happened plus what could have happened plus what might have happened plus what should have happened plus what never happened."

The main goal of the 1974 Seminar was to foster open discussion between faculty and industry representatives concerning "Problems and Solutions in Broadcast Station Management." Faculty participants were assigned to one of four workshop groups (identified as Iota, Rho, Tau, Sigma) and were asked to develop alternative solutions to the real-life management problems. The groups were supervised by a discussion leader, (a broadcast professional), whose task was to keep discussion lively and, most important, productive. The leader was assisted by a faculty rapporteur who kept notes on all useful ideas that emerged. A team of station executives were assigned to each group to present an actual management problem and to provide their professional input and personal experience. Each evening a dinner speaker addressed the group on a subject of particular concern to broadcasters.

After three days of discussion, a plenary session was held on the final morning in which each group's rapporteur presented the substantive ideas developed in response to the managerial problems.

The editor is grateful to Howard Coleman for his editorial assistance on the news and economic discussions. A very special acknowledgment is made to Eija Ayravainen for her patience, tolerance, support and very worthwhile assistance. Also, the editor thanks Robert Boulware and Aaron Cohen for their help. Finally, a very special thank you to Gene Accas, without whose efficiency and tremendous organizational ability neither the Seminar nor this book would have been possible.

This book represents the editing of thousands of pages of dialogue. Although a substantial amount of material has been cut from the actual discussions, the editor has made an effort to maintain the flavor, style and essence of each of the faculty/industry interactions.

Participants in the group discussions are identified by their surnames. A brief biography of each faculty participant is included in alphabetical order in the Appendix. Omission of anyone is inadvertent and is regretted by the editor.

Robert H. Stanley

New York, N.Y.
April 1975

Introduction

WHEN I WAS ASKED to write the Introduction to this volume, I was appropriately flattered, but unable to put words on paper. I tried to analyze the problem and realized that there was a point of view missing from the Tarrytown sessions whose expression might be more appropriate to a foreword than my own.

The principal groups at the Tarrytown meetings in 1974 were faculty members, and experienced broadcasters. Among the missing were those ex-students who were now young broadcasters. How about their attitudes now that it was no longer theory? Were they dissillusioned? Was it difficult for them to make the transition from campus star to station rookie? Were they finding professional broadcasting inspiring? Frustrating? Worth the trouble? Was anybody bothering to teach them, or, for that matter, equipped to?

I went to three new broadcasters, Peggy Cooper, Steve Jacobs, and Jan Thomas. Their cumulative experience in commercial broadcast stations is about three years. They are bright over-achievers, anxious to have an effect on the world and impatient with whatever frustrates them in so doing. Read what *they* have to say and come back to it every so often as you work your way through the Tarrytown dialogues, monologues and dissertations:

First, Steve Jacobs, early 20's, veteran of campus radio at Cornell, fired from a medium-sized radio station when he refused to change a local news story to suit the management, unemployed four months, now working both radio and television in Washington:

JACOBS: Gone through the documentary stage yet? The point where your ambition is to produce significant, well researched exposés that show just how shallow those two-minute quickies on the six o'clock news are? Well, you get out of school and find that no one is going to make you a documentary producer. In fact, no one is going to make you much of anything.

Leaving school, you find that you've been sold a bill of goods. For most of your 20 years, you've been told that a college education and some part-time experience will land you the job you want in San Francisco. Don't believe it. Most likely your B.A. and summer work will land you in Poughkeepsie. Or maybe you'll end up in Montgomery, Alabama where I had my first job after school.

What's the first job like? Like a first date that turned out to be a dog. Or worse. All the expectations and hopes battered to hell. Hours so long and pay so low that the labor department should investigate. Management that thinks of the "public interest, convenience and necessity" only when it's time for license renewal.

My station manager was a super salesman. After he sold his own soul, he tried to barter mine. The day after I refused to kill a news story on broadcast political spots, I was packing. What did I think after being fired from my first job? What would you think?

After four months of gainful unemployment, I landed at WTOP in Washington. I'd like to tell you that I was hired because I am competent, but I was hired because I found the right people. If I hadn't, I'd probably be in Poughkeepsie myself.

Welcome to Washington. The bigtime. Bright, young, imaginative people doing some very creative things. But doing some very silly things as well. Things have improved; however, I've traded the old frustrations for some new ones.

Change. Broadcasters do not like radical change. Nor do they like to be told by a 23-year old what to do. They can stall and equivocate just as surely as any Senator filibustering through the night.

The system. Call it rationalization, call it maturation, but parts of the system make sense. When you've criticized and criticized, it's frustrating to admit that some of the conventional wisdom is wise. And that some problems, though easily seen, have no easy solutions.

If you can deal with the limitations and the frustrations, the system rewards you. You lose part of your idealism but gain the power to influence the medium. The real trick is to retain part of the idealism; you have to keep the gut feeling that there's something wrong with the system that turns out TV news shows that look more like Sonny and Cher re-runs. You have to get along, but just don't go along.

I hope I can do that; I hope you can, too.

*　*　*　*　*　*

CHASEMAN: Jan Thomas, New England born and bred, began in Hartford less than two years ago as a continuity writer, became a production assistant on the station's local daily morning show, and is now assistant producer. She's also attending graduate school at Trinity, hoping to be a network producer for CBS-TV's "Sixty Minutes" or NBC's "Weekend.":

THOMAS: There can be no other means of communication that reaches as many people as often and as realistically as television does. The material presented on television is made up of every element of human experience: actions, emotions, thoughts and sensations, and as a result, the people who produce it have an awesome influence over the way people think.

The opposite is also true, or at least it should be. Good television is the product of a very special exchange between viewers and broadcasters. Television must reflect the attitudes of the viewers, which means that the broadcaster must anticipate the needs of his viewers far in advance of their expression of their needs. He must be ready to answer their questions when they ask them.

One example of how this has been done successfully is in the difference between the kind of situation comedies on television today, and those that were made 20 years ago. Because of a growth of social awareness, the ironic and often satiric humor in shows like "All in the Family" has taken the place of the slapstick humor of shows like "I Love Lucy." At one time "All in the Family" was unconventional, but it proved to be timely and it rapidly became the standard for the kind of situation comedy that people want to watch.

This process is important in all areas of television, especially where it affects mores, stereotypes, political bias, and religion. It is the broadcaster's responsibility to recognize the changes that are happening around him, and to translate his own ideas about change into programming that is not unrelated to the world in which he and his viewers live. He must always keep in mind the direction in which he is going, and constantly be able to relate it to where he has been. If he can do this, he will respond to his viewers' needs with material that is just what they want, when they want it. His material will not only be popular, but it will set meaningful standards for other programs.

*   *   *   *   *   *

CHASEMAN: Peggy Cooper's bio is self-contained in her essay. What she doesn't tell you is her dedication to straight talk and effective action. She's a born leader. I only hope we can keep her interested in broadcasting long enough for her to contribute all she's got. Peggy has a way of making things work better:

COOPER: I am black. I grew up in Alabama. I had a great deal of difficulty reconciling the equal treatment I received at home with the biases I faced outside.

"You don't understand, but you really are equal," said my father.

"Things will change when people change." He taught me that the best way to change people was to influence the way they think. I concluded that the quickest way to affect the minds of others was to become a politician. In high school I ran for every student office. For college I came to Washington, majored in political science, and became deeply involved in the arts and education. I went to law school and then spent a very selfish year as a fellow at the Woodrow Wilson International Center for Scholars reading and reassessing.

My interest in politics continued, but so did my reassessing. My child's eye view of politicians as societal saviors was radically changing.

Two years later, Washington got home rule and the right to elect its leaders. I wanted, still, to lead, to influence. If it was to be through politics, now was the time to move. But the fruits of political life, I decided, were not worth its rigors. It was, however, still time to move for my desires had not changed.

Television emerged as a good alternative. It could be an even more potent instrument of change than politics. I spent a few days regretting the fact that I had overlooked this great American mind-molder during my students years, for I surely would have charted my studies differently.

I wanted to learn television and eventually be in a position to influence programming decisions, so I sought and found a job in management. That was seven months ago. I have made many observations but few conclusions. Some general observations follow: These observations, like my experiences, are limited to local television.

Many of the thoughts I had as a viewer about television and the people who make it were ill-conceived, but I am still convinced of its awesome power. Power demands responsibility. This demand, too often, remains unmet.

Except for top management, local television seems to attract few really intelligent people. Even those who appear to be basically intelligent seem much less knowledgeable and educated than their counterparts in print media. Perhaps this is because their education has been narrowly defined, too technically oriented and without a strong liberal arts undergirding. There results a dearth of the kind of social sophistication which derives from a full awareness of one's surroundings. I have often felt that too many of these people are alien to the communities which they serve. Knowledge of community is important to most jobs in television. Schools should stress it, and TV personnel offices should require it. We should constantly sharpen our feel for people and their priorities.

I am surprised by the lack of creativity and artistry in television. The local television director is a very mechanical person. Neither he nor the producer does much work with the talent in terms of drawing out everything the talent has to give. I submit that both producers and directors could gain from exposure to some of the techniques of the theatre director.

There's also a lack of artistic creativity in programming conception. Even within the limits of local television production budgets there should be more room for the creative mind. Television creativity might be enhanced if we developed a closer relationship with our local community of artists.

Programmers, producers and directors work under great time restrictions. Even if they had the capacity to be more creative, I question whether or not time would allow it.

In light of the demands of time, management, perhaps, had concentrated too heavily on hiring those who can cope with the pressures of working in television as opposed to those who can contribute to the development of the medium.

The major conclusion I have made during my television tenure is that in retrospect I would not change my educational sequence. Although I sometimes feel like a technical idiot, most of what one must learn about television technically can best be learned in a practical or clinical situation. But in all aspects of programming, I think it is critical to have broad interests and knowledge areas. Even beyond a strong liberal arts education, law school, etc. continual learning must take place. Listening, reading, feeling—and above all, staying in touch with one's surroundings.

I am oftimes frustrated, but I am very excited about the prospects for learning and effecting change. The major challenge I have is to bring these generalities within specific parameters.

*   *   *   *   *   *

CHASEMAN: Those are three of the stories. They should help fill the gap between undergraduate, faculty, ad grizzled, perhaps jaded broadcaster. The first few years can be the toughest, and many drop out—often precisely those individuals whose energies, talents and drive would have been most useful in moving the industry along.

The Tarrytown meetings are dedicated to the idea that we can learn from each other. I hope these additional points of view have contributed to that process, and I'm grateful to Peggy, Jan and Steve for being so candid.

February 1975   JOEL CHASEMAN
                                                                 President,
                                                      Post/Newsweek Stations,
                                                             Washington, D.C.

Television News: Strengths and Weaknesses

TODAY, TELEVISION is the preferred news source for most Americans. More people view one of the three major network evening news programs than read all of the daily newspapers combined. Television news, unlike newspapers, is restricted by time. The average network news program, excluding commercials, presents less than 20 minutes of news information. Consequently, television cannot treat any event in depth. It is primarily a headline medium. All of the words presented in a network newscast would not fill even one page of the *New York Times*.

Since television is a visual medium, it tends to concentrate on visually realizable occurrences. Only a tiny fraction of the world's actual events are transmitted by television each day and those events are shaped by selection, emphasis and suggested inferences. Television uses closeups for what it deems important and leaves the apparently unimportant in the background. Segmented happenings can become an artificially exciting, unified, continuous event. The medium itself helps to shape the events that it reports.

Despite its technological bias, television news at its best can substantially broaden the human experience. Television, with relative immediacy, can capture the significant sights and sounds of history unfolding around the world.

Mr. John Chancellor, the NBC Network News anchorman, in his Dinner Address, examines the role of television news in reporting and shaping world events.

JOHN CHANCELLOR

JOHN CHANCELLOR *brings to his job as an anchorman more than two decades of journalistic experience in the United States and overseas. He has been an NBC News correspondent since 1950.*

In 1972, he received the Overseas Press Club's award for the best radio interpretation of foreign affairs, based on his reporting from China, the Soviet Union and Washington. Mr. Chancellor shared the NBC News anchor position in 1972 with David Brinkley.

Mr. Chancellor has wide experience in reporting. He has reported on the Apollo Space flights from Cape Kennedy; he has covered the Senate Watergate hearings; he accompanied former President Nixon to China and Russia; he covered the solar eclipse from the Okefenokee Swamp in Georgia and much more.

His reporting has won him a national Sigma Delta Chi Award, a Robert E. Sherwood Award and an Emmy Award from the National Academy of Television Arts and Sciences.

Address by John Chancellor, IRTS February 13, 1974

I'm going to talk briefly about some things that are on my mind dealing with journalism in America, peripherally with television journalism, and then I'd like to ask you to fire questions at me—because I get a lot more out of that. This talk is about credibility. We were late this evening because the driver had to wait in line to get gas. I find one of the fascinating aspects of covering the gas shortage story, which is a real one, is that so many people in this country think it's a fake!

A lot of people think the energy crisis is something made up by the oil companies; that the government is deceiving us about it; that there are pockets of collusion we've not been able to find.

I think the energy crisis is real. I think it's stupid that we're in it. I think we could have been warned about it a long time ago. But what I do find most distressing, and a sign of the times, is that the people think there's something phony about it. And I think that's very bad in a country like ours that depends, to operate its government, upon credible information being persuasively presented to people who believe it.

The Harris poll was out this week, showing that the job rating of the Congress now is worse than the job rating of the President. Which is, in statistical terms, a great condemnation of the Congress at this stage in our history. Only 21% of the country said they had confidence in the way Congress was doing its work. The President is at 29% in Gallup. Lou Harris wrote of his poll that it seemed to him we had come as close as we could in a republic of our kind to a total lack of confidence in both the executive and legislative branches of government.

And I'm worried about journalism as it involves the public in these matters, because to a considerable degree American journalism is a passive instrument which transmits information about the society to the audience— to its readers, listeners, viewers, whatever. When it's good it does what Walter Lippmann once said was the goal of all journalism—it gives the people a picture of the world upon which they can act. When it's doing its job normally it simply transmits the information it soaks up from many different sources, passes it on to people, and they make certain judgments.

But what sort of journalism do we have? And what kind of country do we have when, in reporting on the President and the Congress, the oil crisis, the settlement in Vietnam, all kinds of things, there is this level of disbelief in American society? In the long run this is probably one of the most difficult periods for American journalism and journalists that we've ever gone through—because of this lack of belief in what our institutions do.

There's one factor that influences that lack of belief: I think that in the United States we have the informational mix, to use a technical term we use in our newsroom, *reversed*. Newspapers are very good at giving the facts. Edwin Dale can write a complicated story in the *New York Times* on the economy, and it can have a lot of dates and numbers in it, percentages, and you can read it two or three times and get a lot of facts from that day-old story.

Television, in the words of Reuven Frank, is very good as a transmission of experience. It can take you to places where you cannot be. TV has taken us to the Berlin Wall; it has taken us to Vietnam, for better or worse. But television is really terrible when it comes to presenting the facts to people. And I worry, because more and more people are taking their news from television, which is rotten at transmitting the facts.

And I worry that the newspapers in the country are turning into journals which are better at giving you the transmission of experience, or analysis—they are staying away from some of the facts because they're carrying a heavier load.

That's the reverse I mentioned. I think that's a factor in the American people's scepticism—scepticism I hope, cynicism I don't hope—about the media. We are working, those of us in all kinds of journalism in this country, with audiences that are increasingly pessimistic. I worry that we're in this reverse mix that I see no end to. I see shorter and shorter radio and TV newscasts. I see newspapers going into all kinds of gimmicks because of the competition from television. And I see the people of this country being very badly served indeed by this informational mix.

Another problem is that about 30% of the people are dead on the side of the President. I see this in my mail, I talk to them on the phone, I also have—I think—a reporter's intuition about them. Many of these people are perfectly willing to believe that the bulk of the President's problems are caused by a media conspiracy against him. Thirty per cent is one in three. If that lasts, a generation of Americans will go on living with the conviction that the business I'm in is not only conspiratorial but crooked.

Which is why I think the President has to stay in office. I think he should go through the process of impeachment and be vindicated or convicted. I think that resignation for Mr. Nixon would allow him to go back to San Clemente and begin poisoning political wells. One of the very first things he would start to do, it seems to me, is to begin to say that the press is one of the elements that turned him into a martyr with no charges proven against him, a sitting President driven from the White House. I don't want that. I want to see him tried, acquitted or convicted.

Another problem we face in journalism is that, despite all the brave words about the press and Watergate, we are being manipulated more by government officials in Washington, in other countries and in some local communities, than we ever have before. The devices being used by government press agents to get around some of the traditional openness of American journalism are increasing in sophistication and in number. And it is now common for big business to begin to adopt the techniques long in use in Washington: the *backgrounder,* the *no-attribution story,* the *carefully-handled leak.* (If we're talking about leaks in the question period, I have some anecdotes.)

One of the other things that bothers me very much is that in this wonderful land of ours—with all the jet planes and all the AT&T long lines, and all of the other transportation and communications things we have— we are beginning to develop a journalism which is very flat. At NBC, we can put a man on a plane out of Washington in the morning and send him to Columbia, South Carolina on a breaking story. We can have film shot down there and put that story on the air for the program I front the same night. Now that's nice in one way, because you got the story quickly. And in a competitive world that's good.

What's wrong is that it gives that reporter on the jet plane trip about two hours to cover a complicated, lengthy story. *No* time for reflection. The reportage has few anecdotes, little sense of local coloring.

And if you think NBC is bad, think about the *New York Times,* think about the AP. A lot of us have this problem. "I just got in from the airport" is a report happening more and more in American journalism, and I don't see any answer to that.

I also worry these days a great deal about the First Amendment. In the Pentagon Papers case, we won, but I really think you can make an argument that we lost. There are more hidden pitfalls for journalists of the future in the decisions of the *Times* publishing the Pentagon Papers than even First Amendment types like me care to think about. I think those decisions will haunt us. I think they have, in fact, limited our freedom. We had in the Pentagon Papers case the first instance of prior restraint;

of a court in America telling an independent publisher in America, a free country, that something couldn't be printed in the paper. Terribly scary.

So I think we should not have had that Pentagon Papers court decision, because I think we may lose our freedom. In an interesting way, President Nixon's problems with the courts on the confidentiality of his own documents and tape recordings, which the decisions in the courts against Nixon served to hearten people who wanted that information out, in the long run could have serious effects on the confidentiality of *any* information. I am not at all sure that we are going to be able to protect our sources in the future the way we have in the past. And if American journalists cannot protect their sources, then one of the great correcting forces in American life will be closed off.

Which is why I am, with terrible reluctance, in *favor* of the National Shield Law to protect the First Amendment. It's a rotten way to go about it, but it's a rotten problem we're facing, and we've go to do something about it.

Many people are saying that the Watergate case helped American journalism; that it proved how good the press in this country really is. What it proved to me was the *Washington Post* had the courage of its convictions. That the *New York Times* tried to catch up but couldn't. That a few other papers had a tiny end-hold on the story. That the television networks came along in their most passive mood and carried hearings.

American journalism can, by no means as far as I'm concerned, call the Watergate family of scandals its finest hour. I don't believe that at all. I think of the nonexistent investigative staffs on all kinds of newspapers, on many magazines, and on lots of networks. The number of good, fulltime, fully-prepared-and-staff-supported investigative reporters in this country can be counted on these two hands.

The *Washington Post* should get every honor in the world; they have, and they're delighted. But they were alone, and it was very cold out there for a long time. And we're a country with more than 1,600 daily newspapers.

One of the things that Watergate has done for us is that it has destroyed certain institutions in which I place great value. President Nixon was well on the way to abandoning the regularly-scheduled press conference in the White House, on or off television, when Watergate broke. That absolutely sealed its doom for this Administration.

Also, I'm not sure, whether we have a Democrat or a Republican next time, if that next President will feel the responsibility of communicating with the people through the device of the press conference.

I think the government itself, and the people, foreign governments, and many others, have been sadly served by the lack of information coming out of this Administration—which in our society can and should come from the President himself through the press.

We may have ruined some careers in terms of the press and in terms of men who cover the White House through various associations. There has been so much bear-baiting of Ron Ziegler, there have been so many statements declared inoperative, there have been so many deceits and evasions on the part of the White House that some members of its press corps are beyond redemption. They're furious; they've been hurt so many times; they've been forced to lie to their readers and listeners. We're going to have to restructure that entire relationship, because it's not working well at all.

Those are some of the things I think we ought to be very sober about in our business. We can list as credible, perhaps, that we're all watching public officials with a closer eye than we did before, and that can only be good. A lot of editors and reporters in other communities are taking closer looks at the governments they cover, municipal and state as well as federal. I believe that, because of Watergate, the group of wrongdoings that we've come to call "Watergate" couldn't happen again. At least not in our lifetimes. I think that's positive.

I believe we've seen a stiffening of resistance on the part of broadcast executives, for which one can only bow his head. They have been tested and challenged. They have had Clay Whitehead nipping at their heels. They have had Spiro Agnew thundering about them in Des Moines. We have had the President yapping about us on national television, saying that we are no good. And I do think that I have seen morale on the executive level—at least in the organization I work for—strengthened; they've had their feet put to the fire and they've come out fairly well. That's not so bad. I can't tell you about tomorrow, but I'm satisfied with today.

And the general *level:* well, to use my favorite phrase, which is Spiro Agnew's phrase, it's the "new post-Watergate morality!" Do you suppose that we could in reality get a "new post-Watergate morality"? Do you know what they'd call it if we got it? *Morality,* that's what!

But it would be marvelous if we came out of all of it. I think our institutions have been damaged severely in the last few years. The government bureaucracy in Washington has been damaged by Watergate; Congress has been damaged by it; the President; and the press.

I go back in this assessment to Lyndon Johnson deciding not to run again, resigning, in fact, from the White House. Our Presidents haven't had too easy a time of it. Yet, at the same time, we *have* come through this bad experience. The price was too high, but I do think some change for the good has come about and people are thinking about problems in the United States in a different way than they did before. There's less complacency about where we stand, about what our institutions are like. You've probably heard it said that Charlie got to be a better man after his wife died. I think the price has been too high.

I want to read you some T. S. Eliot. There's a poem about information that he wrote that I've always liked. He said: "All our knowledge brings us nearer to our ignorance. All our ignorance brings us nearer to death. But nearer to death, not nearer to God. Where is the light we have lost in living? Where is the wisdom we have lost in knowledge? Where is the knowledge we have lost in information? The cycles of heaven in 20 centuries bring us farther from God and nearer to the dust."

QUESTION AND ANSWER SESSION FOLLOWING CHANCELLOR ADDRESS

Q. I have an hypothesis on broadcast journalism that is untested, and I'm not sure it's even original. An earlier speaker here reported research that indicated that the American public has substantially lost confidence in government, mainly the social institutions that have been inviolate through the years. The hypothesis is that the average "J.Q. Listener" to broadcast news is listening not so much to find out what *has* happened in the world but to find out what *hasn't* happened. Would you comment on that?

Chancellor: I understand the question to be negative because of my own bias. I've always believed that certain kinds of broadcasting—hourly newscasts are the prime example—exist to reassure people, not to inform them. I really believe people want to know the dam hasn't burst or the rockets aren't on the way. And we've thought about this in the presentation of our own programming. I firmly believe that certain coverage—let's say the network evening newscast—serves a different function. I think people do make an assumption that they will have an informational function and not one of reassurance.

But I find myself, in the car or at home, checking in at the top of the hour, just to make sure. And I always have that little feeling. I wonder if anything terrible has happened. And I don't propose that broadcasters come on and say, "Nothing terrible has happened"—although it's a thought. What worries me is that if people have little or no confidence in their institutions, do they have confidence in the journalism that describes those institutions? This is a question of great profundity that nobody is dealing with. In the last Gallup poll on that subject we may have gone down a notch or two, but not badly. The poll data do not indicate that there is a great lessening of confidence in broadcast journalism. In some places, quite the contrary.

Yet at the same time, if people think they're getting conned by an awful lot of politicians, etc., we are the ones who have to carry those burdens, and I worry that some day this may start feeding back on us. And as it is, despite what the White House would like you to believe about the national press, we're really the unwitting accomplices of the institutions of the United States. No question about that—the institutions get a better break than anybody else.

Q. Two questions. The first has to do with Solzhenytzen: why did they let him go and why did they not throttle him as they have done in the past with anyone as expressive as he has been? The second is a little more difficult. If there hadn't been a Watergate, where do you think we would be as a country today?

Chancellor: Oh, that's a terrible one. Let me talk about Solzhenytzen first. They couldn't move against him because there was the weight of world opinion and it is both good and bad. I used to live in the Soviet Union, and I know a little bit about that. The way the Soviet authorities worked in this case, and the way we think they're going to work with Zakarof, possibly with Maximov and some others—they're doing it in a much more flexible way because, to use Henry Kissinger's phrase, there's bigger fish to fry. The SALT talks are coming up, a lot of trade deals are standing by, and they got the message from the United States Congress that certain things wouldn't be possible with our country.

I talked with Kissinger about this just this morning, and they just knew that certain things were not possible of accomplishment in our ongoing relations if they did anything that bad to Solzhenytzen. So they exiled him, and they're going to let his family go out. He's got royalties in Switzerland, so he's okay—unless you look at it the other way, which is that exile is really one of the most vicious weapons against an individual that a government can use. Particularly a man who is the bard of your country. The man who wrote more movingly about it, who loved it, who never wanted to go. The Russians have shaped their policies to world opinion for a long time, and they've said and done things which were aimed to attract attention or to help them for many, many years. Solzhenytzen is the latest, most sorrowful chapter.

To the second question: would the country be better off if we hadn't had Watergate and Richard Nixon were President? Where would we be with Nixon and Ehrlichmann and Haldeman? If the guard hadn't been there that night, if the police car hadn't been back in the garage, and all the rest of it?

I don't know. In what we've seen since, there have been some terribly menacing things. Do I believe, as I've heard some people say, that they were going to try to cancel the next election? No way. Absolutely not. Do I believe that they were willing to go on narrowing the limits of individual freedom in this country? Yes. Benjamin Franklin said that people who give up a little liberty for a little safety deserve neither, and I think the American people were in the mood to give up a little liberty for a little safety. People thought they wanted law and order, when really what they wanted was peace and quiet. My guess is that domestically the administration would have played on those feelings heavily, and from what we know, we would have ended up shorn of some of our liberties. We're still okay as a country. We'll have to fight hard to get them back. I don't think it would have been a pleasant time in the United States.

Q. Do you have any projection on what the network news might be like five years from now?

Chancellor: They ask me, "What will we do if CBS news goes to an hour?" And I always say, "Go to 15 minutes." I like it pretty much the way it is. NBC asks people to watch a lot of informational television. We presume that people are going to watch a certain amount of the *Today* show and we presume that they're going to watch a half hour of us in the evening. We presume they're going to watch the local station's late news such as *Eleventh Hour* and things like that. We presume they're going to watch some other local news. That's quite a lot of information coming out of the tube. What I'd like to see in the future is some arrangement so that we wouldn't have to go for a one-hour newscast—which I believe would not be so much a program as a service. I can see headlines at the half hour, headlines at the end—what I *would* like to have is the ability on those news days during the year when we can't get it all in, to have a flexible arrangement with the affiliated stations so that we could have another 10 or 15 minutes if we needed it. And play fair with them so that we would take it only when we needed it. But that's a difficult proposal.

One thing about the limitless expandability of TV news programming. We're going into a two-hour news program in New York. We have a very successful two-hour program in Los Angeles. I can't imagine people watching two hours of anything, and yet they do. I sometimes think of news programmers the way I think of the highway lobby—they're going to have the whole country paved over before they're done.

Q. Why don't you editorialize more than you report?

Chancellor: I think it's breaking the rules. I like the idea that news has a life of its own, if properly treated. I like the idea of working within fixed criteria that are not all that removed from what the AP used when it began to bring honest news to people all over the country, and later UP, of course. I like the idea that we are part of how change comes about in the United States, but we are not changers ourselves.

Maybe I know too many journalists too well, but I wouldn't want to trust anybody with that responsibility, except that we've given a little bit of it to the politicians and that's probably the way it ought to be. But, I feel very strongly that the news, if it's done ethically and fairly, ought to speak for itself and very rarely would you have to do what David Brinkley has to do every once in a while, or used to do fairly often, when he says, "What follows is opinion." I think sometimes you need that, but I would not like to see us emerge as a leading force for social change in the United States. I'm made terribly uneasy about basic freedoms in this country if the national press really got together and tried to do that. Henry Luce, for years, thought of himself as a great, motivating engine of social change in the United States. Well, I don't agree with that. I think journalism ought to reflect what a society does on its own.

Q. I would assume that implicit in your answer to this question is how you feel as a broadcast journalist about Senator McClellan who came out four-square for the application of the Fairness Doctrine and he came out four-square at the very time that the Miami case came up in the Supreme Court. Now suppose the Supreme Court finds in favor of the plaintiff, in this instance the Miami paper, you've got to apply the Fairness Doctrine in the very fashion that broadcasters have to apply the Fairness Doctrine. Does that worry you?

Chancellor: Scares the pants off me! We're talking about the Fairness Doctrine. Just the way I was scared to death by prior restraint in the Pentagon Papers case, I am just profoundly affronted by the idea that people can tell you what to print or what to put on the air in the area of information. That's a foot in the door that I'm desperate about. I would like to say that those of us who lived with the Fairness Doctrine, as it applied only to us, pointed out to many of our colleagues in the newspaper business—the Gutenberg people as they are sometimes known—that this would hurt them someday. Absolutely deaf ears. Now they call me up and say, "Tell me about the Fairness Doctrine." You see, you get to a definition of what printing is, what broadcasting is, in a free society. It's the right or the privilege to make mistakes. It's the right to be outrageous. It's the right to carry all kinds of information in the freest possible way. That's what makes it work and while I agree that a limitation on a Shield Law may hurt us more—you've got an argueable point. I worry that we're going to end up someday having less freedom for the reporters, as well as for the publishers and the broadcasters under the Fairness Doctrine.

The Plight of News in the '70s

IN TV'S EARLY DAYS a senior citizen of news reporting named Cliff Utley offered a nightly news program dominant in the Chicago area: *Facts* on one hand and *inference* on the other were a religion with him, and he set a standard seldom equalled. (The advertising theme of *Newsweek* claimed this same admirable goal a few years ago).

Cliff Utley's credo and style was being recalled at a meeting of the news directors of stations KPPP-TV/AM-FM, owned by the same group and located in a Southeast metro area with nearly 2,000,000 people.

John S. of the television station, was bemoaning the fact that, "Everything was simpler in Cliff's day. The 15-minute newscasts didn't allow for much in-depth reporting and we were truly a headline medium. Now every news program is at least one-half hour and in New York they'll soon be starting up a two-hour early evening report. Can you imagine the size of the staff they'll need to produce that program? And even harder to achieve will be a continuing viewer interest in the program. I was told at the RTNDA meeting that the Los Angeles stations, which telecast the long news shows, have found that unlike radio (where the all-news stations cycle the news approximately every 20-25 minutes) people tend to watch the entire news program. That means that the New York station will have to prepare about 93 minutes of news each night and not duplicate anything that their network will run in its half-hour news, which will follow the two local hours. Think of it as two-and-a-half hours of continuous news."

Gene A. of the FM station, which followed a hard rock format and was one of the five highest rated stations in the market, slowly shook his head. "Compared to that story, we're still in the dark ages. All that we do is the five-minute edition at the top of each hour. And that's mostly "rip and read" copy. Believe it or not, our surveys have found that our listeners forgive us the news interruption of the music, but only because they believe that it's mandatory for the station. Otherwise, they want 60 minutes of music."

"Man, I can't believe what you're telling me," interjected Bill B. of the AM station. "I see it quite another way. In this era of Watergate, when the public is looking to us as the watchdogs of their interests, respect for broadcast news has never been higher. We've been discussing the need to expand our normal news service to include investigative reporting, commentary and more local service. We've even thought of establishing an Ombudsman or a Community Reporter. It's going to be more of a trauma for us, we've got severe budget limitations, and a full rounded news service is going to triple our normal news headline service reports."

"I'm glad you mentioned budget," John said. "Did you hear we've just lost our late news anchorman to a station in Atlanta. He's been with us for only three years and was just recently voted the top late night newsman in the market. Now, we've got to start all over again. We just couldn't match the money they were offering him, and frankly working in our market isn't quite as prestigious—if you're concerned about image and ego. The costs compound themselves since we're doing more local news documentaries and we ask our reporters to narrate these documentaries, or actually go out to cover the major news stories. Bill, I'd love to get into investigative work, but the cost of putting a crew in the field (producer, reporter, cameraman and soundman at a minimum) is prohibitive. And I wish the questions about First Amendment protection were clearly answered, it might also add some impetus to this form of reporting."

"Next to you guys, it sounds as though mine is a bed of roses." Gene hunched forward, "I've still got the problem of being competitive to the other radio stations. Even though we try to improve the news in every way possible, pragmatically we can't expand any of the features and reduce our basic product, music."

DISCUSSION POINTS

Have we become too absorbed in what the public wants in news reporting? Does this help to explain the importance of highly paid consultants acting as news tinkerers? If the polar extremes are "news is what I say it is" (traditional) and "news is what will attract the largest audience in head-to-head competition with my rivals" (contemporary) where along this line should a responsible news department be positioned?

And most all reporting, in any medium, has been under attack as having a strong bias. Can we, *should we,* separate *hard news* from *inferences drawn,* opinion from observable action?

How many all-news stations are "enough" in a market? How much research do you do to back up your intuitive news decisions? Is the research followed or allowed to gather dust while the operations of the department continue unchanged?

Are We Guilty of Making News?

(This writer will claim that for a three-year period every time he plugged into a New York all-news station the lead story was "And in Vietnam today. . .") Which is to ask: who directs the editorial policy? Who selects the lead, the second, the third, stories? Maybe, in another way of questioning, *is* there always that much hard news—or are we guilty of promoting platoon action to regimental level for the sake of filling time?

Are We All Buying the Same Press Releases and the Words of the Same Press Conferences?

What's new? The news director, his shift man, his crew, can't risk missing anything—so they all cover everything. If you are a serious student of TV you set up three monitors and catch it all: if you are one, have you ever seen a night when it wasn't at least 90% duplication? What can you do to be different? Or should you?

IOTA GROUP

Discussion Leader: Frank Harden (State Broadcasting Company)
Industry Participants: Joel Chaseman (President, Post/Newsweek
    Stations, Washington, D.C.); Herb Saltzman (VP, General Manager,
    WOR, New York); Stanley Spero (VP & General Manager,
    KMPC, Los Angeles)
Faculty Participants: Douglas Boyd (University of Delaware);
    Stanley Donner (University of Texas); Philip Macomber (Kent
    State University); Carol Reuss, SP (Marshall University); Charles
    Shipley (Southern Illinois University); Williard Thompson
    (University of Minnesota)

HARDEN: Gentlemen this is a vitally interesting subject and we are going to have a lot of stimulating discussion. Stan, would you begin by telling us about the Los Angeles market.

SPERO: We are literally covering Southern California from the ground, sea and air, as well as domestic and overseas news, with actualities from distinguished journalists and local reporters. It is our opinion that we are living in a very powerful, crisis-prone, changing world. Our citizens are being affected every day by events happening in all corners of the earth. Equally important, though, are the many events in the Southern California area which affect the daily lives of our listeners. A progressive radio station must editorialize when important local and community issues are at stake. The frequency of these reports is determined by the events in the community. At KMPC we have a three-man editorial board, which includes myself, that reviews all editorials. The frequency of these editorials is determined by the importance of the subject, and the editorials normally will be 15 to 20 times over a three-day period.

Editorials usually are 90 seconds to two minutes in length, and are confined to local or state issues. We exclude endorsement of all political candidates.

CHASEMAN: Our number one priority is to attempt to inform our viewers of events, trends, significant matters, which may affect their lives. In order to do that the operating priority is to find people skilled at communicating, professional in their attitude toward news—and then to give them the resources both in terms of hardware and time to do the job. To that end we commit appropriate air time and dollars, often without regard to return. That leads to a different kind of attitude. I think if we were to go around the room and have people write down what their definitions of *news* might be, assuming we have 22 people here, you would probably end up with about 30 definitions of *news*.

SALTZMAN: At WOR we have, if there is such a thing, a philosophy, a policy that news will pre-empt regular programming. We do 15 minutes every hour on the hour in the morning and afternoon drive times, and 5 minutes at the half hour. So 20 minutes of 60 minutes is news. And in the body of the morning and afternoon programming we carry other news features. With any kind of happening in our community, disaster or tragedy, any kind of news that we feel our community has to know about, we will pre-empt the programming to stay with the news story.

We ran an ad in *Broadcasting* recently, stating that we delivered more hard news in a 15-minute newscast than an all-news station delivers in 30 minutes of broadcasting. There are very obvious reasons for that. The news stations just have to stretch a story or do a story in greater depth. We're delivering hard news for 15 minutes.

BOYD: Have you ever, for business purposes, costed out your news to say what kind of return you are getting on your investment? Just for *news*. The price of personnel, helicopter, wire services and the rest. Everybody is a little different in Los Angeles, because they don't get a direct return on that air watch service.

SALTZMAN: We don't either. We don't have it sponsored. We have broken down the cost of the news operation, but not by return. I don't think any of us breaks down the revenues we get as to who sponsors news and who sponsors regular programming, personality programming.

DONNER: Do you think you come out about even on news yourself?

SALTZMAN: We sell, I'm happy to say, very successfully. We've had a very successful operation for many years. I think we come out very well, news being so important a part of the operation—really the corner-stone of the business since we do so much of it.

SPERO: With our helicopter service we are well into the six-figure area for maintenance alone, aside from the mobile equipment and the 15-man news department, the overseas feeds and all the other things. We look upon news as the leader. If you are going to judge by cost accounting you may lose that competitive edge. It's the kind of character and stability and personality and reputation that the news operation gives you that is the critical thing—not the cost accounting.

CHASEMAN: The whole is equal to the sum of the parts. We are a government-licensed business and custodian of the air waves. We have responsibilities to the FCC and to the public. And when you have a competitive situation or you have a crowded spectrum on the dial you've got to give people reasons to tune you in constantly, to resample you. Today, when the world is volatile and changing, people want to know what's going on. If you're going to have that resampling of your basic product you've got to have news. You can't look at it as a separate economic entity—you've got to consider it as a part of the whole operation.

THOMPSON: When we talked with some of the people from stations, we were talking about a market that had gone soft and the problems the manager faced, and what kinds of things they were doing. I think consensus on the part of the professionals was that we would just call our people in and say we're going to have to cut; call the news director in and say you've got to cut 15%. It was suggested that you'd best have a contingency in your bottom drawer that will permit you to do this. What groups would you people lose before you'd cut your news operation, if faced with a tough situation?

SPERO: We would get into the staff organization long before we got into the on the air product. If you don't have the air operation shaped up as your judgment tells you it should be, if you start tinkering with that for economic considerations—that is the worst thing you can do. To answer your question specifically, I would look at the secretaries, I would look at the promotion department, I would look at the supporting staff or-ganizations to the major program. The product would be the last thing I would touch. I might even get into cutting some of the sales costs before I would tamper with the air product—because without that product you don't have anything to sell.

SHIPLEY: This is a day when news, like all programming, is constantly experimented with—the length of the news, the format of the news, the mixture of news and commentary. But I have always been fascinated with the WOR operation because they have the highest priced and probably the most successful morning man in the country or the world. And he has been doing this, just as his father did before him, for lo these many years. And the news operation is the same way.

Lyle Van and all those fellows have been on for umpty-ump years. You are sticking to hard news essentially. You added the weather, the helicopter, and I'm sure you added correspondents. Why have you been so darned successful doing a thing that many stations dropped many years ago? In a sophisticated, multi-ethnic, melting pot city like New York it's old home week at WOR and the money keeps coming in!

SALTZMAN: For a number of reasons. It's habit, responsibility—and we program to adults. I have a letter from a listener, wishing us a Happy New Year. She says a number of delightful things: "I listened to your station from the time I was a young girl, and I continue to do so because it's the most interesting and informative station around. Others have gone the route of news all day; or, even more tedious, music all day—but you have innovated and polished a wonderful program. And now, gem of gems, radio drama plays!" We brought that back in New York. CBS owns it, but the CBS owned all-news station wouldn't carry it, so *we* offer "CBS Radio Mystery Theater."

CHASEMAN: I'll try it another way. I'm going to distinguish between radio and television. We try to do several things, while recognizing that we are not a monthly magazine, or a quarterly, not even a newspaper. As Cronkite once pointed out, all the words in his half-hour show wouldn't cover the front page of a newspaper. So there are certain things we *cannot* be; but we feel responsibility to do the best we can within our limitations to make sure that our news coverage isn't simply that of events, fires, fender benders, the planned happenings of a given day, and that we don't become walking mike stands available to the politician or other person in the community who wants to get his views across without too much opposition or probing questioning. So we do several things. Let's pick economics— the release of a major city budget. Number one, we cover this as spot news. We give those people a chance to say their piece. We seek out, in addition to that, people who are informed within the community—state legislator or city councilman or whatever. We seek out those people who don't necessarily agree with whatever the established wisdom is, the conventional position. So we get spokesmen of two different kinds: the presentation itself, its proponents; and then the people who *don't* agree.

MACOMBER: One of the things that I believe happens very often, and particularly at the smaller station, non-major market level, is that the manager is negative about his news operation. Ask why it isn't better, why doesn't he do a more comprehensive job of local news, and he will tell you very quickly that it costs too much money—I lose money; I subsidize my news operation.

INDUSTRY COMMENT: I think a lot of it depends on the background of the station manager. I'm talking about very small markets. A lot of managers come out of sales, and to do a news job they have to hire a really competent news director, and they don't have the money. But I know of one very

small market where the radio station owner/manager is a former newsman, and he does a tremendous job in local news and has made the station
quite profitable. If you try to isolate how many commercials run in a
newscast you make a mistake. It has to be part of the total picture.

DONNER: It strikes me that one of the great needs of the American
people is to have some kind of warning of what's going to happen. John
Chancellor's response in his speech—which I think was a good one from
his point of view—was that this was not really the function of the newsman.
This gets back to Joel Chaseman's first discussion of how would you
define news. The Donner way involves a whole lot more than just the
recording of events as they happen. Even the very fact that we're in a
cycle of enormous change alters our lives every day. And I can't find any
place where this is discussed very much in any of the media. So my
question, then, is what responsibility should news departments or stations
that are interested in the news have in trying to look ahead to give some
kind of early warning of gasoline shortage or of any other events that may
be off on the horizon?

CHASEMAN: Broadcasting is just a medium. It's another medium.
It's more transitory, but with sight, sound and motion it's more effective.
People remember it better. And I think it is in the ingenuity of the assignment editor; it's in the definition of the reporting job as distinguished
from general assignment—where the reporters never know enough about
the assignment to ask intelligent questions. It demands people who are
thoughtful, who are well read, who aren't simply the reporters of fires and
fender benders and the cataclysm of the moment in the state legislature.

SALTZMAN: And also the freedom to describe a thing like it is.

CHASEMAN: That should be fundamental. Freedom both at the station and in the society. People have to want these things and if they want
them they will protect them.

REUSS: One of the topics suggested was that we are guilty of *making
news*. I would like to extend that to ask: are making guilty of making
or *expanding* news?

CHASEMAN: I think by definition in this society there is no question
but that the mass media put a lens to many unsavory things and made
them the common coin. It's a regrettable but unavoidable part of their
function in the society. It's different from any society that ever existed,
and part of that difference is in the lack of time to react, to marinate, to
think about. The fact of this type of instant communication, both locally
and world-wide, has created a whole new kind of diplomacy, economics,
the warp and woof of the way we live. And we are part of that. We
have yet to learn sometimes what these sensitivities ought to be. We're not
sure what effect we cause. As a citizen and a broadcaster, I fear what will
happen with this Symbionese Liberation Army kidnapping of Patricia
Hearst in San Francisco; what the results of the reporting will be and

what the societal effects of the whole thing will be. I'm not sure all of them will be negative. As the father of a 15-year old daughter I'm sacred to death of parts of it, and I wish it had never happened. But to say that we should not report it or that at times it isn't the lead story is to run away from reality, I believe. The danger is in generalizing and in assuming guilt rather than in trying to understand the societal forces that are at play and how we become part of them as viewers and as listeners and as perpetrators and as citizens.

SALTZMAN: I believe what Joel is saying poses this question: what steps do we take to be free from bias? A news show is written and a news editor sits over that news writer and carefully examines the copy. If he thinks there is too much on any one side he has the freedom to make the changes he feels . . .

FACULTY COMMENT: What about the news editor himself?

SALTZMAN: The news guy is a performer. In general, he is *not* in the role of commentator, with that kind of freedom. I'm setting apart opinion from the processes of news writing and editing. Two different things. The newsman, the air guy, will possibly change a word or two. It's difficult to control that. I think Joel's point is that there is no one who comes into any situation without any particular bias.

INDUSTRY COMMENT: True. So everybody gets edgy about this to some degree, but again everybody turns around admitting that there are certain biases which the newsman passes on to the public.

CHASEMAN: I know our time is up, but I can't let that pass without some response. I think you must distinguish—or perhaps not, if you have no responsibility except to yourself—but others must distinguish between deliberate bias and differing points of view.

RHO GROUP

Discussion Leader: Robert Henabery (ABC-AM Radio Stations)
Industry Participants: Richard Adams (News Director, Post/News-week stations, Washington, D.C.); Ed Allgood (Vice President and General Manager, WDVA, Danville, Virginia); George Carpenter (Sales Manager, WHO, Des Moines); Suzan Couch (Sales Manager, WXLO, New York); Charles Harrison (Manager-News, WGN-TV, Chicago)
Faculty Participants: Kenward Atkin (Michigan State University); Wesley Wallace (University of North Carolina)

ALLGOOD: I've been manager of WDVA for six years, and in that time we've won 12 Associated Press awards. Three of those were for the best editorials in the state—we editorialize every day of the year. We call ourselves the "News Hounds." We all look for news. All of my salesmen wear these News Hound badges—everyone. We have 48 newscasts a day. We have Mutual Network, and we also belong to the Tobacco Network. Of those 48 newscasts, 12 are from Mutual; of the other 36, 12 are five minutes and the others are one minute. We have adopted the old Gabriel Heatter thing. We say: From WDVA's 24-hour newsroom, you are now hearing the best news you will hear all day. We're not saying it's *good news*—we're saying it's the *best news* you'll hear all day. And for the one-minute news we billboard it with "Here's our Minute Man news." Incidentally, of the 36 local newscasts we have daily—we have 24 each on Saturday and Sunday—every one is sold—which I think is a little unusual. The five minutes we sell individually; the one minutes we package six at a time. We're 24-hours country music, which in our town is it. We're tobacco and textiles; 46,000 people; five radio stations—so we work hard to be number one.

ADAMS: From my perspective, working in the very strange city of Washington, D.C.—where what everybody considers national news is also local news—creates serious problems in terms of allocation of resources. To what extent do you serve the community as a local community, and to what extent are you expected to report the national scene? What do we do to be different? Probably nowhere in the country, except maybe New York, do you see gang journalism at work as in Washington. Film crews standing shoulder to shoulder shooting the same talking head; and scores of reporters who've been turned into little more than walking microphone stands, lurking around the halls of the Capitol and everywhere else in town.

What we've done is to use the power we have in swaying peoples' minds and in teaching people things, to teach them to expect things from us. We created our own monster in that we've taught our viewers to expect a talking head; to expect the news conference—and, as a result, we all cover it. We're afraid not to, because the competition will have it, and our ratings might slip because we're not giving our viewers what we taught them to expect. To change is to risk losing some of the ground that you've built; there's always the fear of "maybe it's too unusual for the market." It's a problem we're wrestling with right now.

CARPENTER: We want to have the reputation for the best newscast in the market, if not the state, if not the nation. This may be more for pride than for anticipation of economic gain. Perhaps because our air time is so filled with network and syndicated programming, we see news as the area where we can project an image—and we go to great lengths to do this. We also know that most stations that are number one in their six o'clock and ten o'clock news strips are also number one from sign-on to sign-off. We've been number two in news—a fact that, unless you're Avis, you don't shout about. We've nudged our competitors at times in the past, but we've never been able to come across the way we aspired. We've made a lot of changes, but mostly of a cosmetic nature: new sets, new formats, new promotions, new personalities. But we were doing this based on what *we* thought the viewers wanted; and our management group had a lot of input from the "influentials" of the city club, the country club, and other social spots— they'll always tell you exactly what you should have on your news.

We commissioned a research company to determine what the opinions were in our market toward news. Did the viewers want more reporting of national stories, or did we have too many local stories? Were we covering the state legislature adequately, or did they want more ambulance chasers? What about sports—first, last, not at all? What did they want to hear about weather? Editorials? And what about our air people and the competitors' people? Are they thought of as presenters or reporters? What's their credibility? Would you want to live next door to them, or have them marry your daughter? The research showed very clearly that our top competitor was thought of as *the* news station. Although by actual count we carried more stories, more local stories, more film—the viewers thought our competitor ahead in these and every other category tested.

We could only conclude that our viewers were dumb or our packaging was bad. And since Iowa has the second highest literacy rate in the nation, the answer was easy. While we were recognized as a bona fide, legitimate disseminator of news, apparently it wasn't packaged attractively enough, excitingly enough, interestingly enough, to get viewers to change their habits. We retained the consulting services of the same group that had done the research and delivered the opinion study. We viewed over a hundred tapes before finding our Mr. Superman—Mr. Super Anchorman. From many more tapes we devised a new set and a new weather format. We've added new equipment and lots of motion. I detail this because it is happening with many stations now, and I have a feeling it's going to be even more widespread in the very near future.

COUCH: I'm going to come off sounding militantly feminine—and that doesn't become me because it's not altogether where my head is—but I think the question deserves to be asked: Why do we go on a search for an anchor*man?* I loved what you were saying, and I know what your problems are because I would like to have more sales people who are female—and they don't necessarily exist. But why do we look for an anchor*man?*

HARRISON: We've also had some experience with consultants: most of the information you paid $25,000 or $50,000 for was information you already had. You already knew if your anchorman was accepted, the sports man weak, and the weather man should stay sober more often. Consider what can happen: we have one consultant firm, then two, then three— there are now six. And they're all doing the same thing, and suddenly on 700 television stations potentially you have three minutes of sports, one minute and 47 seconds of weather, two minutes of access from the public— and it's all so packaged and it's all so sterile that nothing can come to life. *That's worse than talking heads!*

ADAMS: We have a consultant right now, doing a community survey, so it's a sensitive point with me. I'm interested in knowing how our news is perceived, is thought of, by our viewers, and I will refuse to let this consultant become the news director of WTOP-TV. It's a very imminent danger. He *talks* like the news director of WTOP-TV sometimes, and the temptation is there to say, "Well, he's been out there surveying . . ." But I like to think that all of us as professionals do, or should, know more about our market and about how to use our techniques than our consultant. And if we don't, we've got to hurry up and get that way!

COUCH: I want to tell you very specifically what implementation of some kinds of consultants' recommendations can mean from the business aspect. We had a very expensive, 18-county New York market-area survey done. One of the things we discovered—only *one*—was *immediately* implemented, and that was that in New York people will stay tuned to the news *through the weather*. We moved the weather to at least 23 minutes into the half hour telecast, picked up two rating points in the second 15 minutes, and were able to get more money out of the news because the ratings went up. Whether to implement the consultant's findings and recommendations very properly belongs within the control of the station. But when you consider the unit cost per spot you are able to get in a well-rated news show, it can really mean dollars and cents in the coffers. I want to make the point loudly that broadcasting is a commercial business, and news is a large money maker at a large television station.

HARRISON: But the news people never come out and say that the news is entertainment. They will . . .

COUCH: No, wait a minute. Nobody faults the *New York Times* because Charlotte Curtis does a wicked coverage of a party. Yet it's entertaining; it's mildly, knife-in-the-ribs entertaining. Yet we're not faulting the quality of the news in the *Times* because of a Craig Clairborne or a Charlotte Curtis. But with the so-called "Happy News" we have taken such lumps! This might well be because we're trying to force people who are not natively amusing, but natively articulate, to be amusing. When you try to force something that somebody tells you somebody else wants on somebody else who can't do it, the result is a disaster. But to have someone who is natively entertaining deliver in his own natural style—there's nothing wrong in that. *If* you're true to what it is you've got in the first place. The question I would raise is do we really know? Have we taken stock? Do we have an inventory? Are we honest about what we've got before we start to package it?

ADAMS: A very good point. We've discussed anchormen—anchor-persons—like they were small fuzzy animals that we kept in a cage and let out at 6:52 P.M. These are human beings, and I think that in all the research or whatever we do to get our community input, what we find people saying is: "We want to see human beings who, because of their training and background, have some knowledge and expertise in this field, and they use this medium of television to relate it to us." Whether they be black or white, male or female, when we put them on the tube we shouldn't ask them to be any more than they are.

WALLACE: I'd like to move to another topic, and that has to do with the role of news on a broadcast station—radio or television—as *agenda setting*. That's a kind of fancy way of saying that whatever I say is news *is* news, and that is what the people in my community are going to talk about.

HENABERY: One question: what is news, and how do you define it?

WALLACE: Maybe I'll start with a practical definition, and that is that whatever goes on a newscast *goes on*—I mean, it's news, no matter how you define it.

HENABERY: I think it's a very important question. I'd like to ask some of the working news directors how they critique their new news reporters and what definition they give them. To tell them that this story they brought in is or is not news. What criteria do you supply them?

HARRISON: I'd like to back into that through the subject of ascertainment. In our shop, the most recent example is in the results of questionnaires and interviews covering community leaders and the general population (we did, I believe, 1,500 interviews with the general population). We were a little bit surprised to find out that the citizens of Chicago and the suburban areas had distinctly different problems that were bugging them. Their idea of what was news differed from ours, at least in order of priority. What we thought was number one ranked fourth in the city and about twelfth out in the suburbs. What we thought was number two vacillated, depending on the geographic area. Immediately, when that happened, our community affairs department stopped having luncheon meetings at WGN. Now we go down to the South Side, to 79th Street near Cottage Grove, and we meet with people who live in that community; or, if we're going to meet with the Appalachians on Broadway and 4500 North, we go to a restaurant up there. This of course is a public affairs activity, but the feedback comes back in written form and the news department gets a copy. As a result we're getting news stories that we never got before, and we're getting them from people who never had a voice before. The reporters go out on a story better informed, and they are in charge.

ATKIN: Chuck Harrison, how do you differentiate in your news gathering and news dissemination operations between the *Chicago Tribune* and the broadcast outlets?

HARRISON: It has been an amicable divorce, I'd guess you call it. There's common ownership, no doubt about that. But in the operation and up to and including management level, it's a complete divorcement. They do their thing and we do ours.

ALLGOOD: What are the differences? You're both in the same business, news.

HARRISON: We're in the same business, yes; yet our newscasts may not bear any resemblance to their front page. We may go one course and they go another. We may have an editorial on the problems of the Rapid Transit Authority for the Cook County area, and our editorial opinion may be 180 degrees from their approach to the same subject.

ALLGOOD: Let me take a minute to tell you about the worst newscast I've ever heard in my life. I was driving to Florida on vacation and I went through Douglas, Georgia. I always—like I guess most of us do—tune for the local station, and I hear an announcer come on and he says, "Now is the time for the Obituary Hour." And until I ran out of his signal, which was about 35 minutes, he was still reading obituaries!

HENABERY: Ed, we had the same kind of program on a small station where I started in Pittsfield, Massachusetts, in the early '50s. Every day at noon we'd give the birth and death notices, and it was most certainly very dull radio to have to plow through all those names and addresses and next of kin and whatnot. I remember that one day an announcer started out and said that there were 24 births in the Pittsfield hospitals in the last week, and there were 12 deaths. And he then read through all the names and other details, and concluded: "Net gain for the day, 12."

TAU GROUP

Discussion Leader: John D. Kelly (Storer Broadcasting)
Industry Participants: Joel Chaseman (President, Post/Newsweek
    Stations, Washington, D.C.); Stanley Spero (Vice President
    and General Manager, KMPC, Los Angeles)
Faculty Participants: Susan Cailteux (University of Kentucky);
    William Hawes (University of Houston); John Kittross (Temple
    University); Jeffrey Lowenhar (University of Connecticut); Lucius
    New (Texas Southern University); Daniel Viamonte (University
    of Hartford); Irving Webber (University of Alabama)

KELLY: I happened to be listening to WCBS radio this morning as I drove downtown. They were in the business news section of the all-news grind, and the reader was reporting the story that for the first 10 days of February the figures were out on automobile sales. He said it something like this: "The figures are now in, and in the first 10 days of this month General Motors car sales are down 22%. As you know, General Motors is the largest manufacturer of big cars—which nobody wants anyway." Then he went on to give the downward trend in car sales for the other major car manufacturers—without any further editorial comment. I damned near drove off the road. "Which nobody wants anyway!" If I had been the manager of WCBS radio I would have driven right back to the studio and had a little talk with that man. It was an irresponsible remark; potentially damaging; in effect, it was negative advertising for the poor people who have got their life monies tied up in automobile dealerships who are trying to move Oldsmobiles and big Pontiacs. It's not their fault that there's a gas shortage, and in my opinion the fellow had no right to make the remark.

But let's turn to our case study, and see if we can make some decisions on the questions in the syllabus. Can we, should we, separate hard news from inferences drawn, opinion from observable action? Are we guilty of making news? Are we all buying the same press releases and the words of the same press conferences? Are we simply playing the game of gang journalism, with all of our cameras in a row, pointed at what Rich Adams has called the "talking heads"?

CHASEMAN: Our number one priority is to help the people who watch us or listen to us to know more about what's going on in the world and how it affects, or might affect, their lives and their futures. A subdivision of that—we're not simply talking about events, we're not simply talking about the matters of crisis, we're not simply talking even about fact—we *are* talking about analysis, interpretation, comment, helping make it fit, putting the facts in perspective, establishing a context: all that risky stuff that we look at when we contemplate what is fact and what is opinion. Anyway, that's our first priority. You can't do all of that unless you have the people. So another top priority is finding the people, the professionals, people with judgment, stability, understanding, respect for the opinions of others. Hopefully they'll have the ability to follow a story wherever it leads them without regard to outside criticism or from those who may be hurt by the story or who disagree with it.

Next, we give those newspeople the commitment that the effort deserves not only in terms of time and dollars and support and hardware and so forth, but important time on the air. The toughest thing of all is a kind of intangible: Can you, when you make this commitment and do these things and find these people, can you be fair in your assignments, in your treatment, in your reflection of the community—as you attempt to present the material in context? Can you be fair? When you make a mistake are you big enough to admit it? When you blow it, can you go back and fix it somehow?

KELLY: There was a lovely gentleman by the name of George S. Kaufman, a fine playwright and I think an even better wit. One time while he was playing bridge he said: "Gentlemen, may we review the bidding *with the original inflections?*" What I'm actually doing, of course, is picking up on what Joel Chaseman just said: *can we be fair?* Are we sometimes, as managers of radio and television stations, forgetting to arbitrate unfairness of our own people on the air? Ergo, the Kaufman idea of the inflection of the voice, the tone of the voice, and what it means to a news story. I'd like to hear from the broadcasters and/or the academicians about this subject. Are we being properly concerned as broadcasters? You people who are sophisticated broadcasters, teachers of broadcasting, have you noticed this? Does this ever bother you as a viewer?

HAWES: Well, it seems to me that managements in general, as I've observed them, are in no way committed to the extent we'd heard described. I have the feeling that the managements of the several stations are doing what they can in what they consider to be the budgetary restrictions they must impose on their news departments. Therefore, this in itself limits the news coverage and news service very, very substantially—and that brings some perspective to the question of whether they can be fair and complete, under this kind of budgetary restriction. Yet the kind of station Mr. Chaseman was describing seems to me to be ideal.

CHASEMAN: It makes mistakes. It has problems.

HAWES: When you have a management commitment that deep it surely borders on the ideal; and I think that it is not typical of the stations I know anything about.

SPERO: Are we talking about radio or television?

HAWES: I'm thinking primarily of television in this case, but I think it pretty much applies to radio as well—aside from some of the all-news, all-talk stations.

SPERO: Well, I have to disagree with that, because there are radio stations that aren't all-news around the country who have substantial news and are dedicated to news. If you don't have a good product in news then you're not going to be a program leader. And even though you may not in your cost accounting prove to derive the income from news—or sports for that matter—that you do out of your basic programming, you've got to equate the overall picture. All these parts—the disc jockey formula, the news, the sports, the service features—must be weighed as contributing to the overall ability to perform.

KITTROSS: British commercial television, *commercial* television, operates on a different basis than our networks do. Programs that go out on the networks originate at the local stations as they would at a program contractor's. I visited a number of those station origination points in Great Britain a year ago, and every one of them I talked to said: "We push like the devil to get programs out on the network." Why? Not because they make money, actually they lose money frequently that way, but because it's so good for staff morale and it shows up in the local programming where they do make their money.

The other thing I would like to mention comes down from your personal point of view. I would like to attack it from a slightly different angle of the Kaufman inflection. We are expected to be much more than a conduit. We don't just plug into whoever is giving a news conference—and I say *news* conference, not *press* conference—we don't just plug in there. We are *standing in* to some extent for the public. That's our job. We are interpreters. If you will, we are the guy who says: "Hey Joe, what happened yesterday?" We find out and tell what happened. And to be fair does not mean having to be a eunuch. I hope that the emphasis on fairness doesn't get translated somehow into meaning *just be an inhuman conduit*.

CHASEMAN: Are you equating fairness, judgment, with bias?

CAILTEUX: "Prejudice" is really unfounded judgment that there is no factual basis for. "Bias," you do have an opinion but you have no reason. There is something in back of it. There are opinions. Judgment might be slightly removed from that. But any time you make a decision somehow— you try to be fair and you try not to prejudice.

WEBBER: All the news media have to lend themselves to the management of news by newsmakers. That's really what you're saying, because what else can you do. You have assignment editors, you've got to send people somewhere and they've got to cover the things which they judge to be important at a given time. I don't know how expandable it's realistic to think we can be. Where do you go? Where do you stop? Radio and television are commercial media, as are the newspapers. They can only do so much. But I think this is a very fundamental aspect of the whole problem we're talking about.

CAILTEUX: John Chancellor said in his talk that he was afraid the performance by radio and television as conduits for our major institutions, relaying information that subsequently is altered or called back as *inoperative,* is going to affect the credibility of the news media and their news. I'm posing the question, what are you going to do about this? Are you anticipating this as a problem? Because when you're given information from whatever institution and you put it on the air, when somebody keeps making those "inoperative" statements, how are you going to handle it?

WEBBER: And another closely-related question: how can we assure this thing called fairness? Jack Kelly was asking us how we deal with the question of facial expressions and inflections and so on. It's important. I'm going to say something and see how many people will disagree with it. I don't see how we can come to grips with this whole problem except by saying that we get the very best trained, most mature, cautious, thoughtful, creative people we can in the important editorial and reportorial spots from the point of on the air presentation, and we supervise them well and hope for the best. I don't see how you can reach any other conclusion.

KITTROSS: There's a professionalism question that ties right in with that. Where do young journalists have the required course in ethics, for example? They have it on the job if they're lucky. What do we have by way of practical example? We've got the *Mary Tyler Moore Show,* which occasionally gets into the question of broadcast news ethics. Remember the business where she was suspended for two weeks because she wrote a funny obituary? And that probably talked more about the ethics of broadcast journalism than anything else we have. And a fun question rises out of that: should Walter Cronkite have appeared two weeks ago on the *Mary Tyler Moore Show?*

VIAMONTE: John Chancellor said he was shocked. I threw a little joke at him and said that I understood he was rehearsing for the *Mary Tyler Moore Show* but holding out for more time. He said: "No, there is no truth to that rumor, but I am shocked that Walter is out of character."

In an earlier meeting, when we talked about fairness the group brought out the observation that maybe we should get rid of fairness and put in access. Might this be a factor in news coverage: that rather than limit news reportage to a select few, the news be given by a great many—some of whom are extremely professional, some others who are there with a particular partisan focus, but all available to a diversified audience? The question is why have news to begin with? And the answer is the people have a right to know. Then fairness is a weak answer. Access is the answer.

CHASEMAN: I have lived long enough to have some opinions. One is that I have discovered some things that have really changed around me. And I am part of that change. Our emphasis, our need for news, is incredibly greater than it was even a few years ago. One of the problems is that our need for news, and hence the kind of sophistication that we are talking about, has far outstripped the ability to find the kind of professional people with the qualities we are looking for. Part of this might be that a lot of managements haven't caught up to it yet. It's partly, I suppose, greed; it's partly commitment; it's partly sheer knowledge—and it's partly because we don't share Dr. Webber's concept of the sophistication of the society. Most of the people who are operating news media today were raised in another era and they are not quite into this one; just as some of the younger people in this room 20 years from now will have been raised in another era and won't quite get into that one. I caution you—it happens to all of us.

SPERO: We have been talking primarily about national news and international news and some sociological aspects. I think, however, we have to do something about the local situation, as important as these larger problems in the national and international field are. We've swept under the rug for as many years as I can remember the problems of the big cities. We're finally getting into environmental problems. Mass transportation is just beginning to have light put on it. We're exposing some of the problems of the ghetto.

LOWENHAR: I would like to reclarify a simple point. You probably know from behavioral science that people hardly ever remember specific things over time. They remember a sort of *gestalt*, the general picture of a kind of *rapport*, a feeling which is usually called an attitude over time, sort of goodness or badness.

The normal consumer doesn't really know what 4% inflation is, 6%, a 1.7% increase in wholesale prices. They know that over time they are spending three dollars more a week at the grocery. They get general pictures of things. That is probably the responsibility of all of us in terms of forgetting and doing away with the great detail that mesmerizes a lot of us in terms of statistics and numbers, which we all like to see because they have a meaning unto themselves. We should try to remove that certain amount of detailed information that I think clogs ourselves, clogs our ability to get what the general picture is across to the various mass media audiences.

NEW: It's a challenge: we really have to put it all together. National and international news doesn't mean anything to us unless we can show our audiences exactly how they are affected. Affected number one as individuals, number two as Houstonians, number three as Texans, number four as Americans, and number five as world citizens. In other words, we must make an honest attempt to localize, to personalize—"This is the broad picture, but specifically this is how you're going to be affected." And I think it registers and has meaning.

SIGMA GROUP

Discussion Leader: Philip Spencer (WCSS, Amsterdam, New York)
Industry Participants: Richard Adams (News Director, Post/ Newsweek Stations, Washington, D.C.); George Carpenter (Sales Manager, WHO, Des Moines); Charles Harrison (Manager-News, WGN-TV, Chicago)
Faculty Participants: Albert Book (University of Nebraska); Knox Hagood (University of Alabama); Ken Harwood (Temple University); Dorothy Johnson (Marshall University); David Lange (Duke University); Arthur Savage (Ohio University)

ADAMS: When we talk about a news operation we think of ratings. We talk about changing our sets to improve our ratings, changing anchor people, making what I think is described as cosmetic changes in the news operation. The question suggested, and a very good question indeed, was where does news itself stand in the priorities of running a news department, and how much do we get involved in dealing with some of the peripheral issues? Another question that we might want to address ourselves to and was discussed at some length, is the extent to which we allow consultants to run our news departments, to tell us who we should hire as anchor people, tell us how we should present the news, tell us even the kinds of news that we should present. This morning the group more or less determined that it was our general feeling that consultants are valuable in that they can bring you input by virtue of an extensive community survey that you don't have time for or really just don't have the facilities to do, to bring you information about the attitudes of the community. But you have to stop short of actually allowing them to make the policy in your news shop. It might be interesting to see how you feel about that.

There was some discussion about the fact that news is a business. And the point was raised that many times students of the news—and those of you who are teaching, this is directed particularly to you—students of the news are not made fully aware of the fact that news is a business and that we are involved in an economic operation that doesn't exist solely for the sake of pure journalism. My personal feeling is that I think in some cases students come out of a school thinking that. And there is a rude awakening when you get into the real world of the business.

CARPENTER: Commercial television stations share two things that they all agree on. One is that the competitors are always underpricing their rate cards. The other is that they want to have the reputation for having the best news in their market, if not their state, if not the country. And best includes the most popular, the most widely watched, the highest ratings. This is more a result of pride than anticipation of economic gain. News is the one area that we feel we can project our image, where we can get recognition for our efforts. So much of our other time is filled by networks and by syndication. Also, not incidental to that, we are aware that stations that are number one in news in their early and late evening newscasts are most often number one sign-on to sign-off.

HARRISON: The students that you have in the colleges are facing a whole set of criteria and circumstances that, honestly and frankly, I never had to face until very, very recently. Broadcast news used to be fun. Broadcast news had explosive growth. When I started out in 1940 I guess there were about 200 radio stations in this country, not many more at best. And it surged to 7,000. I started in television in '49 when there were just a handful of stations across the country, and now we have reached the optimum figure. There is no more growth, or at least very little. Along with it there have been some changes and there are confrontations that are brand new, and there are problems for the broadcaster in merchandising and packaging his market that are going to make it a little less fun.

I don't think that the five-minute newscast on radio is the big problem it was set out to be in the formal presentation. If that's all a station does they've got trouble or else they're doing a specialized type of programming. But as your students go into the craft of journalism for radio and television they will soon find out that in addition to the hard news of the five-minute newscast, your station probably does, if not traffic reports on a regular basis, it does specialized weather and business reports. It does in-depth discussion programs of two hours that can cover any subject under the sun.

I hope that your students as reporters can concentrate on objectivity, which may show a generation gap, but I'm deadly serious. I think that is an imperative. A reporter covering a courthouse or the White House, when he knows in his gut that he has information that the people should know and yet he cannot label it by any fair criterion as fact, that it will be properly labeled either by introduction or by a little slug on the video side so that the audience will know that, OK, we will want you to know this but we're not telling you that this is who, what, when and where. We're getting into that nebulous area of opinion. Stations' and networks' personal opinions should do much more, I think, to give us a better plateau from which to evalute that which is said in a newscast.

BOOK: I would like to ask all of you gentlemen in the industry: How do you feel about on-the-air commentators delivering commercials? And why do you feel whichever way you feel?

CARPENTER: We will not allow it.

HARRISON: I've done it both ways when I was on the air over a period of many years. I was personally uncomfortable working for people whom I respected and were personal friends. I don't feel that a newsman should have the luxury of that extra money in his pocket when, if he does a commercial for a gas station or an oil company or a bakery, he might face tomorrow or next year the need to talk about bread prices or additives in bakery products or the oil shortage. But if you're running a little television station in Ottumwa, Iowa, and your staff is 10 people, the economics of staying in business may declare that you depart from what is proper in another market.

BOOK: But Mr. Harrison, the Omaha-Lincoln area is comparable to Des Moines and you don't have it there. Is it because you have the right kind of principles there, which I'm willing to concede, that they don't have in Nebraska?

HARRISON: I would expect that within another couple of years you wouldn't see it in Lincoln either. It has been pretty commonplace in the business for many years in many markets, regardless of size.

ADAMS: At Post/Newsweek it is not allowed. There is nothing in the union . . . I don't know if you other gentlemen have such tight strictures with unions, but Washington is very tight and AFTRA is very tight there. There is nothing in any individual performer's contract or in the house contract that prohibits it, but our Post/Newsweek policy discourages it and no one does it.

HAGOOD: Last night, I think it was WCBS I was listening to and they backgrounded the story of the Hearst girl up to the point of the demands. They had an insert, Mr. Hearst and his reaction and a very tearful message from Mrs. Hearst. They capped this story off with "And Mrs. Hearst turned and walked into her mansion." The word mansion hit me right between the eyes!

HARRISON: I'm just kind of wondering, because of the time difference between the west coast and New York, if that stuff didn't come down the pipe maybe eight minutes before air time. Someone in a hurry wrote a lead-in and a lead-out and had looked at a Photofax or Unifax picture of the couple standing in front of their huge mansion, and just out of nowhere wrote a closer. Probably I would love to rewrite that and just say she went inside. Now a more important problem that we have in radio and television in the presentation of fact is the startling situation of an age group 18 to 25 who do not read news magazines, who do not read daily newspapers, who get all of their input from radio and/or television newscasts. And I say that is a very poorly informed citizenry. With all-talk radio it still is not enough.

HARWOOD: The 18 to 25s, at least many of them in the colleges, recognize that they don't do much news listening or news viewing and particularly not much news reading. And they account for that, many of them, by saying that they read so doggone much and are absorbed so very much in their studies that if it comes to a little recreational time out of the books they would like to have a little background music and forget it.

SAVAGE: I would ask this question in the area of broadcast economics of the news from all three of our industry representatives. A little background. Ten years ago the average station manager that I talked to indicated that his news was a losing proposition as far as the station was concerned. It cost him far, far more than he ever got out of it in revenue. I had on our campus last week a station manager from a group-owned station in the midwest and he indicated to me that 19% of his total revenue is now coming out of his news operation—which just flattened me, from 10 years ago or six, seven, eight years ago—the idea that with most news operations, if one had to justify on the basis of what they produced for station revenue, there was no possible way it could be done. And now this individual is telling me that 19% of his revenue on his television station comes from his news operation. Now how do you gentlemen react to that? Is your news operation profitable? And you may address it from one or two aspects, that is the commercial business you run in the news pays for the news, or the fact that you can use news locations to hook the rest of the business. Having been in the rep business for a long time, that was one of our favorite dodges. We could sell damned near anything if the station would clear two spots in the news, we would get the client right next to The Star Spangled Banner six nights a week if the station would give us a couple of news spots. So from either aspect, either that which runs in the news pays for the news or what business you attract totally to the station because of the news—is it still a revenue producer for you?

SPENCER: Two ways, George Carpenter, how much percentage direct from news and then what percentage of your gross comes because of your news?

CARPENTER: I couldn't give you a percentage, because you get into cost accounting here and how you want to charge it off. I would say this in answer. If we were to strip *Truth or Consequences* at the same time instead of the news we would net more money.

SPENCER: What about your income percentage of news, Rich?

ADAMS: Again, I don't think I can break it down into numbers. I really don't think that you could possibly, realistically, pay for your news operation with the spots you sold in it. You would have to put too many in and charge too much. It's really hard to say. I guess the best thing to say is that we consider our news as a quality product which, by virtue of the fact that we hope it attracts a large number of viewers to the station, can be used as a saleable commodity and thereby increase the total input to the station. But certainly it could not be self sustaining if we had to run the news operation on what we took in in spot revenue *only* within that news block. You couldn't, and I don't think any station could. I may be wrong but I just don't think you can. It's a very difficult thing, because as you make the point, most of your entertainment programming is virtually all revenue unless it's locally produced. And when you're talking local production costs then you're getting into a whole other thing. So it's really hard to give you a precise answer. I'm sorry I can't be more definitive.

SAVAGE: You're either red or black ink on your news.

ADAMS: I think we're doing all right. I think it's a hold-the-line thing and it fluctuates, of course, depending on what we have to cover. I'm not trying to be evasive. I just think that's about as precise as I can be.

HARRISON: I will give you some things that I am relatively sure of. I believe we're making money on our radio news and about breaking even on our television news. It is difficult to answer because my people, unlike every other station in my market, work for both radio and television, and it is kind of hard to "carve" bodies. But it's also a pleasant way in which to work. It's also complicated by the fact that our drive-time program host, Wally Phillips, and Berg in the afternoon have fantastic audience numbers. And the higher income for our radio news is partly attributable to their audience on the air which is delivered to us on a 24-karat platter. We make money on it. We're spending uncomfortably close to $2 million a year for news. I consider that to be a tremendous amount of money even in a major market for an independent. But that money comes back. I'm not talking about image. I'm just talking about the money that comes back.

JOHNSON: When do you get gutsy and say, "I'm not covering that?"

ADAMS: We created the anti-war movement. There was an issue there, granted, and we can't deny that, but we created it. When it became the determination of most people in major market local news and at the network level and at any college or university level where you had that issue, when it was determined that it was no longer news in our judgment to cover this, or when we became aware that we were being used and stopped covering it, the issue, or at least the people who were screaming and hollering, faded into the background except for those who had a legitimate purpose. But the people who were obviously out for publicity disappeared because they discovered that they could no longer use the media. I saw that in Chicago—when the lights went on the police began to react like that. So the gist of it is I think you cannot set a rule. You cannot set down on a piece of paper and pass around to your staff what to do in case of a volatile situation. If tomorrow we were faced with that I would have to just urge my staff to use common sense. That sounds very vague, whatever that is, to use common sense. That's really about all you can say.

LANGE: Rich, just to put it shortly, I think that your statement that you in the media created the anti-war movement is overstated. It's a profound overstatement to say that you created it or to even say that you were predominant as an instrument in it. There is no question in my mind that the media influenced the course of events, but it's not the kind of media effect that you are suggesting except in a sort of anecdotal way where people actually held up placards.

ADAMS: What about the creation of personalities? People who wouldn't be leaders except that they could be accepted by the media as leaders?

INDUSTRY COMMENT: The point that Mr. Adams made about the fact that you could turn on a couple of lights and attract a crowd and out-of-town camera crews coming it . . . it's disturbing when we realize that. There is one news consultant giving out advice that what we need is more reporter involvement in stories. There is, in fact, a tendency for a lot of stations making a lot of money to take that advice. And it goes for everything—maybe this wouldn't apply to Washington—a routine fire story for the reporter has to have him almost in flames. When he is given a feature on the trampolines out in City Park, there he is jumping up and down on the trampoline as he is trying breathlessly to give his final words.

HARRISON: Let him be an observer, not a participant. If he does get involved there are areas where this is quite proper. A reporter goes to Ringling Brothers Circus and interviews a clown. He puts on his makeup which is a rather interesting feature. The last 20 seconds of the report is the reporter sitting in front of the mirror and putting clown makeup on one side of his face, and as he does a close-out from a normal reporter side view he turns 180 and suddenly becomes a clown. He got involved in something I think that would be perfectly acceptable. But if you become physically or emotionally involved within the story then you are a participant and not a reporter any more, in my definition.

ADAMS: All right, let me just make an example and tell me if you think this fits that criterion. Given an interview situation where you have a man—let's just take a member of Congress. You can interview him in his office, or the reporter and that Congressman can walk down the Mall together discussing the same issue—but visually it's a more appealing story. The reporter is a human being, physically interacting with his news source. I would consider that the kind of reporter involvement that I would consider acceptable. I think the clown would probably be the limit, and in that case it would be clearly defined as a feature story. You have to delineate the nature of the story before you can draw an example of a case. So if involvement implies that the reporter is a human being interacting with another human being in a reasonable way, a way in which he would normally do so, I would say that's acceptable. If it becomes artificial or staged and it becomes overly theatrical, *certainly not*.

License Renewal: A Critical Problem

THERE IS, PERHAPS, no topic more significant to a broadcaster than license renewal. The most valuable commodity a station owner possesses is his broacast license. The stability of the entire broadcast industry rests on the assumption that licenses, once granted, would be routinely renewed.

Consequently, few Federal Communications Commission decisions have caused as much alarm in the broadcast industry as the WHDH case. The Commission for the first time in its history, in applying comparative criteria in a renewal proceeding, ruled against the incumbent license holder and awarded the frequency to a challenger.

WHDH-TV, owned by the Boston *Herald Traveler* Corporation, was granted a construction permit for Channel 5 in the Boston area in 1957. In 1962 its license was renewed for only four months. Finally, in January of 1969 the FCC in a 3-1 vote failed to renew WHDH's license and awarded the channel to a challenger, Boston Broadcasters, Inc.

Fearful that the WHDH case would establish a dangerous precedent by creating a rash of license challengers ("strike applicants"), the broadcast industry urged Congress to enact protective legislation. Senator John Pastore of Rhode Island, Chairman of the Commerce Sub-committee on Communications introduced S.2004, a bill which would require the FCC to ignore competing applications for licenses until it had decided that the present licensee should be denied renewal. Citizen opposition measurably slowed the progress of the "Pastore bill." Then, without any formal rule-making proceedings the FCC, on January 15, 1970, issued its own license renewal "Policy Statement."

The 1970 Policy Statement provides that the renewal issue must be determined first in a proceeding in which challengers are permitted to appear only for the limited purpose of calling attention to the incumbent's failings. The Commission stated that it would give preference to the existing licensee over a competitor if the licensee can demonstrate that his programming has substantially met the needs and interests of his audience. The Senate bill was thereafter deferred in favor of the Commission's "compromise."

The Commission's Policy Statement was challenged by the Citizens Communications Center in the U.S. Court of Appeals (D.C. Cir.). On June 11, 1971 the Court repudiated the Commission's 1970 Policy Statement finding it unreasonably weighted in favor of the licensee it is meant to regulate, to the detriment of the listening and viewing public.

Since the problem of license renewal is both historically and currently of paramount concern to broadcasters, the Seminar's producers invited Mr. Sterling "Red" Quinlan as a dinner speaker. Mr. Quinlan is the author of *The Hundred Million Dollar Lunch* which traces the extraordinary occurrences that resulted in the WHDH decision.

STERLING "RED" QUINLAN

Mr. Quinlan began his broadcast career at an early age as an actor, announcer and writer in radio. He began his television career in 1947 and spent 17 years with ABC in Chicago. For 10 of those years, he was Vice President and General Manager of ABC's owned Chicago channel. Mr. Quinlan also launched an independent UHF television station (WFLD) for Field Enterprises in Chicago. Under his hand, that station became known as the most innovative UHF station in the country. Since then Mr. Quinlan has continued his career as one of the chief executives in IDC Services Inc., a company that provides research and electronic monitoring for major advertisers. Mr. Quinlan attended college at New York University, Western Reserve in Cleveland and Roosevelt College in Chicago. He has written four books: The Merger, Jugger, Muldoon Was Here and most recently, *The Hundred Million Dollar Lunch.*

Address by Sterling "Red" Quinlan

How do you lose a VHF television license in the nation's fifth largest television market, Boston? How do you eliminate one of that city's four major newspapers, the Boston *Herald Traveler?* How do you blow one hundred million dollars? Two thousand jobs? Sixty million in stockholders profits? That's the WHDH story.

The WHDH case has more twists and turns than a whirling dervish. Were I, or anyone else, to try to write this case as fiction, I am sure it would be turned down on the grounds of lacking credibility or believability. A former FCC Commissioner said that not more than 25 people in the country really understood the case.

The story begins in the year 1947, when WHDH Inc. first filed its license application. Others, of course, filed against WHDH. An FCC moratorium on granting further TV licenses delayed action for almost seven years. Finally, in 1954, a comparative hearing began under Hearing Examiner James Cunningham. Two years later, after that comparative hearing, Cunningham ruled not for WHDH, but for Greater Boston TV Corp. The other losers were Dumont Television and Massachusetts Bay Telecasters, Inc.

Cunningham ruled against WHDH Inc. on the grounds of diversification. Its owner was the Boston *Herald Traveler,* which owned a radio station and two of the City's six newspapers. One year later, in April of 1957, the FCC overruled Examiner Cunningham and awarded the license to the Boston *Herald Traveler* Corporation which within eight months put WHDH-TV on-the-air.

In April, 1958 the case was still under appeal by the losing applicants. While these appeals were being considered by the Circuit Court of Appeals in Washington, evidence came out via a chance remark before the House Subcommittee on Legislative Oversight that two men had a certain luncheon at a time when it was entirely *verboten* to be having such luncheons. The two men were George C. McConnaughey who, at the time of the luncheon, was Chairman of the FCC and Robert B. Choate who, at the time, was Chief Executive Officer of the *Traveler* and the Radio and TV Stations. The Court of Appeals became considerably interested in the news that these two men had been breaking bread together, and three months later on July 31st, it acted by remanding the Channel 5 license case back to the Commission with instructions to look into the matter and to investigate it thoroughly. Did the lunch constitute *ex parte* activity? How much hanky-panky was there? All parties could participate, said the Court, including the Attorney General as *amicus curiae*, "friend of the Court." It took the FCC six months to react, but finally on December 4, 1958, the Commission, with John C. Doerfer as Chairman, ordered the case reopened and a new hearing held. The hearing was conducted by Special Hearing Examiner, Horace Stern. Stern wasted little time in getting into the matter of that luncheon. It turned out to be not one, but two luncheons. But, as can be expected, both Choate and McConnaughey had very poor memories.

At the hearing, all of the major participants were conspicuous for their rather poor memories and conflicting testimony. "I remember only one," said McConnaughey, "It was at the Statler or Mayflower, and I can't remember which." "No, it was two luncheons," corrected Choate. "The first one was late in '54, or was it in '55? Our mutual friend, Charley Mills, was with us." "I don't remember the first luncheon," said McConnaughey. Choate refreshed McConnaughey's memory. "The first one was at the Raleigh or Willard Hotel. I don't remember which. Our second luncheon wasn't at the Mayflower. It was at the Statler and it occurred about April 1956 and Charley Mills was with us that time, too." "Anyone else?" asked Examiner Stern "Yes sir. Tom Joyce." "Who is he?" "Thomas M. Joyce, a lawyer for our company. But he wasn't present in any legal capacity." "I shouldn't think so," Stern commented.

After the dates and locations were finally established, Stern got into the more important matter of who said what to whom. Neither Choate nor McConnaughey remembered much of what was said. "He was obviously trying to size me up," explained McConnaughey. "And letting me size him up. Everyone tries to impress a Chairman of the FCC."

"Mutual friend," Charles F. Mills, had a somewhat better memory. The first meeting, he said, was indeed at the Raleigh and the conversation was general and of a social nature. He did recall that Choate asked about the FCC procedures; how long Colonel Cunningham would take to reach his decision; and what would the procedure be afterwards? Regarding the second meeting (which Mills, again, thoughtfully arranged), Mills recalled that he heard Choate say something about Cunningham having already reached his decision, and that it was negative against the *Herald Traveler:* so now, what was the procedure to follow? Could the matter be reviewed, and, if so, by whom?

Choate and McConnaughey remembered nothing about this, prompting Mills to add quickly, well, he wasn't really *that* interested in the conversation; he had just come along for a friendly meal and wasn't that interested in what was being said. Examiner Horace Stern found nothing wrong with this. "Judges," he said, "were frequently consulted on procedural matters and such conversations were distinctly not of an *ex parte* nature."

Choate, Mills and Joyce remembered much more about the second luncheon. This was the time they said that they brought with them an amendment to a bill they wanted to get passed. A very important bill to newspapers everywhere in America. "We called it the Dempsey Amendment to the Harris-Beamer Bill," explained Choate. "Senator Jack Kennedy introduced it for us to the House Subcommittee and he likes it. If you read it, we think you'll like it, too."

The Harris-Beamer Bill threatened to hurt newspapers in the "diversification" issue which was raging then, as it has ever since in the Commission's list for deciding comparative contests for TV licenses. There were some "myopic" souls within the Commission (as there still are) who felt that the concentration of media in the hands of a few was not necessarily in the "public interest, convenience or necessity." The newspaper industry was vocally fighting the Harris-Beamer Bill. The American Newspaper Publishers Association was lobbying effectively to have the bills killed and, of course, Robert B. Choate wanted to do his part.

Ex-Chairman McConnaughey, however, turned a deaf ear to his plea. "I can't discuss this," he said curtly. So, the amendment was not discussed. They talked social chit chat and went their separate ways. One thing they had to say about the chairman; he was an inexpensive date at lunch. He ate sparingly, but drank good Scotch. He was a skinny little man, weighing not more than 110 lbs, with a waffled, craggy, prune-wrinkled face and wiry short frame that made him look like the number one gnome in Santa's Mafia. He was considered a loyal and staunch friend of AT&T, having procured for them several sizeable rate increases during his term.

Some time after this second lunch, Choate admitted that he had invited McConnaughey to go with him to a Washington Gridiron Dinner, but the Chairman had turned him down. They say that the Chairman did not have much of a sense of humor. Maybe he had too much on his mind.

Hearing Examiner Stern learned that several people were after these TV licenses and that they were also having luncheons with McConnaughey.

Dr. Allen B. Dumont had lunch with McConnaughey at the Raleigh Hotel. Forester Clark, director and vice president of the Massachusetts Bay Telecasters, admitted to Stern that he had been extremely active. In the space of a few days, he had seen Henry Cabot Lodge, Senator Saltonstall, Sinclair Weeks, Robert Cutler, Leonard Hall, Representatives Bates and Curtis, and others. His purpose was very simple. He told Stern he merely wanted to make sure that all of these gentleman remained neutral in the bitter Boston case.

Did Forester Clark have luncheon with McConnaughey? "Of course," he admitted to Stern. Only he had handled it in a much better style. Clark lunched with McConnaughey in the privacy of his suite at the Mayflower.

The heads of the Boston *Globe,* the Taylor brothers, William and John, were equally busy trying to make sure that the *Herald Traveler* Corporation did not get a license. Their personal *blitzkrieg* of calls to Washington included Senators Saltonstall and John Kennedy; Congressmen Martin and McCormack; Max Radd; Senators Payne and Bridges; Sinclair Weeks and Vice President Nixon's secretary. The brothers also talked with Sherman Adams and perhaps they complimented Sherman on the fine vicuna coat he was wearing (which the world would later learn had been given to him by his close buddy, Bernie Goldfine).

So, what was the result of Examiner Stern's hearing? Well, he concluded that no one was guilty of anything. Not Choate, not McConnaughey, not any of the others. This, apparently, was part of the game and the way you played the game back in those days of what I call "The Whorehouse Era" of the FCC.

This seemed to clinch victory for WHDH except for one darkling cloud on the horizon—the Attorney General of the United States, one William P. Rogers, who had been participating as a Friend of the Court. His brief rattled thunder from the sky causing a number of persons to begin looking for the nearest gas pipe.

Those luncheons were certainly improper, Rogers said in his very strong brief. Choate was certainly trying to influence the FCC. Forester Clark was trying to do the same thing on behalf of his group. Both WHDH and Massachusetts Bay Telecasters should be disqualified. He stated that from the moment an applicant ceases to depend upon the justice of his case and seeks discriminatory and favored treatment (he) is fortunate if he loses no more than he seeks to obtain. The grant of Channel 5 to the *Herald Traveler,* he concluded, should be set aside. A new comparative hearing should be initiated by the FCC. This put the FCC in the middle because, remember, it did not have jurisdiction over this case. The Circuit Court of Appeals held that singular honor—an honor it stubbornly clung to for the next 13 years. In fact, it never once relinquished jurisdiction in this case. John C. Doerfer, Chairman at this point, did not need this kind of problem because he had a lot of problems of his own. The House Oversight Committee was having a field day disclosing some of Doerfer's personal problems, such as padding his expense account on trips, getting paid twice and sometimes three times for his trips, taking vacations as the guest of major broadcast groups who had cases pending before the Commission, and so forth and so forth. The press quaintly called these "pecadillos." I think it is a marvelous word. Watch your pecadillos!

One of the last things President Eisenhower did before retiring from office was to request that Doerfer resign. He did so eagerly and probably with a great sense of relief.

John F. Kennedy was President now. One of his first appointments was Newton Minow as Chairman of the FCC. What Minow saw when he came to Washington literally gave him heartburn. The real Whorehouse Era of the FCC had largely passed because Richard Mack had gone as a Commissioner. (He later died of acute alcoholism.) His buddy and attorney-fixer, Thurman Whiteside, had committed suicide. Attempts at influence peddling at the Commission had, more or less, subsided but there was still much that Minow did not like, such as Charles Van Doren confessing to the fix of quiz program "Twenty-One." Another thing that Minow surely did not like was that decision his colleagues had reached concerning Channel 5 in Boston.

Despite Attorney General Rogers' strong brief, they came out and said that station WHDH should retain Channel 5. However, they did ask the Court of Appeals to remand the case back to them so that they could convene a new hearing and they suggested October 16, 1961 as the date for this oral hearing. Minow had already exorcised himself of some of his disenchantment by delivering his famous "vast wasteland" speech in the Spring of that same year. So, now the oral hearing was held in the Fall of 1961. However, it took another full year before the Commission reached its decision and what a pixillated decision that was! Or, at least, Newton Minow thought so, for the decision was that WHDH should be granted a license, but it would be a license for only 4 months.

Commissioners Hyde, Lee, Ford and Cross voted this way. Minow could scarcely understand this. He wrote a dissent that made Attorney General Rogers' brief look like greasy kid stuff. Now, this strange decision, however, did have a peculiar *caveat* which went something like this: "Since you at WHDH have been operating for five years on virtually no license at all and since licenses are supposed to be renewed every three years, it might be a rather nice gesture if you filed a license renewal application, and we would appreciate it if you would do it posthaste." Well, you couldn't fault this logic. Some Washington wits were saying that, in terms of licensing, the most permanent license was a temporary one. By the time the Commission gets around to looking at your problem, a decade can fly by.

At any rate, WHDH-TV got to work and filed its renewal, I think in about a month. The Commission, with Newton Minow securely in the driver's seat, had something else up its sleeve. As soon as WHDH filed, the Commission opened the door to new challenges. Any new group could put together an application and file for Channel 5, which meant, of course, that there would be another comparative hearing. But this time it was going to be the final, final hearing to which everyone said "Hallelujah and Amen." Some of the old contestants, however, ran out of gas. Massachusetts Bay decided that it had had an expensive enough lesson in FCC litigation. Dumont had already dropped out. Only Greater Boston TV of the old group decided to hang in and now they called themselves Greater Boston II. In addition, two other new applicants accepted the Commission's challenge or invitation and, in retrospect, I think it is rather strange that there were not more new contestants.

One of the new contestants was Charles River Civic Television. The other was BBI—Boston Broadcasters, Inc.—which ultimately won the Channel, nine years after that. Robert Choate, however, now suddenly complicated the whole case. He did a very unsporting thing because he died. The poor old fellow gave up the ghost after all this notoriety. He died a very bitter, unhappy man. He lost face within his own group. He was demoted and given an office in the back of the station's new studio building and he definitely was the victim of some corporate hi-jinks in his own corporation, which is another story, but he hung on. Incidentally, Choate's son is now the guy who is very active in the consumerism field and has earned a reputation in Washington as self-appointed "protector of nutrition"—Robert Choate's son.

So, when Robert Choate's remains were gently lowered into his grave, his colleagues probably breathed a giant sigh of relief for now those damned luncheons in Washington with McConnaughey which had proven so embarrassing, those damned *ex parte* challenges would now be moot and irrelevant. At least, that is what the *Herald Traveler* Group thought and George Akerson was now the head of the company.

On June 27th, 1964, the longest comparative hearing in the history of U.S. regulatory agencies began in the old Post Office Building. The Hearing Examiner, Herbert Scharfman, was one of the most erudite, lucid and respected of the approximately 15 gentlemen who specialize in this work at the Commission and he was assuredly the writer of that group's best prose. Thirteen months later, Scharfman concluded, despite all that had gone on in the past, WHDH still was the best qualified applicant among the total of four.

Suffice to say Scharfman had a lot of doubts. In fact, he had doubts about the very judicial system he had to serve. He opened up to me as I am sure he has never opened up to anyone in the past. I think you will get some very revealing insights into a very complicated, sensitive and gentle man. More than that, the prose of Scharfman's decisions, his turn of phrase, his imagery, are alone worth the price of admission, in my opinion.

Regardless of what one may think of his decision, he was a master of judicial prose. I think that one of Scharfman's problems was that he could not believe either River Civic Television or BBI. There was a credibility gap to him. Not that members of both groups were not credible, but they had put together such paper-perfect proposals. Each group was loaded with so many innovative ideas, plans and policies and each consisted of such star-studdied casts of intellectuals, educators, community leaders—Charles River, for instance, had not one Cabot, but two Cabots. BBI had practically every member of its group bring in one kind of Who's Who or another. There was Oscar Handlin, the Pulitzer prize-winning author and a professor of American History at Harvard; Dr. John Knowles, the famous doctor and general director of Massachusetts General Hospital; Dr. Leo Beranek, world famous acoustics expert; Robert Gardner, anthropologist, filmmaker and Professor at Harvard; and on and on and on. Just great credits behind their names. I think all this was a little too much for Herb Scharfman—too much overkill. For instance, Charles River Group was going to put their profits into a Foundation—the whole station was going to be a non-profit Foundation. You know, he probably thought what kind of heresy can this be? Here this was the country's 5th TV market where the profits for each station had to be even then $5 or $6 million before taxes. BBI, for example, was to plow about 90% of its profits back into operation. It was going to operate 24 hours a day—7 days a week. Twenty-five per cent of its station was going to be vested in its own employees. It was going to offer local live programming for 36% of its 160.5 hour per week schedule. Whoever heard of that kind of rank heresy? Scharfman had to be thinking something like that. So frankly, I don't think he believed either Charles River or BBI. In the longest hearing decision in history, 226 pages, Scharfman granted the license to WHDH-TV for "the regular period," three years.

After seven years of being on the air without a permanent license, WHDH-TV really thought it had won the ballgame. BBI and Charles River also thought the ballgame was over. Each one of them came within a gnat's eyebrow of throwing in the towel. But, BBI had an attorney named Benny Gaguine. It will embarrass him because he happens to be here in the room tonight. Excuse me, Ben, while I tell them what I think. He's a tough, gritty little Frenchman who's as hardnosed and pragmatic as he is talented, and it was Benny Gaguine and his colleague, Nathan David of the BBI Group, who persuaded BBI to hang in for one more crack at the big apple. This would be an oral hearing which wouldn't cost more than an additional few thousand dollars and since they had already spent about $300,000, why not take that final shot. Now, an oral argument at the

Commission means that, as a lawyer, you get a few minutes on a given morning to talk to the FCC Commissioners who are interested in hearing you. In this case, only four were interested enough to show up. At an oral hearing, you talk for about 30 minutes about why the hearing examiner made a wrong decision. You cut the other parties to ribbons and they do the same to you, and then you all go out and get stiff. As for the original hearing examiner, he isn't even there. He's on another floor hearing another case which will later result in another oral hearing. When your time is up you get a blue light flashed in your face which means "Stop Talking." This, I think, is a rather barbarous ordeal for attorneys, and not too many are good at it. It can be a sure route to an ulcer.

After an oral argument, the Commissioners convene and try to come quickly to a consensus of who did the fastest and best talking before that blue light came on. However, for whatever reasons, this was not done in this case. Considerable time was taken to discuss the case. Two of the seven Commissioners had already removed themselves for good and sound legal reasons. They were Ken Cox and Lee Loevinger. But, now unexpectedly, the Chairman, Rosel Hyde, also removed himself from the case which left only Commissioners Bob Lee, Nick Johnson, Jerry Wadsworth and Robert Bartley to vote.

Only four men, the barest of bare quorums. If one guy got sick on a given day, the quorum was destroyed. If one guy was too constipated to show up, the quorum was out. Well, these four august gentlemen did, however, reach a decision eventually, but it took a while. How they arrived at that decision is one of the more quaint and memorable bits of FCC folklore in recent years. While the Commissioners are remarkably reticent about disclosing exactly what happened, I think I've got the story about 100% right.

The decision went to BBI by a vote of 3 to 1. Bartley, Wadsworth and Johnson voted for BBI—Robert E. Lee voted for WHDH-TV. So, you ask yourself why did BBI get the Golden Apple? Because of its extravagant proposals? Not at all. Just the opposite. BBI actually received a demerit for gilding the lily so to speak. So did Charles River. Bartley, Johnson and Wadsworth did not believe all the things both groups said they were going to do. They ignored the old issue of *ex parte,* completely— all but Wadsworth, who later rather confusedly said, "Yes, the *ex parte* issue was really what he was voting for."

The reasons given on the record in that decision were diversification and integration of management. The decision was the biggest shocker in the broadcast business. Wadsworth's vote was a great shock. He had been expected to aid the fellow Republican, Robert Lee, and make it, at least, a 2 to 2 tie. Chairman Rosel Hyde's refusal to vote was another shocker. It still has not been satisfactorily explained. To say that the industry was stunned was a megaton-sized understatement. The nation's first major market VHF-TV station was taken away. Sol Taishoff (Publisher of *Broadcasting*) predicted that this would mean the end of broadcasting. The NAB went into hysterics. Major broadcasters began making trade deals with psychiatrists. Business really picked up for the television station brokers. Worse even than the decision was Nick Johnson's concurring statement which really rubbed salt in the wound. "Come one, come all," said Nick Johnson. "It is now open season. Everybody get together and file on top of your nearest friendly TV station. Claim jumping is the thing—the new fad." "Break up the broadcast monopoly."

That bomb was dropped on January 22nd, 1969 and for WHDH, it looked like the end of the ballgame. BBI would certainly be on the air within a year or slightly more. However, legal rubrics being what they are, much more was yet to happen. After all, WHDH had massive industry support. It also had now as its leader one Harold Clancy, who proceeded to put up one of the most relentless fights imaginable. He used every legal tactic in the book and some, perhaps, that were not so legal and he admitted that he was doing so because, after all, a $50 million franchise was at stake. That franchise supported the *Herald Traveler* newspaper which, too, then would go down the drain. Thousands of jobs were involved. It was the only Republican voice in heavily Democratic Boston. Clancy cried that WHDH was the victim of an unconscionable injustice—the very words that Chairman Dean Burch was later to use. Burch, at this point, was relatively new on the job. To put it mildly, he was dismayed at what he saw. Here was the Boston decision already made and he was helpless to do anything about it.

There would be appeals by losing parties, of course, but they would be made at the Circuit Court of Appeals which still held jurisdiction over this crazy case. How to get it back is what went through Burch's mind, I'm sure, day after day. But, far from trying to get it back, irony of ironies was that the FCC had to defend its decision before the Court of Appeals and this job fell to one Henry Geller. Dean Burch must have surely been hoping and praying that Geller would fall on his face. Henry Geller was then the General Counsel of the Commission. He's a mild mannered, unassuming little guy who can charm the rattlers off a diamond back. He is so disarming, so beguiling, that you want to help him along to get across the street, so to speak. But along with this curious package of equipment goes one of the sharpest legal minds the Commission has ever known. Geller realized that the decision, as written, was very badly written. He came out and said so. The issue of the Choate-McConnaughey luncheons never should have been taken out of the case, he said. That *ex parte* issue should never have been removed by Scharfman even though Beanie Choate, to be sure, was resting in his grave. That was all Henry Geller really wanted to do on that oral argument before that 3-man panel of the Circuit Court of Appeals on May 26, 1970—and he put the luncheons back in with a passion and a vengeance and a conviction. He called this Paragraph 40. Those original luncheons had been feeding WHDH 12 years, he pointed out—12 long years—and it was high time that someone made them pay the bill. Five months later, on November 13, 1970, the Circuit Court came out and did exactly that. They upheld the FCC decision. The Court accepted Geller's reasoning on Paragraph 40, and Beanie Choate. It said Geller had demonstrated an "attempted pattern of influence" and its decision ended with the chilling words referring to the 3 to 1 decision to grant Channel 5 to BBI, "There was no error."

Obviously, Henry Geller had done a real number on the Circuit Court in that 30-minute argument and one of the Judges is reported to have said later that Geller had turned him completely around. He was not prepared to go so far as to be the first Judge to take away a major market TV license, but after listening to little, mild-mannered Henry Geller, he could vote no other way.

Well, you would think that would be about it, but not quite. BBI did not sign on the air for another 16 months as the *Herald Traveler* pulled every conceivable legal trick. Both sides pulled out every stop. There was corporate espionage. Wiretapping alleged by both sides. Dirty tricks alleged by both sides. Harold Clancy, for instance, freely admitted that he had assigned his best investigative reporters to the case. They traced BBI's garbage to a refuse dump in Quincy. They went through that garbage night after night, not because they were hungry but because they were looking for carbon copies of letters, memos, and so forth.

BBI, on the other hand, was convinced its phones were being tapped so they put out phony stories on those phones and sure enough the phony stories began playing back to them. Clancy went a step farther. He put on his brass knuckles and gave an exclusive interview to a New England advertising publication called *Ad East* and that interview, by itself, is remarkable reading. He threw the entire book at BBI, at the FCC, at everyone he could think of. Yes, he admitted, the luncheons between Choate and McConnaughey had occurred, but hadn't Judge Stern absolved Choate of any wrongdoing? Hadn't Scharfman done the same thing? And wasn't that poor bastard in his grave and how much longer must WHDH wear his albatross? Then he went after Rosel Hyde. Why had Hyde not voted? Was it because BBI's attorney was Benny Gaguine, who had formerly been Hyde's legal assistant? Did Benny have something on Hyde? As for Bartley, that guy was a total hypocrite. In the meantime, Clancy's investigators were busy, busy, busy. And soon they had begun to strike pay dirt. Most important was the charge that BBI's Executive Vice President, Nathan David, was a very bad boy, indeed. David was being sued for fraud in violation of Federal Security Laws. He held stock in a company called Synergistics and had not informed the Commission. There were charges against others in the BBI group, but the Nate David matter seemed to be the most bothersome because they knew that Chairman Burch was looking for just this kind of ammunition to get the case back from the Court of Appeals. While the Commission considered this new information, WHDH went to the Supreme Court. BBI was now up to its eyeballs in payroll, its studios were under construction and Benny Gaguine asked for a termination date of September 26, 1971.

Suddenly a calamity struck again at BBI. Nathan David was indicted by a Grand Jury for selling stock without a license, the cost of which was a mere $10 and in which the law, for some 50 years, had never been enforced. He was fined $200 on each of five counts, but imposition of fines was stayed pending appeal. Nate David was sure he saw the sinister hand of Harold Clancy behind the scenes, but on the other hand, Nate David had now become a liability to BBI. They desperately needed something to bolster their spirits and that came on June 14th of 1971. The Supreme Court did act. It turned down WHDH's appeal by a vote of 8 to 0, Chief Justice Burger not participating. One would think now that delaying tactics was all that WHDH had remaining. That, plus a miracle. The miracle seemed to come a short time later. The Securities and Exchange Commission filed some serious charges against Nate David. According to the *Herald Traveler's* graphic prose, they raised questions about "misconduct, moral turpitude, possibly even the commission of State and Federal crimes." Dean Burch was looking for exactly this kind of angle. He convened the Commission on August 18th and (1) tried to get a consensus to ask the Court of Appeals to remand, and (2) withdraw BBI's construction permit. Burch got his way on his first objective. He failed, but only barely, in his efforts to rescind the construction permit and, had he succeeded on this, he very likely would have put BBI out of business for this group now had $2 million tied up in various stages of construction and installation. Its payroll numbered at least 35, and came to more than $300,000 a month. I'm sure the First National of Boston would have turned a deaf ear for more money. So, after that, it became cloak and daggers all the way with a crisis a minute for all concerned. BBI was trying to get on the air before it went broke and WHDH was trying to stall long enough to see that BBI did go broke. However, to show you what a stubborn bunch of fellows they have at the Court of Appeals, that Court once again refused to remand the case to Dean Burch. Surely, they knew what would have happened had they done so. There would have been a new hearing. A different resolution and probably, very likely, WHDH would have been on the air today.

The Court of Appeals decision came on October 2nd, 1971 and after the inevitable appeals, the Court said no once again on December 29, 1971. This time it was emphatic. Straighten out the problem of Nate David, the Court said. Separate him from the case. Get the show on the road. Put BBI on the air. On March 19, 1972 at 3:00 AM, BBI went on the air with its call letters WCVB-TV.

QUESTION AND ANSWER SESSION FOLLOWING QUINLAN ADDRESS

Q. After a certain number of years, should stations be granted permanent licenses?

Quinlan: No. I really can't say that I think that it would be good for the industry to have perpetual licenses. It's an antagonistic system. I think there's got to be continual pull and tug between the industry and the government. A longer term of license I would go for, but not a perpetual license. I'm a practical broadcaster—but we need some government. We need some pushing and tugging. We need some criticism. We need gadflies.

Q. What are your feelings, Red, about the current system of license renewal? Are there any shortcuts which could be implemented by the FCC at the present time?

Quinlan: I don't want to radically change the present licensing system. I think it's sincere. The Commission today is basically honest and far different from what it was in the "whorehouse era."

Regulation: A Full Nelson, or A Strangle Hold?

PETER T., President of the AAA Broadcasting Group, is a broadcasting pioneer, having spent more than 40 years in the industry. At dinner with friends one evening, he paraphrased the old line, "Any similarity between regulation as practiced today and its original conception is purely coincidental. Back in the old days, the FCC only told the industry how to operate their technical equipment, what their wavelength restrictions were, in what manner they should identify themselves and how often. Where have the good old days gone? Now the industry is dictated to by the FCC, the FTC, the Congress, ACT, and it doesn't stop there. No matter how hard you've honestly tried to serve the community, it's a free-for-all at renewal time."

"Now wait a minute, Pete, don't you think you're pushing it just a bit?" asked a friend. "You seem to be doing pretty well, just how do all these groups affect the way you run your stations?" Pete smiled, "If you've got three days to listen, I'll fill you in. But let me give you a rough idea about the four main areas that are affected, namely: license renewal, the Fairness Doctrine, equal time and advertising restrictions."

"Let's look at license renewal. Do you remember the Maine? And do you remember WHDH-TV? They were both victims. Or were they? The growing public awareness of the right of any group (e.g. minority, private interest, citizens) to issue a challenge for any one of my stations' licenses has made the process of renewal into an industry unto itself. It's a full time job year-round. Like Topsy, it grew, and you just can't satisfy every group. The process is time consuming, expensive and non-productive. And stretching the period of renewal from three to five years is not enough of an answer."

"Let me tell you about Fairness. There doesn't seem to be any such thing. Oh sure, when we do an editorial we invite members of groups with opposing views to voice their opinion, that's fair. But have you followed the trials of NBC-TV in relation to their program on pensions? The case may go to the Supreme Court." "What about equal time? There is a great notion. On paper. But how has it worked? The Democrats now get an hour of prime-time to respond to a Republican President's State of the Union Message. Candidates of the United Chimney Sweeps Party ask for and receive equal time with the Democratic and Republican candidates. And the records that must be kept to justify our performance fill warehouses every year. Thank heavens for ¾ inch videotape, we now record our total broadcast for FCC record purposes."

"You're all familiar with the steps leading up to the restrictions on cigarette advertising on the electronic media. And you may have read about the hearings on the use of proprietary drugs. You've also read about the effect of the ACT group on the structure and content of children's advertising, and you've read about proposals for counter-advertising. Well, while you've been reading about these things, I've been living with them and watching my revenue potential being eroded and further threatened. And there is very little I can do to stop it."

DISCUSSION POINTS:

License Renewal:

Can steps be taken to buffer stations from irresponsible challenges? Without disrupting station activity, what is the easiest way to cope with license renewal information collection? Does it benefit a station to have a consistent dialogue with community leaders and organizations? Would a change in the time frame of renewal be a boon or a bust? What is an ideal license renewal formula?

Fairness Doctrine:

If we must live under the fairness doctrine, who is to be the final arbiter of what is fair? Can a national standard of fairness be established or do local situations make this an impossible task? If a subject were to be labeled editorial or commentary, who is to make the final judgment in the event that there are several seemingly valid requests for equal time?

Equal Time:

Should equal time provisions be automatically waived during local, state and national elections? Can it be left to stations to balance the time alloted to candidates and spokesmen of opposing views or must it continue to be regulated?

Counter or Non-Advertising:

Published statistics prove that cigarette consumption has increased despite the ban on advertising of the category on the electronic media.

Does this stand as sufficient evidence of the uselessness inherent in trying to regulate the public involvement with products even when proven to be harmful to health? Could the medium survive under a program of controlled commercial content?

IOTA GROUP

Discussion Leader: Frank Harden (State Broadcasting Company)
Industry Participants: Russell Barry (Vice President and General Manager, KNXT, Los Angeles); George Spring (Station Manager, WRGB, Schenectady)
Faculty Participants: Douglas Boyd (University of Delaware); Peter Clark (University of Michigan); Stanley Donner (University of Texas); Joseph Johnson (San Diego University); Philip Macomber (Kent State University); Peter Pringle (University of Florida); Robert Schlater (Michigan State University); Carol Reuss, SP (Loyola University)

HARDEN: Probably no problem causes the broadcaster more frustration, more money, more man hours, more paper work and more legal fees than license renewal. It's a complex subject, but I don't know of a more timely subject because, facing us now as broadcasters, is the question of license renewal. License renewal legislation is being proposed in this current Congress.

SPRING: I inherited, as I walked into my new job, the license renewal problem of the three stations that I run. Our stations are in New York. As you probably know there are different years in which licenses are renewed in different States throughout the Country. Our were renewable in 1972. We don't mind license renewals but it is *a propos* at this point, that the Commission has just given us new guidelines regarding the procedures that you must follow to renew your licenses. It is a perfect subject of conversation, right now. We have already started working on the license renewals for 1975. That's the massive type of job it is and the amount of work that is necessary. Really, untold man hours have to be spent on it. There is one profession that really gets rich in the radio television business these days, and that happens to be the lawyers.

HARDEN: Thank you very much George, for giving us a first hand touch on license renewals. I think most of us are either entering into license renewals or we have just finished.

BARRY: I have gone through seven different renewals, including several challenges. We did not get a strike application against us in that period of time although CBS does have one now, in Philadelphia. That will probably end up costing us several million dollars and the litigation will go on for seven or eight years.

HARDEN: At one time, not long ago, some of the attorneys were saying around Washington that if you wanted to play safe or be relatively safe in your next license renewals, you should be sure that your application and all the attendant exhibits weighed so much. In other words, if you passed a certain weight limit, you were okay—they just didn't check it. Do you think there's any truth in that, really?

BARRY: I'll just give you one little anecdote. My second renewal for WCBS-TV and WCBS-Radio was written in really a remarkable prose fashion by an editorial writer and they made him re-write the whole thing because it was too easy to read.

SPRING: When we did our last renewal for the television station, we did approximately 375 face-to-face interviews. That's sitting down and talking like we're talking here, for approximately half an hour to an individual, a community leader.

BARRY: All within six months, it should be noted.

SPRING: Yes.

BARRY: They only count during the last six months.

SPRING: Now, fortunately, you've got a year to do it, but you've got to do it all year long.

DONNER: I've thought a lot about this license renewal business over a long period of years because we do teach about regulations. What happens when you do 1,500 pages and it's done by all the broadcasters in a single State? This stuff pours into the FCC, wheeled in trucks. There are only seven commissioners aren't there? Well, they're not going to be able to handle all this information. It will be read by their staff.

INDUSTRY COMMENT: There's a $34 million budget for that staff.

DONNER: The whole thing becomes so absurd that you, on one hand, are spending time and money and at the other end they are facing the same problem because you've done it. I suggest a kind of 1040-A form in which every station in the country, every year, would file which would consist of two or three pages, something extraordinarily simple. The Commission receives these and they are read. There can be the same kind of spot-check that the Internal Revenue Service makes. If your station is spot-checked, then you have to go back and do the enormous amount of work to defend what is said.

BARRY: We're defending against the various special interest groups that come in to examine and/or make copies of our public file. We're dealing with a multitude of special interests and pressure groups, and we're serving as many masters as there are in this room. You have to have something for everybody. That is one of the problems. The Commission itself will not come back at you with a license problem unless there is an obvious and rather noteworthy deficiency in your application.

DONNER: People would still be allowed to write to the FCC or anybody they wanted and a dossier kept on these stations. If there are accumulating protests of some kind, then maybe these should be the stations to be spot-checked.

MACOMBER: How many special interest groups look at your license?

BARRY: That's hard to say. I don't know off hand how many we get to come in and look at our public file. There's a considerable amount of traffic in there, and it will accelerate during the next several months. The Annual Report that the Commission is requesting now for television stations is a response, in a sense, to the Donner Plan. You talk about the programming that you're doing and you're only allowed to go five pages.

SPRING: I think your Donner Plan would be sensational. We would still continue doing all the work and have all the background material sitting there in our public files to show them what we've done. But the plain, license renewal application could easily be one sheet.

SCHLATER: I want to play the devil's advocate on ascertainment for a moment. I would like to suggest that philosophically many stations in this country don't have the slightest concept of who their audiences are or what their audiences' needs are. I think it's a magnificent audience feed-back to a station, to be required to do some face-to-face interviews with community leaders. I could care less whether anybody reads the 1,500 interviews. I think it can certainly be very valuable in your concept of what your community is.

BARRY: I've spent as many as three or four meetings a week with various community leaders.

CLARK: I think that most of us would agree that the Fairness Doctrine has had very evil effects on public affairs programming. All of us would agree that the process by which much of the regulatory machinery is undertaken is extremely cumbersome. There are many bad effects of the equal time provisions, etc. I am wondering if you as broadcasters, think that these evils have been visited upon the industry by under-employed bureaucrats or whether there were some real problems in broadcasting that necessitated the establishment of ascertainment?

SPRING: I'd say that there were a lot of real evils in broadcasting as far as not being fair. There are still quite a few. There are responsible broadcasters and unfortunately nonresponsible broadcasters. It is a business like any other business. There's a lot of good guys, some fair and middling guys, and a lot of bums.

CLARK: I'm wondering if there is anything in the machinery of a trade association that could be brought to bear against the negligence of those who are causing this pain?

SPRING: Well, they are self-owned-and-operated businesses and all you can do is suggest and guide. You set up standards like the National Association of Broadcasters.

DONNER: I think that you have your finger on the whole point of the matter and that is that most broadcasters are fair minded and do an extraordinarily good job, but there are "schlock" operators and everybody knows it, and everybody in the business knows who they are.

BARRY: I just want to respond to that. I think that there's a reluctance on the part of Government and, perhaps, special interest groups, to allow the marketplace to wash out these schlock operators.

MACOMBER: I wish to say a few words about the schlock operator and the bad apple in the barrel, that we've been talking about. Most often, isn't this bad apple in a highly, parochial and protected environment? He's the one station in a one-station market where you can't get to him competitively to drive him out of business. You can't be a schlock operator in your market because somebody will get you there, your competition, the other stations. But you get out into Ohio or Indiana where you've got one-station markets or two-station markets, there is a relatively low level of competition.

FACULTY COMMENT: Do you think you might simplify things if you go over to the five-year license period? I think it would probably be easier for you to fight for a five-year renewal rather than to get the FCC to change all these forms to something simpler. Would that help any in the industry?

BARRY: Any extension of the term would enable you to better use your resources. Instead of spending every three years, you spend them on other endeavors over five years. We have a Community Relations Department that is responsible for license renewals. There are seven people in it, and in all honesty, in the next six months, because of license renewal preparation, they cannot spend their time visiting community leaders and identifying the problems.

INDUSTRY COMMENT: If you propose a five-year renewal to the FCC, they'll want additional guarantees.

SPRING: There are right now in Congress several bills and one industry-backed bill to go ahead and extend the length of the license.

JOHNSON: It was mentioned a while ago here, about schlock operators, and there was the feeling that in some of the strong markets you don't have schlock operators. Channel 13 in Los Angeles is a schlock operator. There are a whole lot of radio stations in Los Angeles who are schlock operators. But, maybe in somebody else's terms they are not. I'm not sure.

I think broadcasters already have a license in perpetuity. You have to account every three years in a formal way, but the history of broadcast regulations in this country indicates that with a few rare exceptions, those really are licenses in perpetuity and a three-year time frame is really not unreasonable. We really have a bad system but I wonder what the alternatives are. I hear a lot of alternatives being kicked around and everybody seems to think that the alternatives are worse than what we've presently got. People feel awfully uncomfortable about this phrase "public interest, convenience and necessity." The FCC doesn't know what it means and you don't know what it means. It seems to be some kind of framework around which people can show good faith and good intentions. You have some kind of negotiation process with a minority group, you go out into the community and do your ascertainment, you feel very insecure about this whole thing. I would really like to hear some constructive alternatives that are better than the present system.

HARDEN: Does anybody have any alternative proposals to kick out?

BARRY: Well, I'll just make a couple of comments. I think you're right. I mean, it's not so much insecurity as it is frustration. If you adopt an annual programming report, a report of the problems as you perceive them and how you've responded to them, it would seem to me to be more than adequate. It would satisfy the bureaucrats and would enable them to monitor us more closely. It would give the community groups more up-to-date information and would not place a terrible burden on the licensee. It would relieve us of the three-year renewal and replace it with the yearly short form.

SPRING: I'd really like to see the elimination of the irresponsible, threatening, non-thinking person or group who attacks you without valid reason or, frankly, tries to hold you up.

PRINGLE: This is a most interesting and stimulating discussion, but are we going to make any realistic attempt to deal with some of the other things before us? Just how realistic is it to expect that there is such a thing as a public interest? Many publics make up the great audience. These pressure groups represent the vested interests of a few people who have the money and who are outspoken. They've got the gimmicks to attract attention and the public sits by because we don't like to march and pressure and protest and be held up for ransom. How are our interests going to be served?

REUSS: I think that one of the things that you're going to run up against in the future if the regulations stay as they are, is that the pressure groups are becoming more sophisticated in using you. We saw that with the demonstrations. I think that Congress should find out about these things. Something has to be done.

SCHLATER: I'd like to make the simple point that you are unique broadcasters as we look at the stations across this country. You represent multiple-station owners. There are an awful lot of single stations in rural areas across this country where we find schlock operators. It seems to me that the regulations now require them to improve their service to the public. You've always been operating in the large markets where you have competition, but I'm wondering if anybody has proposed in the Congress or the FCC that we look at ascertainment by market size? In other words, the guy who does ascertainment in Adrian, Michigan for his one little radio station, is not going to have quite the big job that you in Los Angeles have because your ascertainment potential is so enormous.

SPRING: I think the ascertainment is going to get easier for stations in Adrian, Michigan or Dominance, Ohio or places like that.

SCHLATER: But I disagree with that point. I would like for it to be just the opposite. I would like to see the FCC get easier and easier on you and a little tougher and tougher on the people who are in single-station markets.

CLARK: Just a couple of observations and a question. One, I think, rather than FCC action, the thing that has led most to citizen participation is the ruling in the Jackson, Mississippi case where Justice Burger, for the first time, opened the door to challenges by people who did not have an economic interest in a competing license or a competing corporate entity. That's what has opened the gates and transformed our lives much more than the ascertainment rules or any other FCC requirements.

BARRY: I consider ascertainment a useful process, per se, now. I really do. We try to have our whole staff sensitive to the needs and problems of the community.

SPRING: One of the things that has come up in our industry is counter-advertising, particularly as it relates to television. What do you think about the fairness of regulation of advertising on the electronic media and not on any others?

BOYD: One of my concerns, not only as a broadcaster and an educator, but as a parent, is the type of advertising that appears and has appeared for a number of years on children's programming. We've tried to deal in specific terms with this question, to look at the nutritional value of some of the things like Tasty Cake and the nutritional value of General Mills' and Kellogg's cereals, which are 75% sugar. I'm just wondering, if we don't need some guidelines in this area? If, in fact, groups aren't doing some good in terms of looking at this? I realize this is not counter-advertising, the subject you brought up, but we have an attempt by several groups not to take your license away but to influence what you, as broadcasters, do in terms of advertising. I don't think ACT wants to pull licenses; I think that what they want to do is try to improve some aspects of advertising within the program.

BARRY: Yes, I agree with that and I think that their motives are very sincere, I really do. I think that they and other groups, feel very strongly about what they're trying to do. Again, though, I think that they're trying to replace, in some instances, their judgment for ours. Children's advertising is a difficult and sensitive subject and I personally feel that if you are going to relegate the television set to a baby sitter then don't ask us to assume the responsibility of influencing these people. I cannot help but be rather upset about the cigarette thing where here we are talking to adults and we're treating them like children. It seems to me that the Government and a great many of the special interest groups are determined to protect us from ourselves. We can't be allowed to run free because we're going to commit suicide, and I reject that. I think that the audience, at large, can make intelligent and discrete decisions.

SPRING: I just jotted down three quick observations of what the industry has done by themselves without any pressure group whatsoever getting after us. Number one was the beer industry. No way have you ever seen, in the last 10 or 15 years, anybody drink a glass of beer. I'm talking about the commercials. Number two: we, ourselves, invoked the non-acceptance of liquor advertising on radio and TV. That was strictly done by us. We, ourselves, alone went ahead and said no more doctor commercials. Nobody had to pressure us on that. That was all done and changed by ourselves. I'm saying that the old trite phrase still applies: Rome wasn't built in a day. We know of the things that are still lacking and I think we can go ahead and do it ourselves over a period of time. I'm not saying that your ACT group, regarding the cereals shouldn't prod us, but don't regulate us. The cigarette ruling has got to be the most nauseating piece of legislation that has ever come down the pike. That was forced through Congress by a bunch of guys who wanted to get a big batch of headlines out of it. The latest industry data and the tobacco industry show that people are smoking more cigarettes now than ever before. We're arguing against regulations, regulating advertising on the air—in other words, telling us what we can and can't run.

PRINGLE: It seems to me that what the broadcasters have been trying to tell us, and I think that we've been quite sympathetic, is that they object to the great amount of time, detail and effort and diversion of resources that is required to do ascertainment to the satisfaction of the FCC or the FCC staff. They have a stinking suspicion that they don't have the time to do justice on all the work.

RHO GROUP

Discussion Leader: Robert Henabery (ABC-AM Radio Stations)
Industry Participants: Wallace Dunlap (Vice President, Group W, Washington, D.C.); Jack Tipton (Station Manager, WMGH-TV, Denver)
Faculty Participants: Kenward Atkin (Michigan State University); Bertram Barer (California State University, Northridge); Robert Crawford (Queens College); Gordon Gray (Temple University); Allan Mendelowitz (Rutgers College); Keith Mielke (Indiana University); Maureen Milicia (Marshall University); Wesley Wallace (University of North Carolina)

DUNLAP: I'd like to begin with a comment on the title of the problem —REGULATION: A FULL NELSON OR A STRANGLE HOLD? There's a question mark following that. I guess my one word answer would be neither. But first of all, I have a disclaimer to make: I do not come here as an openminded, objective person.

GROUP: Join the crowd.

DUNLAP: I have a built-in bias which is a product of many, many years of introspection in the operation of stations and companies that have been very good to me, and I think that it reflects the philosophy of the company that I work for now. People like to give things titles. We're living in an era that I refer to as the "new reality," and once you accept the concept of a new reality, the answers to the questions asked here, which might at first seem obvious, become quite debatable.

Certainly, there has been a move on the part of the Executive Branch that is now in office to get into the broadcast world and do damage, or at least, mischief. But the idea that "Washington is out to get broadcasting," is a dangerous over-simplification which does not take into account the existence of the public in relation to the broadcasting field. The public is going to become increasingly more involved. I think broadcasters, and people who are being taught to be the broadcasters of the future, rather than being given a cynical or negative attitude toward the new reality should be talking about how to live with it. How do you go about this? How do you attack these various problems in light of the fact that there is a new reality in the relationship between the licensee and the public. Washington is only a catalyst; it's required by law that they be there and they act on behalf of the public—not on behalf of broadcasters. That's the way the law was written and until we change the law, I think we have to learn how to live with that and with the public pressures (if you want to call them that). Public pressure can be frightening. Obviously, when you open up yourself and your license and your business (because we *are* in business) to public pressure, it gets pretty scary. But, I don't think it has to be if we learn how to deal with it.

TIPTON: I like the realistic approach. The pressures are all there and I don't think there is a darn thing that anyone of us can do to eliminate them. I'm not sure that it's all bad because in living with this type of thing we're in, we may become better broadcasters.

MENDELOWITZ: Before anybody sheds any tears for the license holders, I think we should admit that the preponderance of precedents and the preponderance of financial resources hardly indicate that your discomfort with license challenges is justified. If we go back to the WHDH case, they made $5 million in advertising revenue during the decade they didn't even have a regular broadcast license. Any group that challenges a licensee, is at a tremendous disadvantage. They have to struggle over a very long period of time before the FCC and the courts without the financial resources of the advertising revenues that the licensee has. Given past experience anyone who is willing to spend the hundreds of thousands, and even millions of dollars, necessary to challenge an existing licensee is almost crazy. He's got to have a few million dollars lying around for which he has no use, because the chance of getting any return on this investment is essentially zero.

BARER: I think that there is one factor that we really have to lay out on the table and face up to, we have to be careful that we don't characterize the challenger as the hero in overalls. We have experienced thoroughly irresponsible charges and fraudulent documentation. Licensees are vulnerable because there is always an implied element of truth that you haven't done enough. All of us haven't done enough. How do you answer we haven't done enough? The preponderance of broadcasters are responsible, and they have to live with the fallout of the marginal operators. I personally feel that the National Association of Broadcasters has exercised poor leadership in trying to instill professionalism to the industry.

HENABERY: Wally, would you like to comment on the NAB's effectiveness?

DUNLAP: I certainly share Bert's view that the NAB has failed to exercise a position of leadership which we feel is adequate, either in representing our industry to the Government or in leading the industry.

WALLACE: I feel we should take the position of Justice Burger in the June 1973 obscenity cases and apply it to broadcasting. In the *Miller* case he said that the concept of national standards is meaningless, that after all, communities are different. One of the characteristics of broadcasting is that it is local—that is to say, it is founded on the principle of localness.

DUNLAP: In television, at least for the forseeable future, if you arrive at a reasonable standard, I see no reason why it can't be applied to all stations.

CRAWFORD: Is there any information to indicate the motivations of these people who are submitting the petitions to deny? In other words, how many of them are doing it just to embarrass you or to raise a little dust in the community? How many actually want your license?

TIPTON: I can only speak from my own experience. Two or three of our challengers were asked: "If you won the license, what would you do?" And they said: "We'd be scared to death." But I don't want to imply that everyone who challenges is irresponsible.

BARER: We were challenged, and we are a public radio station. We started investigating the whole situation and we began to find that this organization that called itself a corporation was never chartered by the State of California as a corporation. The people listed as on its board of directors were not informed that they were on the board of directors. So, we started spending a lot of money that we really didn't have, firing off letters to Washington. Anyway, the bottom of the line was that these people were turned down and we had the impression that their main intent was really to generate publicity for themselves.

DUNLAP: We should make one very important distinction. The distinction between people who are irresponsible, and people who are guilty of irresponsible acts. I know Everett Parker and I know Nick Johnson; I know Al Cramer; these are not irresponsible people, but they have done irresponsible things on occasion.

HENABERY: What is the percentage, in rough terms, of people in broadcasting—to the best of your knowledge—who are responsible and who are not responsible, who are making these strike applications at this point?

DUNLAP: I don't know of any very frivolous ones. I'm sure there are some but it would be a very small percentage. I would say that less than 5% of the petitions to deny are frivolous. Some of the competing applications which are now being litigated are opportunistic, and may or may not have merit.

MENDELOWITZ: I think you have to differentiate between the types of licenses being challenged. The motivation for challenging a public license is quite different from the motivation for, say, challenging a commercial license in a major area. I personally believe that a license of a network affiliate in a large market, is essentially a license to steal. The license confers upon the license-holder a monopoly profit. The rate of return on capital of a CBS affiliate in a major market is probably one of the highest rates of return on capital in the economy, primarily because a license gives a license-holder a monopoly of profit. WTIC, in Hartford, was sold for $32 or $35 million. I don't know what the capital stock was but I'm sure it was less than $10 million. I can see people being motivated to challenge commercial licenses in large markets for economic reasons.

I think that if you look at other regulated sectors of the economy that have a legal monopoly position such as telephone, the rates are set for customer use by the regulatory body, supposedly guaranteeing what's known as a fair rate of return on capital stock. Only in the broadcasting industry does the license-holder have a right to make as much profit as he wants. This profit is a direct result of the legally conferred monopoly position.

ATKIN: I just want to get some clarification. How many licenses have been lifted by the FCC since 1934?

HENABERY: Yes, Bert?

BARER: Edward R. Murrow made a statement that is engraved in my mind. He said that "there are two kinds of coercion: the threat of coercion and actual coercion." Even if it is the threat of coercion, despite their economic health commercial broadcasters are in a terribly sensitive position. The irresponsible behavior and actions of challengers set in motion the kinds of things that are really destructive to the broadcasting industry. I find this very worrisome, because then people act out of intimidation and they don't really act out of a need to do a good job. An attitude develops of "We'd better do this because Washington wants us to do it," or they run scared and then what they do is make the kinds of arrangements with these groups that I personally think are outrageous. They sign a contract which says that they're going to put on certain kinds of programs. Now, those of us who've run stations know that in the final analysis the only one who knows how to run a station is the person running it. I tempered my idealism with the realities of 24 hours-a-day of programming.

CRAWFORD: Let's assume that a station has to be responsive to the community—and you might want to argue this point—but let's say that these groups that work up these petitions to deny are exercising their right as members of the community to question the practices of the station. Now, on the surface that could be a reasonable thing. In some instances, these people are, as you mentioned, filing on lack of data. I mean, they are out of date on this, and maybe it's a matter of trying to find out what is the actual situation of stations. Maybe the stations ought to promote themselves more and provide these data on a regular basis so that there wouldn't be these challenges or, at least, the incentive for these challenges.

TIPTON: The most frustrating thing in the world is to try to get a group of people to come up with one opinion. You get a group—black and brown and white—in a room and say: "What are we doing wrong?" And you can sit there for hours and walk out a schizophrenic. You can't even get one opinion from two Chicanos.

WALLACE: I believe very firmly in the Fairness Doctrine in principle. On the other hand, when the FCC's staff recommended that it had to be incorporated into a single program, I departed from them. Fundamentally, I'm opposed to rigid standards. If we were faced with a choice between an attempt to revise the Fairness Doctrine or to eliminate it completely, or to have more rigid control of it, then I would have to opt to eliminate the Fairness Doctrine and go in the direction of complete freedom of the licensee to make decisions about how that should be carried out.

HENABERY: So, Wes has made a point that fairness should exist on the station, but not necessarily in the same program.

WALLACE: Absolutely.

MILICIA: We should take the intimidation out of the Fairness Doctrine by releasing it from the direct control of Congress and the Executive Branch. It was Congress' baby in the first place but they are always referring to the Executive Branch and not holding up their end of the bargain.

DUNLAP: I haven't any problems with the Fairness Doctrine. The

Commission has ruled time and again that fairness applies overall, not within the body of a particular program, and as long as that exists, I don't see any problem with fairness.

CRAWFORD: How would you evaluate one station against another as to their ability to be fair? I mean, are there no groups of stations that fall into a certain category?

HENABERY: Can I answer that question? Someone in the consulting business whom I talked to recently was saying, "How do you get by with these station operators?" And he said, "Well, a third of them pay their bills; a third you have to ask for the money and a third you have to ask your lawyer to get your money." Now, I think that you're talking about that level of performance in terms of license or in terms of any human endeavor. Your broadcasters are going to be just as human as anybody else. You're going to find excellent people, medium range people and lower level people. Albeit, the standards are set, hopefully, by the leaders of the industry.

TIPTON: My boss, Hugh Terry, had a perceptive expression, he said: "There are more doctors and lawyers in the penitentary than there are broadcasters." Think about that. I don't know of many broadcasters who are in the penitentary.

BARER: It seems to me that the FCC has traditionally insisted that the judgments are station judgments. Even when it comes to religious matters, it is the station's judgment as to whether the program is controversial.

WALLACE: There have been an awful lot of FCC decisions which support station judgment.

BARER: I think it's unrealistic to try to set up national standards for fairness and local standards for fairness. Once you do that, you formalize it and then it becomes rigid, and then you have even more trouble.

WALLACE: I agree, but when you get into the argument at what point does it get decided? By whom? By the courts?

HENABERY: Could be.

WALLACE: Well, but is that the proper place?

BARER: The courts have traditionally ruled in favor of the broadcasters. I think it's a first-rate happening when the FCC reviews provided they are not operating under political pressure. We know this is a reality of life in Washington and I feel that this kind of underhanded activity has got to stop.

GRAY: It is a political world and you're not going to remove the politics from it, but what you can do is mount your own political attack. In other words, we must continue to call attention to the fact that there are certain areas of activity that are improper for Congress and the President. We've got to continue calling attention to some of the chicanery of the OTP.

BARER: I happen to think that, historically, there have been some outstanding people appointed to the FCC. We certainly have a lot of disagreements with Dean Burch, but he is not a foolish man. He's very intelligent, and a very talented individual. We happen to have some different philosophies but I think that he has done as good a job as any of the Chairmen in recent history. Unfortunately, the climate in which the Commission exists is one of Congressional neglect. That's why it is vulnerable to White House and other pressures.

HENABERY: Let's talk a little bit about the counter-advertising issue— the whole area of citizen's groups and others having the right to respond to commercial advertising with counter-advertising.

DUNLAP: Right now the talk on counter-advertising is very quiet. There are still people in both government and out of government who have a great interest in it. Bob Choate is obviously going to continue to press for it. He has very strong convictions along those lines. The cream of the National Communications Center people are quiet on the subject right now, but I have the feeling that it could come up again depending on the political future of Nick Johnson. I think it's something that broadcasters have to be alert to. I do not subscribe to the idea of counter-advertising. I think it is counter-productive. It goes to the heart of a system which could be very seriously injured if it became the law.

TIPTON: Counter-advertising scares me to death. You end up like a bunch of "piranha." I often wonder how much effect anti-cigarette commercials had that were running at the same time as when cigarette commercials were running? I believe in the power of television, I think it's the most powerful thing that's ever happened. Maybe our counter-cigarette advertising had more effect in keeping smoking down than we thought.

MIELKE: I wonder if the anti-smoking spots were constructed with the same kind of sophistication, prior marketing research and budgets as the smoking commercials were? I wonder if, indeed, they were evaluated as the pro-smoking or pro-Winston or whatever are routinely evaluated by the advertising agencies?

TIPTON: I always thought the counter-smoking spots that were produced by the American Cancer Society and the American Heart Association were outstanding.

DUNLAP: Yes, very creative and very persuasive.

MIELKE: The power of the television commercial is in its very ability to exploit innuendo and the power of suggestion.

MILICIA: I think that the anti-smoking commercials were direct and to the point. The commercials for cigarettes dealt with things like selling manliness. If you smoke a Camel, women will flock into your room. I don't think they were out to sell cigarettes. I think that advertisers, and many of you who are in the business will agree, don't really sell a product, they sell sex, love, kissable lips, skin you love to touch and this type of thing. It would be very difficult to make a study comparing what happens psychologically to people when they watch these advertisements.

MENDELOWITZ: I think that the first point that has to be made about advertising on the broadcast media, especially television, is that the rules of the game for television advertising cannot be the same as the rules of the game for other advertising. Television advertising has such power, that it needs to be watched much more carefully than other media. The primary problem is not counter-advertising so much as it is untruth in advertising. The line of attack should be to remove untruth from advertising. The amount of disreputable advertising that takes place is unbelievable. Almost nothing is sold on television on its own virtue. The basic responsibility of advertising in a market economy is to inform the consumer rather than to confuse him. My wife told me that when she was in high school she had a biology teacher who used Listerine as a solution in which to grow bacteria.

The call for Government intervention should be led by the broadcast industry, because you can be sure that Ralph Nader, the Congress and everybody else will if you don't. The Federal Government is just getting off its feet in this. Carter's Little Liver Pills were taken off the air. This was the grossest example because they had nothing to do with the liver. I think this is the most powerful example of television's impact. My son is now 19 months old. His second word was bird; his first two-word combination was "big bird." At 17 or 18 months, when I read the *Sesame Street* book to him, he would point to the big bird in the book and say, "big bird," and I'd say "Where's the big bird?" and he'd sing the *Sesame Street* song.

DUNLAP: The law already provides for the protection of the innocent adult as well as child, you have the Federal Trade Commission, the Federal Drug people, and so forth. Most broadcasters would like to insure against carrying false advertising or misleading advertising. However, there is no way in the world for us to do laboratory testing. There are instruments available and public challenges are being used more and more. More pressure is being put on the FTC and on the Food and Drug people to stop it at the source.

MIELKE: We lack the analytical tools to discuss with a great deal of confidence the analysis of advertising messages. We are not even close, for instance, to being able to analyze a commercial with the precision that a group of lawyers can analyze a contract or a group of logicians can analyze a printed argument.

BARER: Research now shows us that there is a cause-effect relationship, on a general basis, with certain kinds of stimuli. For example, people will be persuaded if there is a certain appeal to the survival motive. If you can show it is to their self-interest, they're interested, and they will be persuaded on most levels of behavior. We know that to exist. It is unrealistic to expect any kind of persuasion—advertising—without that kind of appeal. The reality of human behavior is that they will be persuaded if you appeal to basic motives, basic drives. I'm sure we're all aware of it and that is one of the things that we must come to terms with in criticizing advertising.

HENABERY: Let's spend the remainder of our time discussing Section 315. Are we going to have any Congressional action taken on equal time?

DUNLAP: This is a guessing game for anyone in Washington, but I don't see any change coming in 315. There are several bills in the hopper now that would either suspend it or do away with it completely, but I see no chance of passage, at least, not during this session. I can live pretty well with 315 the way it is. It's the most orderly process we have of dealing with a very disorderly process—our whole campaigning system in this country. I think that under 315 the broadcaster has a certain amount of protection.

WALLACE: I don't think that you can get any change in 315 given the fact that every member of Congress—Senator and Representative— has a vested interest in maintaining 315 precisely as it is. It's for his protection more than for anything else. It benefits the "in" rather than the "out" to a significant degree.

BARER: I don't think there is such a thing as equal time because there is no such thing as equal impact, and the title itself can be terribly misleading to the layman who starts making demands for equal time.

Tau Group

Discussion Leader: John Kelly (Storer Broadcasting)
Industry Participants: Russell Barry (Vice President and General Manager, KNXT, Los Angeles); George Spring (Station Manager, WRGB, Schenectady)
Faculty Participants: Richard Barnhill (Syracuse University); Susan Cailteux (University of Kentucky); Louis Day (Central Michigan University); William Hanks (University of Pittsburgh); William Hawes (University of Houston); Raymond Habiby (Oklahoma State University); John Kittross (Temple University); Jeffrey Lowenhar (University of Connecticut); Lucius New (Texas Southern University); Jon Powell (Northern Illinois University); Daniel Viamonte, Jr. (University of Hartford); Irving Webber (University of Alabama)

KELLY: Our subject is regulations. I think the meat of the discussion should center upon the three elements that are listed in the discussion section—license renewal, Fairness Doctrine, and equal time. Let's keep in mind those questions as we're discussing the whole topic. I would prefer, if the group agrees, that we not discuss license renewal first. Let's save that for the last part of the conversation, and get into the matter of the Fairness Doctrine and equal time.

SPRING: The equal time rule, in my and most broadcasters' opinion, is a horrendous mistake. I think we can go back to the days of the lenient equal-time rule when we had the tremendous, wonderful Nixon/Kennedy Debates. Prior to that waiver, when you had two absolutely outstanding major party candidates on, you had to allow time for all other legally qualified candidates. I remember the pig farmer in Secaucus, New Jersey who was a legally qualified candidate for the presidency of the United States. He requested time whenever a major party candidate appeared. Under Section 315, all qualified candidates, regardless of their chances of winning, get the same amount of time. I frankly see no problem with the Fairness Doctrine. We actively seek both sides of a story and present both sides of a story. We as a company are truly in agreement with the Fairness Doctrine. We think this is what a responsible broadcaster should do to remain a licensee.

KELLY: Does your company editorialize?

SPRING: No, we do not. The reason for it, to be perfectly frank, is that we are owned and operated by the General Electric Company. As you all probably know, the General Electric Company is the fourth largest corporation in the world. If we editorialize we always have to identify ourselves as the General Electric Broadcasting Company, WRGB, WGY and so on. We know that the vast majority of times this may be interpreted as the position of the company, meaning the overall parent company of the broadcasting operation.

DAY: You mentioned waiving Section 315 for the national elections. What about local elections? It seems to me you have two alternatives to Section 315: Either do away with it and prohibit any access for political candidates, or leave it up to the local licensee to provide access. Now, what alternative would you provide for Section 315 at the local level? How could it be handled so that candidates could have equitable representation?

BARNHILL: Under the Fairness Doctrine, do you give both sides within each show?

SPRING: No, you don't have to. It doesn't really have to be equal time as far as the Fairness Doctrine is concerned. Quite often people approach us under what they think is the Fairness Doctrine "right" to speak. And when you turn them down, boy, do they complain.

BARRY: Equal time only applies to candidates during an election campaign. It only applies to non-news broadcasts. Fairness is not a problem per se, because I think an interesting point came up today in relation to the fact that broadcast journalism seems to be recognized by the public as the best source of information. Perhaps, because we have the Fairness Doctrine imposed upon us and are forced to provide balance over a period of time, the public views us favorably. Newspapers have a tendency to be more opinionated in their approach.

LOWENHAR: I would submit to you that in our organization—and this may sound arrogant, I don't mean it to—the journalists observe fairness because their professional credentials would require it.

CAILTEUX: My question now is, do the journalists have control, total control, over programming. Who controls? Is the licensee the one who determines content?

KELLY: The *licensee* is ultimately responsible for everything that goes on over the air.

LOWENHAR: That's right. We all understand that. That's why you hire professional, good journalists.

CAILTEUX: You are saying we have good journalists, and the journalists are supposedly professionals, but the journalists are not the ones in the ultimate decision-making position.

SPRING: I see your point. We accept responsibility. We delegate it. I'm sure that George has not had any problem with General Electric telling him what to put on and what not to put on the air. I've lost advertisers and revenues because of things that have been done by the news department. I don't say that makes me a hero, but I think there are far fewer checks and balances within the news department.

CAILTEUX: You're in a very good position where you have control. It's when you get into some of the smaller markets that you do have people coming in and saying, "You are going to run this bank commercial, and you are not going to run anything on the news opposing banks because I run this bank."

HANKS: A point of information for the notes. Did you say earlier that it was the station that decided not to editorialize, or it was the company that thought it was best not to editorialize.

SPRING: The station.

HANKS: You can editorialize if you want?

SPRING: Sure.

HANKS: But it's your choice as a station, not company policy.

SPRING: Absolutely.

HANKS: In other words, KDKA, that's Westinghouse, makes decisions to editorialize. But you as General Electric don't.

SPRING: General Electric Broadcasting Company.

BARRY: I would observe, too, that I make mine totally independent of the corporation. I can even come out against company positions on issues.

KITTROSS: Equal time is Section 315. That's written into the Communications Act. Next down the line in terms of being able to put salt on the tail of it and know what the hell it means, are the Personal Attack

Rules. Those are, however fuzzy, in the FCC Regulations. Then we come into the real ground of Fairness Doctrine which is controversial issues. The Commission has never been able to sit down and write those and the case law is as muddy as you can imagine. When we talk about the whole area of fairness, I think we've really got to split ourselves and talk about those things that we might be able to do something about, namely the controversial issues. I don't think that Congress is going to change Section 315.

POWELL: Section 315 was put into the Act as a political move. It was enacted by the politicians to protect themselves. We have been cheated by Section 315. The government has forced a profit-making organization into doing nothing rather than risk the dangers of breaking the law. The result has been that the viewer, the listener, the audience and the public have been denied the opportunity to share a very important facet of our American political way of life. Section 315 rather than assuring equal time, has assured no one time. I think it should be abolished.

KELLY: Hear! Hear!

HAWES: WRC-TV, Washington, was petitioned against in September of 1972 on three grounds: programming, ascertainment and employment. In programming, part of the issue involved the Fairness Doctrine. For the first time in history, that I know of, the role of women as portrayed in news, public affairs, and entertainment programming was defined as a controversial issue by the parties here. Could you see the role of women in society as portrayed in entertainment and programming as a controversial issue in which only one side is generally portrayed on the airwaves? If so, then you agree with the Fairness Doctrine's interpretation of the National Organization of Women. If not, then you're taking the side that WRC-TV took.

KELLY: Let's look at the whole question of license renewal.

BARRY: I am now involved in the operation of a television station under the new FCC ruling. We are currently in our six month ascertainment period. The last license that was filed by a CBS station weighed 8½ pounds and was 1,500 pages. It was boring reading with a lousy plot. The time dedicated to that in terms of money, management time, diversion of resources and personnel from perhaps more productive enterprises can't accurately be determined. The ascertainment process is odious in its formality. The idea of it, I think, is very beneficial and very important. I'm new to Los Angeles so I'm finding it a fascinating way to become acquainted with the city. But I think the only people that really benefit from the license renewal process are paper merchants and the lawyers. I just think that's too bad because, again, I think it takes us away from more productive uses of our time and resources and undermines the value of the ascertainment process.

KELLY: Are the seven FCC commissioners and the hundreds of people on the staff really qualified to make a judgment in the matter of a license renewal? Is it feasible that we transfer the determination of a broadcast license to the public, directly?

INDUSTRY COMMENT: In answer to the public judging you, the public will judge you according to whether they like *I Love Lucy* or not. Most of the programming that you do for the public, such as public affairs or public service, isn't watched. I'd be afraid to be judged by the public based upon whether they like my sportscaster's face.

HANKS: I'll respond very briefly to your question, Jack. It seems to me, although it is a provocative question about public determination in license renewal, that it would be antithetical to the public interest and also to broadcaster's interest. Renewal becomes a popularity game and inhibits a broadcaster from being an advocate on issues that he is concerned about. He might take a very unpopular stance just to gain general support.

KELLY: I was thinking in terms of the elimination of frivolous strike applications. Some of you may have read an editorial in *Broadcasting* magazine about four weeks ago, which pointed out that many attorneys in Washington today are actually soliciting and organizing groups to hold up licenses. They make that a living. They're being funded by trusts.

HANKS: I would like to know, since you've raised the point, if you know of one public-interest law firm that does that. I would like to know because I think I know almost every public service lawyer in Washington, and I can't think of one guy who has actively solicited business for personal profit.

KELLY: It would be very difficult to prove, Bill.

POWELL: It seems to me that the FCC ought to do the ascertaining, not the broadcaster. We have put the broadcaster in a situation now of defending himself to his own detriment. He is guilty until proven innocent. I'm not saying that there aren't broadcasters who violate the public trust but I am saying that we have now complicated the bureaucracy to the point where in the 8,000 stations we have we have in effect 8,000 mini FCC's. What we've got to do is work out a system where the broadcaster can broadcast, and the FCC can do some ascertaining as to whether he's responsible or not without putting the broadcaster in the circumstance of forever defending himself. When I think of all the millions and the hours that are spent by broadcasters defending themselves on documents that weigh 8 to 15 pounds, that are never read, I think we have reached "Alice in Wonderland."

HAWES: I tend to agree with that view. I sympathize with the mountains of paperwork that the broadcaster has at license renewal time. Why is there all this work? Why is there all this regulation? It seems to me that it's because the public has lacked the opportunity to actually talk to the vice president/general manager of the several radio and television stations. This man, for many years, lived in an ivory tower. We around this table know a lot about ivory towers. I think that as a result of this paper work and this saber rattling from the FCC the general managers and vice presidents make it their business to listen to the dissidents, to any little guy in the community who takes the trouble to come over to the station and make an appointment to visit him about his problems.

BARRY: Anytime that the FCC gets involved in any of the discretionary areas in terms of ascertainment, the problems of the community and the interests of the community, then I think we've given up the ghost in terms of broadcasting as we see it here. I would fight that.

KELLY: How accessible are you to the public?

BARRY: Reasonably accessible. I answer the phone—whoever calls. I mean, there's a limit. I'm in the community a great deal. Probably not enough. The people who work at the station are indeed out in the community making contacts and working with groups. Now you may presume that the sword is hanging over us and that's why we respond. We would respond anyway as responsible businessmen and citizens of our community. I don't apologize for what we do. But I think we can do more. But I think there's impatience, the impatience of "Let's get it done today," and "Let's protect all those people from themselves." That's the attitude which is mixing up people. The idea that they're not intelligent enough or honest enough to make decisions themselves. Regulation does not treat people as adults.

POWELL: We have, in effect, a bureaucratic effort to assure fairness and access. We tend to think in terms of formula. We arrange a pattern and then we try to interpret everything. Now, our pattern this time is ascertainment. We have a way of getting at the broadcaster through the renewal process—a sword of Damocles. I'm not saying that is good, or bad. What I am saying is that there is another method. We must stop saying: "We'll make you do more because you're going to write more." That is, in effect, what we're doing. We're chasing a bureaucratic dream. This is what the Federal government has done for years. The government creates more paperwork to assure better service. Have we had better service? I don't think so.

KITTROSS: The British did something in 1956, the mere mention of which makes American broadcasters have a heart attack. When renewal time came up for the first commercial television program contract, which is the equivalent of our stations more or less, the governing board, which was the Independent Television Authority said, "You and you are out. We don't think you were doing a good enough job." "B.b..b...but...on what grounds?" "We don't have to tell you. Out." They made it stick. Can you imagine how that would be in this country?

HAWES: I was wondering how it would be to eliminate the present system of license renewal with all the paperwork until you had the protests or whatever from the public. At that time your station would be called to show cause why you should continue.

KELLY: Bill, isn't that where we are now?

HAWES: Now, whether or not you're protested against, you have to file every three years.

KELLY: What you're saying is just discontinue the license and do your work and make sure you've got your homework done. You've got your public file, it's accessible and available. Why go through all the hundreds of thousands and millions of dollars of the filings, and the lawyer fees, and so forth and so on. When somebody in the community thinks that you're not doing the job based upon what you have said you were going to do, then you present your case.

HAWES: If you, as vice president and general manager, cannot resolve it with that group, and you go to the FCC, then you must fully show cause why your station should be renewed.

BARRY: I think most broadcasters sit down with community groups and try to negotiate in good faith, aware of their own inadequacies. If the groups will do the same and will follow up, I don't see many problems, personally.

HAWES: A good broadcaster will not have those groups coming in to him because he has got members of his staff who belong to those groups. He works with them and consults with them.

HANKS: One of the questions before us on the outline, is how we reduce frivolous challenges. It seems to me that you're throwing the FCC right back into the question of how do you decide what is a frivolous cause? The minute you say a legitimate group or a legitimate cause has challenged the license, the Commission must make the determination as to whether that is a frivolous cause. How does the group feel about going to a five-year license renewal?

WEBBER: Why would an extension two years beyond the present refiling period make that much difference? It escapes me how this could make any difference at all. It seems to me that the interests in the community still can make their ideas known.

NEW: Suppose you just eliminated renewal dates and said "anytime." The Commission could really study a situation rather than be besieged by tons and tons of paper during each renewal period.

CAILTEUX: There is an underlying assumption that there has to be some group—some organized group of people—that would raise objections. I don't think that is necessarily the case.

HABIBY: What's wrong with a perpetual license. Why can't it work like a newspaper.

KELLY: Would you move that this group put to a vote the question of perpetual licensing and then we will amend it as we go along? Could we get something down on paper.

HAWES: It doesn't seem to me that there's a real necessity for forcing the many stations throughout the country to go through license renewal and spend all of that money and all of that effort if there has been no public contest in regard to the continuation of that service.

KELLY: I don't think that you'll find any good broadcaster who would be in favor of lessening the power of the community—a community group—I don't think there's a single broadcaster I know.

BARRY: When you have a service that is as broadly based as ours is, it is absolutely required that you be involved in your community and that you be aware of it (the community).

WEBBER: The goal of license renewal is to make sure that the stations know what the situation is and that they're being responsive to it. That they're carrying out what they said they would do. What we're discovering is that this thing is dysfunctional in that it is apparently taking away people from positive, constructive programming efforts and putting them to work on what is essentially a deadend job. The people who have to do it are the people who are right in the middle of your operation, and very important to it. My reaction on the basis of what I've heard here is that the stations are very sensitive to the dangers on non-renewal.

KELLY: Frightened is the word.

KITTROSS: There is one thing about the ascertainment process which hasn't really been talked about. We've talked about promise versus performance. I think we all agree that this is a touchstone we're going to have. We say we're going to do something and we should do it, whatever it is. The thing about the ascertainment process is that it enables you to better know what to promise. Before the ascertainment requirement you may have looked as good as you could when you were in comparative hearing for the initial license, but after that you really didn't have to say much of what your promise was for the next three years. There was a presumption that it would be reasonably good. The ascertainment process enables you to promise for the next three years. I have no objection to five years, myself, at all. It enables you to make better promises, promises you are better able to keep. That is an advantage of ascertainment that I think has been neglected in this.

SPRING: Obviously there's going to be a compromise. There's got to be something done to change this license renewal procedure with or without the length, because it is getting absolutely ridiculous. My contention is that to a good broadcaster who knows what he is doing and who follows reasonable ethics, the ascertainment of a community, the community problems, is totally ridiculous. I, as a good broadcaster should, my manager should, my news department should, my directors should, and my program manager should, know what is going on in the community every day.

HAWES: The broadcaster has become sensitive to the community and the community's problems.

KELLY: Is it the general consensus, then, of the group that the current system is somewhat stultifying to the broadcaster? The immediate solutions are not as apparent as any of us would like them to be.

VIAMONTE: I was just wondering if we would consider Hawes' statement. Is there a way that we can suggest how we can get rid of some of the bureaucracy?

NEW: I go along with the five-year license but I have some conditions. First of all, I think there should be local media monitors to deal with ascertainment continuously. These need not be affiliated in any way with the FCC. If there are no challenges there should be automatic renewals. If there are challenges, these should be sent directly to the media monitor. The FCC would still have the final authority. During this five-year period there should be continuous and close cooperation between local media monitors and the licensee. During the third year of the five-year period formal monitor reports should be filed with the FCC. If there are grounds for a challenge the local monitors would negotiate with the licensee on behalf of the challengers. We must, for the most part come up with guidelines for challenges if it's going to be effective. During the fourth year, if the issue has not been resolved then the licensee would then have to show cause with the FCC.

KELLY: On the media monitor proposal, does that include the newspapers too? Are we going to license the newspapers?

NEW: Of course.

KELLY: You're going to license the newspapers? It won't fly, Orville.

CAILTEUX: I want to say one thing about Lucius' proposal. He said that automatic renewal would occur if the station was not challenged. That is something that I would reject. If there are no challenges, but there is some kind of fraudulent practice that was uncovered, I don't think that that should be automatically renewed.

KELLY: Fraudulent practice is a challenge.

SIGMA GROUP

Discussion Leader: Philip Spencer (WCSS, Amsterdam, New York)
Industry Participants: Wallace Dunlap (Vice President, Group W, Washington, D.C.); Henry Marcott (Manager-Editorial Service, WNBC-TV, New York); Jack Tipton (Station Manager, WMGH-TV, Denver)
Faculty Participants: Richard Goggin (New York University); David Lange (Duke University); Bruce Powers (Niagara University); Arthur Savage (Ohio University)

SPENCER: The subject of this discussion will be regulation. As you know, regulation is a two-pronged problem. Today, broadcasters face not only regulations from the FCC but regulations from Congress as well.

DUNLAP: I think the biggest problem broadcasters have is a lack of recognition of the era we're living through and the conditions we're living with. The existence of the various pressures on broadcasting that are coming from citizens groups and individuals shouldn't be treated with a raised eyebrow. They should be treated constructively. They're here to stay. As a matter of fact, a lot of people don't realize that citizens have a right to protest against a licensee under the Communications Act. It's on page 9 and it says, "Any party may appear before the Commission and be heard." Now the way they're being heard is through petitions to deny, impeding applications in a few cases, and the other pressures that broadcasters are feeling. These are people exercising the right which is guaranteed them in the Communications Act. We don't have to like it, but we have to realize it and deal with it on a reasonable and sensible basis and possibly even turn it to something constructive for ourselves.

TIPTON: We just filed our license renewal application the week between Christmas and New Years, and it was in three volumes and weighed over 30 pounds.

DUNLAP: I'd like to add something to what Tip just said about the poundage of the license renewal applications. We had a golden opportunity but we may lose it now that Burch is going to leave the Commission. He testified before the MacDonald Committee that they don't want all that paper. This was the Chairman of the FCC speaking. "We don't want all that paper. We never asked for it. The broadcasters themselves decided to send it to us."

TIPTON: After reading Burch's comments and talking with our attorneys we decided to considerably reduce the size of our renewal applications. However, we're going to have that much back-up in the files. You still have to produce the material.

SPENCER: Let me just go through some areas that the NAB is involved in now, as far as regulation and legislation goes. Maybe that will give you something to talk about. The first priority is license renewal, but they are also concerned with lottery legislation. As you know, radio and TV now are precluded from carrying any kind of information or advertising while newspaper and outdoor advertising media can carry lottery advertising. Daylight Savings Time, as it affects broadcasters, is another issue, also copyright problems. There is a move on for legislation to charge stations 2% more on top of what they're paying the music licensing companies now for performing artists. That's going to be a lot of money. Equal time, of course, you are all familiar with; political advertising; campaign reform; and of course, the real back-burner, counter-advertising are all major issues to keep in mind.

The pressure for regulation is not coming from inside government. The pressure is coming from the public and they are not pressuring radio, they're pressuring television. As long as they keep that pressure on television, regulation will be responsive to it. It's the only cop-out available to the bureaucracy to say to the citizens, "We took action on your complaint. We're making these people accountable for what they do." However, I don't find the regulation process as difficult as some of my brothers in broadcasting. I think it is pretty simple. Radio has become immeasurably easy with the de-regulation process. I'll just give you an idea of what de-regulation means to a small broadcaster like myself. Relief in areas such as taking meter readings every half hour and having full-time engineers on our staff saves little stations (like mine in Amsterdam, New York and in Herkimer, New York) almost $5,000 a year. I don't know too much about television, but I think license renewal is a real problem for the television broadcasters. It is no problem for radio broadcasters except in those few markets where somebody might file against a station.

FACULTY COMMENT: If cable television ever gets off the ground would some relief for the television broadcaster occur?

LANGE: I don't suppose there is any doubt that if cable television were really freed from its present regulatory structure it could relieve the regulatory pressures on broadcast television. The difference is that it would also make broadcast television largely irrelevant. Perhaps that's the kind of paradox you pose. I said broadcast television. Radio has a different place because it serves an audience which simply can't be reached by cable—people in cars. There is another reason why radio has almost ceased to be regulated—people don't view the impact of radio with any real concern. Unless we free cable from its present regulation I frankly do not see much likelihood that the television regulations will become less onerous. In fact, I think that they will become more and more burdensome.

POWERS: I was a propaganda analyst for the government for many years in Central Europe. I've seen how the governments over there reacted to the development of television. I think it is quite obvious that most of the major industrial countries of the world have used television as a propaganda instrument and have set up regulatory boards accordingly. We are one of the few countries in the world where there is a relatively unregulated broadcast system in the sense of dissemination of information. I can see, from a managerial standpoint, how these vociferous, sometimes marginal, groups annoy the administrator of a station. Time is money to him. The broadcaster works on the idea that he's got to make money to keep broadcasting. One major opposition to American broadcasting around the world, particularly in Central Europe, is that it only operates on a profit motive. Broadcasters want to sell goods to continue operating and they don't care what they sell as long as they make a profit. Now I realize that this is untrue. But there is a certain grain of truth in it, as you say.

SPENCER: I think all of the broadcasters here can admit that we have stations to make a profit. I'm in business to make a profit and that's the uppermost thing in my mind. Now I cannot continue to do that unless I operate my station properly or they will take my license away.

Let's go into another area now. Let me ask our guest broadcasters how they find problems in dealing with the public over the Fairness Doctrine, for example. Is there something that you're having problems with? Can you live with it? Do you feel you could better serve the public if the Fairness Doctrine were changed? What about equal time? We're two years away from a Presidential election. Do you feel you can adequately serve the public under Section 315? I would also like to have you address yourself to the problem of counter-advertising. Do you feel that this would serve any purpose if a piece of legislation is adopted?

TIPTON: Well, first of all I feel very comfortable with the Fairness Doctrine. Equal time bothers me a little bit because I think it deprives the viewers. We have had the situation every broadcaster has, where you set up a debate between the Democrat and the Republican, and three other candidates come out of the woodwork and demand equal time. We have no problems at all with the Fairness Doctrine. In fact, we're a little frustrated. We go on the air, like a lot of broadcasters, saying we have made time available for a free speech message. You may go on the air and talk about anything you want to. Just give us a call, come in and fill out a form. Five people came in and talked about the cross on the mountain.

DUNLAP: I have great enthusiasm for the Fairness Doctrine, not as a regulatory matter, but as a statement on behalf of the total industry that the people have a voice in what goes out over the air. I think if you handle it with the right attitude it can be an enriching part of your program scheme. What you must do in order to meet the requirements of the Fairness Doctrine gives you better programming if you handle it right.

MARCOTT: In Buffalo we tried allowing people to come in and do their own commentaries. We were swamped. It actually got to the point where we were doing so many takes, trying to keep people from flubbing, that it got too expensive. So we discontinued it. Now at WNBC-TV we have one hell of a time fishing out people to reply to editorials.

SPENCER: Do you feel that television stations would be able to serve the public better if equal time were to be waived? In other words let's say you do have seven candidates but only two really amount to anything. Do you feel that the present law discourages stations from putting on more debates between candidates because they would be subject to five hours additionally, an hour for each candidate?

TIPTON: Yes, but maybe I'm being overly dramatic because I can remember some bad experiences out of the past. I think it has inhibited some broadcasters.

DUNLAP: I have no quarrel with 315. It gives us' an orderly way to handle what is basically a disorderly process.

LANGE: There isn't enough ideological profile on a typical television station. This is essentially so at a local level and certainly so at networks.

TIPTON: You're saying TV stations don't deal with controversial editorials?

LANGE: That's essentially what I'm saying. But it's a generalization that I'm willing to argue about, because if I'm wrong I would like to be shown how I'm wrong.

SPENCER: You're wrong as far as New York State goes. I know they all editorialize. Jim, I wonder if you could just tell us a little bit about the number of editorial types you get. Are they controversial or are they for "mother, God and country?"

INDUSTRY COMMENT: They are controversial. They raise eyebrows.

GOGGIN: Why is there a lot of flak among certain segments of the television broadcasting industry for a modification or throwing out of the Fairness Doctrine? What are the opposing points of view? You feel comfortable with it. You said it protected you in certain ways. What do you feel the reason is for these positions which are in opposition to yours?

DUNLAP: I just don't know. I don't think anybody has taken a poll. There are a variety of reasons for negative feelings toward the Fairness Doctrine. One objection may be a philosophical opposition to government intervention in the operation of the station. This is seen as a step in that direction. Another may be the fact that in order to meet your Fairness Doctrine obligations you've got to work a little harder. This might be a hardship on small operators in terms of personnel.

TIPTON: I don't feel uncomfortable with the Fairness Doctrine. Of course we're the only station in our market that consistently editorializes. I can only speak for my own station.

SPENCER: In the four years that I've been on the NAB Board we've discussed the Fairness Doctrine only in the context of advertising and counter-advertising. Outside of that area I don't know of a broadcaster among the 45 that I serve with on the NAB Board, who is opposed to the Fairness Doctrine.

FACULTY COMMENT: Juet let me comment on the thought advanced here as to whether broadcasters in editorializing get into meaningful issues. Do broadcasters who editorialize tackle the major issues that come down the pike in their community? The answer, it seems to me, is clearly yes. It would be a rare broadcaster who really is editorializing who would duck those things which do come down the pike. If the question is whether they are fully explored, probably not. That's not the nature of editorializing, particularly to broadcasters. Editorializing is largely a matter, it seems to me, of tackling the major problems of the community.

SPENCER: Would you suggest changing the regulations by which stations have to operate to allow free discussion and the use of any kind of language?

LANGE: Sure. Unquestionably.

SPENCER: In other words, then, the recommendation that you would make is that there be more freedom for stations to carry more outspoken types of things.

LANGE: That's one aspect of what I would certainly suggest. I'm suggesting the conceptual predicates for some changes and regulations which go beyond that. It's a kind of conceptual predicate which suggests to the viewers that the responsibility we need is irresponsibility.

DUNLAP: The direction of regulation is toward more and more confinement. The Democratic National Committee case sets the stage for it. The NBC pension plan case, which will undoubtedly reach the Supreme Court in another year or so, will further increase restrictions under the Fairness Doctrine. You will have, in essence, less and less option to provide the open message forum on a voluntary basis and more and more the requirement to do it without the right of control.

SPENCER: I would like to hear the educators, the economists and the lawyers discuss the question of how a broadcaster goes about not being discriminated against? Let me tell you what I'm talking about. The broadcast media lost $250 million a year in cigarette advertising, but no other media were restricted from continuing to carry it. The newspapers and billboards can carry armed forces paid advertising, radio and television stations can't. The newspapers are getting post office advertising, the broadcast media must carry that stuff largely as public service. Newspapers can sell time to politicians at any rate they want, broadcasters are forced to sell time to politicians at their lowest single unit rate. Outdoor media and newspapers can carry lottery advertising, broadcasting can not. How would you suggest broadcasters go about getting some relief in this area so that they are not discriminated against by either the FCC or Congress?

SAVAGE: The Georgia Association of Broadcasters has a very excellent reputation as a political lobby. The association is not just the social drinking operation which I have found in most organizations. These people can bring tremendous pressure to bear on their own state legislature. The president of the Georgia Association of Broadcasters had a straight line to Senator Richard Russell during the days when he was alive. I would submit that may be one way to do it. There is nothing like the local guys getting Sam Smatz from 138th Congressional District of Colorado backed up in a silver mine. Punch him in the belly and give him the facts of life. If state associations will begin to apply that kind of pressure on the local congressman you would see results.

TIPTON: I think most broadcasters today have a straight line to their Congressional delegation because they look to us for a voice to their constituencies.

FACULTY COMMENT: Broadcasting has decided on its own not to advertise hard liquor. Why?

SPENCER: I can give you the answer in two words. Senator Magnuson. If broadcasters even start advertising hard liquor they will bring the wrath of God down on beer and wine which they now can advertise. He has made that statement publicly for the last 20 years. There is nothing in the law that says you can't advertise hard liquor. It's prohibited by the NAB code. In other words, if I want to go out tomorrow with a Cutty Sark commercial on my station I can't because I, myself, am a member of the Code. The reason broadcasters don't fight it is because Magnuson has promised that if they ever did that he will take off wine and beer.

Let me introduce a new thought: If you could wake up tomorrow and have one regulation changed, only one, what would that be?

TIPTON: From a financial management—and from a "conservation" point of view—I would like to see the five-year renewal put through. I didn't realize until a couple of years ago that it's not only commercial licenses that have to be renewed, *every* police department, *every* fire department, *every* ship at sea has to renew his license every three years, in other words, everyone who uses the broadcast spectrum!

Program Content: Or, What Are We Going To Do To Fill The Time Between Commercials?

A VETERAN PROGRAMMER, speaking before an IRTS audience a few years ago, said: "Some of you may not believe this, but nobody ever sets out to make a bad program." It's like the businessman who said: "Here I am, the head of a non-profit corporation. We didn't incorporate not-for-profit— it just turned out that way!" Lance S. was preparing remarks to be made at a luncheon of the local Lions Club, and thought that these anecdotes would be a good way to ease into his subject, "Television Programs Today." He intended to state his programming goals and relate all of his comments to the goals. Listed on separate cards were the goals along with brief phrases to guide his comments.

> *Audience popularity* (not necessarily identical with top ratings)— faithfulness of listeners/viewers, mail response, clamor for participation on show, ability of air personality to identify with sponsors, personal appearances, etc.

> *Ratings dominance* (should be closely tied to above, but not necessarily in terms of frequency and reach)—if on top of the heap, this in turn makes sales easy for the national sales rep as well as local salesmen.

> *Profitable return* on the program period (and herewith a *caveat:* if the program cost of popularity and dominance is too much, the net return too meager, he might better settle for second best in cost-effort and come out ahead!)

He called in his secretary to listen to his speech, and proceeds from the point of stating his goals.

"And so, the local television programmer scales his efforts, and sets his goals on the optimistic side. The goals are several, some singular, some compatible, some capable of a degree of overlap; others are seemingly in conflict with one another. Remember that the man I work for is incorporated for profit. In following his direction, I never set out to create a bad program, or to assemble blocks of programs that have less than maximum potential."

"Now if you stop to think of the goals that I have outlined, you'll soon realize that essentially they're no different than the ones you set for the operation of your hardware store, or your 200-seat movie theatre, or your beer 'n' burger franchise. You should now ask yourselves if there is any point of differentiation between our businesses. There is, and it's a major one. In fact, it's a point that goes back some 40 years and it hangs over the broadcaster exclusively. Aha, you say, now I know he doesn't know what he's talking about. Television didn't even exist 40 years ago. Right you are. Except that the rules that were formulated for radio 40 years ago, now apply to television to a much greater degree than radio. The key is to perform in the interest, convenience and necessity of your reachable audience. There are new words, like ascertainment, and loud, clamorous, even raucous sounds from minority groups—'minority' doesn't mean only Black any more, but depending on the market, Chicanos, American Indians, the United Church of Christ and the League of American Wheelmen, and any other organized group that wishes to be heard."

"Our station can't afford the services of a religious advisor, or a full-time public affairs director—it must rely on outside advisories from responsible groups. Here in this market alone, we have local and regional councils of churches, ministerial associations, assorted medical charities, state and national advertising councils, and a score-or-more of similar ethical—but biased groups. These are our judges and critics. And once every three years it becomes a contest to see if we have convinced them of our sincerity and honest desire to serve this community well."

"But it is the challenge of creating programs that will satisfy my management, my own creative tastes, and answer the needs of the community that draws me on. The opportunity created by the prime-time access rule gave me a regular slot to fill with new local products. I know we tried, but we couldn't ever hope to fill 7 hours weekly with original local programs. Now we've lost some of that time back to the network. We still have plans to upgrade our access programming. I can announce the signing of an agreement with the Atomic stations to exchange 26 half-hour programs per year, which will allow us to double the number of original programs we had been producing for our special services. The programs are better now, and they will continue to improve."

DISCUSSION POINTS:

The single largest problem is: how to service, acknowledge, give time and pay homage to, the many clamoring voices—without alienating the general audience, losing rating points, and essentially diminishing the potential of profitable return?

One phase of the problem is, then—how do you determine what your local audience *really* wants to see?

How do you estimate in advance the amount of time that you can profitably devote to women's shows, children's shows, local sports programs, news documentaries and religious programming?

Even when you have arrived at this herculean decision, how do you then select which of the possible entries in each category will produce the maximum sales potential?

In relation to the minority programming you do choose to broadcast, how do you know that its message is getting to the intended viewer and that he is reacting to the message?

And last, but certainly (in this day of loosening taboos) not least, are *you* and should you be the censor of programs "in the public interest?"

IOTA GROUP

Discussion Leader: Frank Harden (State Broadcasting Company)
Industry Participants: William Stiles (Spanish International Network, New York); Seymour Horowitz (Program Director, WABC-TV, New York)
Faculty Participants: Robert Haccoun (Ohio State University); John Keshishoglou (Ithaca College); Philip Macomber (Kent State University); Peter Pringle (University of Florida); Robert Schlater (Michigan State University); Charles Shipley (Southern Illinois University)

HARDEN: We now come to the important product itself. What do you have to sell? What do you have to offer to attract listeners and viewers? We have before us a case dealing with one Lance S. who is preparing a speech for the Lion's Club on the subject, "Television Programs Today." Our experts are with us to discuss the important matter of program content, or, to put it another way: "What are we going to do to fill the time between commercials." I don't know who dreamed that line up but I'm sure that in the minds of some people that is the way it should be approached. Yet I, as a broadcaster, feel it to be the most important thing there is because without the program you can't move on to anywhere else. So, let's take it from here.

HACCOUN: Mr. Stiles, the stations you represent cater to the Spanish community. What does that imply for America as a melting pot?

STILES: I think there is a trend today away from the melting pot. There was this feeling in the early part of the 20th century when the waves of Irish, Italians, Jewish and Polish immigrants came in here, the idea was to become Americans. I think that to some degree we now have this going the other way. We have pride in being Italian or pride in being Spanish which you didn't find even 10 years ago.

Now, where does this express itself in the mass media? In the last two years, two magazines with in excess of 6 million circulation folded. It's because they were not meaningful to enough people anymore; they were trying to be all things to all people. Now from that standpoint, with due deference to Seymour Horowitz and the fine organization that he works for, I think that they have to be very careful that it doesn't happen to them—that they don't become a dinosaur for the simple fact that they're too big.

Radio stations, to some degree, are specialized. You have rock stations, you have classical music stations, you have all-talk stations, all-news stations. The reason this has not been happening in television is that there aren't enough channels. The Federal Communications Commission decided on a mixed system of VHF and UHF stations in this country to satisfy the 96 television stations that had been granted prior to the 1948 "freeze." If the FCC had come out with a UHF system in 1948, you wouldn't have the present scarcity of channels, and wide diversity in program types would be possible. There is absolutely no reason in the world why there should not be a Black television network in the United States. It's a damn shame that there isn't. But the problem is the lack of a facility and the difficulty of operating on UHF. The Spanish International Network is *all* UHF and we operate successfully. Fortunately from our standpoint, we have a hard core of probably half of the 11 or 12 million Spanish-speaking people in the United States who are not effectively reached by other broadcasters. They've got to come to us, and as a consequence, we at least have a base. But you don't have that kind of language problem with the other specialized "minority" groups.

HACCOUN: Well, you've made an economic argument here for specialization. Back to my original question: What does that imply for America?

STILES: Why shouldn't you have stations that could specialize in any particular thing that they want? I'm not talking about specializing from an ethnic standpoint but rather an interest standpoint. Why shouldn't you have programs for stamp collectors and programs for dog lovers and programs for people who like needlepoint—or whatever it is.

HOROWITZ: Let me ask you a question: Do you think that the second or third generation of Spanish-speaking people will continue to cling to their life style? Hasn't the general procedure been that people become more Americanized and want to become part of the main stream?

STILES: Well, I think this is the first thing that we're concerned about from an economic standpoint and the second thing is whether this is really a good thing. The Spanish-speaking people in this country have been here longer than we have. In the Southwest, they predate our own so-called Anglo culture. We have very successful stations in Los Angeles and San Antonio, and in those cities the Hispanic-Americans are third and fourth generations.

HOROWITZ: What I'm trying to say here, is this: Can an advertiser support an all-stamp-collecting station? The costs of running a television station versus the costs of running a small magazine are so different. Even your costs, in UHF, aren't the same as ours. If you had the unions and all the talent costs that we do, I wonder if you could really stay in business.

STILES: No. I think you're right, if we had to do things the way you do. I think that's the problem. Some people hold out the hope that CATV will provide this multiplicity of channels and allow people to do things inexpensively. There is no reason that you have to run a television station with $100,000 cameras.

HOROWITZ: What you're saying then is if you want that type of specialized station, you have to pay for it. That's what you're leading up to . . .

STILES: Yes, of course.

HACCOUN: Well, up till now, we've always used the example: Can a TV station be supported by catering to billiard players and stamp collectors? But what if I were to ask you: Can a television station survive if all that it broadcasts is sports?

HOROWITZ: I think that was tried. The Kaiser (UHF) stations tried that and I don't think that they made it . . .

KESHISHOGLOU: I would like to ask Mr. Horowitz a question regarding programming. I live in a market where we have several channels, open channels. We have a cable system in Manhattan which provides additional stations. My question therefore is: How do you determine what your local audience really wants to see in view of the fact that there are so many channels available to him?

HOROWITZ: Well, I think that what you determine is pretty much what your ratings show you. That is the way we have of measuring the popularity of a show. You measure what the bulk of the audience wants. They like movies, they like police programs and so on. You also decide on a certain type of programming because of your obligations. You program for minorities, children and so on. I think that is the best measurement of where you go. You study your competition. You know, of course, that you want to have news; or better yet, you study how much time you have for local programming. The most important area for local programming is between 4:30 and 8 P.M., excluding a half hour for network news. You also study what you have in program inventory. Nowadays, it seems that the 18-to-49 woman does the buying and so you go after her. Therefore, we schedule movies from 4:30 to 6:00 P.M. The movies are specially chosen and we make sure that they appeal primarily to the audience that we want. Even though we may not get the largest rating, we still deliver the demographics we're after.

KESHISHOGLOU: At what particular point, do you address yourself (if you do, indeed, at all) to such mundane problems confronting New York City as crime, drugs, etc. You're reporting news, but you're not doing in-depth analysis.

HOROWITZ: There are several places where it's done. We have a half hour public affairs show in prime-time, 7 to 7:30 P.M. on Saturday, called *People, Places And Things.* That show is devoted to looking into these problems. We also have from 7 to 9 in the morning a show we call *A.M. New York,* which handles all of these public affairs types of questions. We bring people in from all over the city. Occasionally, we do specials in prime-time.

MACOMBER: An editorial comment. I happen to come from the Cleveland area which is one of the strongest ethnic areas in the United States. There are five major ethnic groups in Cleveland. Like many cities, Cleveland is in real trouble because it cannot get, at any given point in time, any more than two of these groups to move in the same direction at the same time. The politicians keep fostering the ethnic characteristics of the city, which in turn, defeat the politicians' ability to solve the city's problems.

SCHLATER: I want to know what WABC does for the Spanish minority audience in New York City? And Bill, what do you do when some national event occurs (i.e. a major presidential address). Do you carry it?

STILES: Yes.

SCHLATER: In English?

STILES: No. We carry him in English and we translate over him. We take him down under to where you can just about hear his voice, and somebody translates, just as they do at the United Nations.

COMMENT: Simultaneously?

STILES: Yes!

SCHLATER: Do you feel any obligation to program for minorities, given that your majority is Spanish?

STILES: No. That is what I was trying to say in the beginning. The FCC tacitly allows radio stations to program to very specific audiences. In other words, you can program only rock and roll music, and ignore everyone who likes anything else and get away with it, if some broadcaster is serving the other portions of the community. I don't feel guilty about the possibility of polarizing the community or perpetuating separateness because we are dealing with a minority that has been in this country for a long time and have a right to see their heritage and their culture, to maintain pride through their own awareness and involvement, rather than through the eyes of the Anglo population. This is the problem the black community has had. The black community is portrayed in all media—movies, radio, television and magazines—through the eyes of white people. Racial and ethnic groups need separateness and need to have pride. Through pride in yourself you can integrate into a community on the same level as everyone else. People should not come into the Anglo culture by being granted entrance. They have this right and they should come in with pride in their heritages.

HOROWITZ: I think that our obligation is to treat the members of our community, and give them a chance to be seen and heard, based on what we promised and are supposed to do. And I would like to do that because there is so much color in the Puerto Rican and Latin communities. The music alone shakes me all up. It's a great area in which to develop programming.

STILES: Seymour is right and I think that Seymour has to program his station that way. But I see his role, in relationship to the Spanish community, as more of an interpreter to the bulk of his audience, which is Anglo. That's where I think that he can serve to change the Anglo attitudes about Spanish-speaking people. We have to speak to the Spanish-speaking people on how you get a better job, how you work up in the world, stay in school, do these things. This is our job, talking to Spanish people . . .

MACOMBER: But this is a duality of responsibility. You're giving him a different responsibility than what you have . . .

STILES: Are you in favor of that or against it?

MACOMBER: I'm calling attention to it.

HOROWITZ: Well, I don't think that we're sharing the responsibility with him at all. Are we?

MACOMBER: He has no responsibility for your audience, but you have some responsibility to his?

STILES: Well, that is for him . . . between him and his maker, the FCC. I think that when WABC got their original licenses they said that they were going to serve the entire community. When I got my license, I said only one thing, I'm going to serve the Spanish-speaking community because nobody else is doing a good job with that. That's the basis on which we were granted a license, and it's foolish for us to think that we're doing anything else because anyone that doesn't speak Spanish is not going to watch our station.

SHIPLEY: I don't think, Mr. Stiles, that this is an Anglo culture; it's an American culture and it's always developed out of the melting pot. I'm really shocked to find that there is a double standard in licensing, and I wanted to ask Mr. Horowitz first of all, if he feels that that isn't an unfair disadvantage that his station must serve a multitude of minority interests whereas a specially authorized network has no such requirement? Do broadcasters of the standard sort feel that they are victims of a double standard?

HOROWITZ: In New York State and New York City, you see signs now, directional signs in the subways and so on, that are bi-lingual—in Spanish and in English—so it is becoming a way of life there. In voting, in New York City, I think the ballot now has to be printed in Spanish and also in English. They went to court over that. So I can't say that it's unfair for us to have to program to Spanish people. I'm not saying this just because it's being recorded. Our obligation of a half hour a week for this minority group is not that much of a strain, and I also think that it serves a commercial purpose. It brings some of that audience to your station, and they might find things there that they don't find on Bill's station.

SHIPLEY: The government is getting into more and more specific types of broadcast regulation. You're getting close now to a quota system of programming. Do either of you gentlemen think that you could operate under a system similar to that used in Scandanavian countries and practiced informally on the BBC channels—compulsory, non-duplication of program types? Do you think that the private networks that we have in this country might come to the point where they are enjoined to have a variety of pro-grams in any given time slot? Would it be beneficial? Would it be operative in a capitalist broadcasting system?

HOROWITZ: From the programmers point of view, I would like to do the programming completely—where to place it, how to place it, where to compete. I would not like to see us regulated that way. That is a personal thing.

SHIPLEY: Would it adequately satisfy the citizen's groups and the multitude of government agencies?

HOROWITZ: No, I wouldn't buy that at all. This is the way for us to go. That is why this television system is the best in the world. Sure, we fall flat sometimes and sometimes our programs are not the best. England might send over a BBC hour that does very well on Public Broadcasting, but I think over-all, we're doing a very good job and the minute they regulate us more and more, we become like the gas company and the electric com-pany and eventually the pressures are so great that you're no longer free television. There is no opinion kept off the air; we offer the full spectrum of public opinion.

STILES: From the standpoint of the law, I'm not sure that we have a requirement to serve the entire community. When you talk in terms of serving other segments of the community, if you really dig into it, you will find the service of the VHF stations in New York is relatively minimal, on a percentage basis for the broad market.

HOROWITZ: The programs that we do for these minorities have more relevance I think, and I don't mean to be derogatory about your programs, because when we do them we go right to the heart of the issue. I think there's the difference. Another thought about Government-guided programming, I think the industry self-regulates its programming.

PRINGLE: There is evidence to prove that there is a growing disenchantment on the part of the people. People are getting just a little disenchanted with the regular program fare that is fed down the line, particularly in prime-time.

HOROWITZ: Which survey found that people were disenchanted?

PRINGLE: Bauer's study found that whereas, 10 years ago, people were looking to television to provide them with an escape from reality, today they are relying on it more and more as an escape *into* reality. In other words, they were turning to it more and more for information purposes and less and less for entertainment purposes. There was a Harris study that was published in *Life* Magazine in the Fall of 1971 which showed that, particularly among the black community, there is a growing disenchantment with prime-time reliance on situation comedy.

HOROWITZ: There are more people watching television now, more than ever before. So, if there is disenchantment, I guess they are finding something there that they do like. Programs like *All In The Family, Sanford* and *Maude* touch, however deeply or lightly, on current life; I think there's a lot to attract many people.

PRINGLE: I maintain that most of us, when we criticize commercial American broadcasting, play by the wrong rules. We're looking towards it as a public service medium, we're forgetting all about its role as a commercial or as a business medium. American television provides a means of moving goods and services. The problem is that we have to put up with hypocrisy. Many of the people who come to the campus aren't as honest as you are and they say, "No, we're here to serve the public." They deny the economic factors—whether it's going to attract a larger audience or make them a greater profit.

SHIPLEY: I have great fun within my classes with my students who are highly intelligent (they feel) and sophisticated. They feel that nothing should be kept off the air because that is an abridgement of freedom, and they look with favor on that Ontario station in Canada, which played X-rated films. What should or should not go on the air, in this day and age?

HOROWITZ: You do not censor anything. Certainly, you do not censor opinions. The only thing that you have to worry about is obscenity, and even that is . . . well, what is obscenity? Also, you must be sure that statements aren't made to slander someone. You must notify the party who has been attacked and allow him a chance to respond to the attack. As far as program content is concerned, we weigh our programs by the time of day in which they are shown. We are moving into an era where I think that with maturity you can handle certain types of programming and certain subjects without offending people.

SHIPLEY: What about a small minority that finds certain program content offensive?

HOROWITZ: Should a small minority determine program content?

STILES: We do censor programming to a degree, because it's a little more complicated for us since something might be offensive in the Puerto Rican community and not be offensive to Cubans or Mexican-Americans. We have a commercial for a detergent that was done by one of the New York agencies in which they used the word, "el sussio." Well, the word "el sussio" is a perfectly fine word for saying dirt in New York, but it means something quite dirtier than dirt in the Southwest. Yes, we do censor because we have a responsibility to do that. We are responsible for what goes on our air, and damn right we will censor it if we feel that it is necessary.

RIIO GROUP

Discussion Leader: Robert Henabery (ABC AM Radio Stations)
Industry Participants: Robert Rice (General Manager, WRAU-TV, Peoria); George Lyons (Station Manager, WZZM-TV, Grand Rapids)
Faculty Participants: Kenward Atkin (Michigan State University); Bertram Barer (California State University, Northridge); Robert Crawford (Queens College); Allan Geoffrey (University of Hartford); Keith Mielke (Indiana University); Allan Mendelowitz (Rutgers College); Maureen Milicia (Marshall University)

RICE: I think the problem is well stated. It is a constant battle; it's sometimes like keeping eight or ten balls in the air. We must recognize that we do have information to look at which should be used. The ratings are a significant tool. In our market, we have three sweeps a year, February-March, May, and November. They give us a pretty good indication of what the public wants. What they generally like against certain competition, and that is a big factor because programs moved in different time periods can sometimes do much better. We also look at what is happening in other markets. Does a particular program in syndication, or feature film, do well in another market? Would it do well in Peoria? Is there application of a show of this nature on our station?

LYONS: I find that in programming a station it's important that the people who run the station, from the News Department down to the foremen, serve the public. Serve the public with a good show to get good ratings and to get good dollars.

MIELKE: I'd be intrigued to know about managerial ability to predict what those ratings are before they come out. If you take your blank book right now and write down the figures, how close would they be to the ones that come in? And through what process would you make those predictions and have you done it in the past and how accurate are you? Are you really flying by the seat of the pants or is there a synthesizing kind of management expertise that can pretty well psych it out?

RICE: If I might, I would like to indicate that I won $2 on some estimates from my salesmen. I think it added up to be $14; $2 a shot.

LYONS: I'll tell you how good I was in syndication. I thought that *Sea Hunt* wouldn't make it because a guy can't stay underwater. But, I think the habit is there; you get a sense; you get a feeling from the years in the business and you watch the audience. What is available at this time? Are there only children in the audience, or are there also adults watching? And then you sit down and flip a coin.

HENABERY: What do you forecast the positions of the three networks to be five years down the road?

RICE: I think it's going to depend on whether ABC is able to attract enough primary affiliates. They still are penalized by not having equal exposure in the major markets. Where NBC or CBS may have a line-up of 200 stations, ABC may have 175 stations. The national ratings reflect consideration of that factor.

ATKIN: Do you have a bottom level in the ratings when you say, "Boy this is time I get rid of this program?" Or do you just die with them?

RICE: I've never established a bottom rating. In fact, I don't even talk in terms of ratings. I talk in terms of shares. If you're getting a 33 share, you feel you're holding your own. If you're in for a 40 share, you're a winner. If you're doing a 20 share, you're pretty nervous. Somewhere in there without a specific figure, a red light does flash.

BARER: In terms of sports programming, what kind of shares are you getting with local sports and national sports?

LYONS: We're doing very well, as ABC was built on sports. We're a sports network and I think we've got the best sports crews in the country and the best announcers. Locally, we have a 52-week sports package in which you pay X amount of dollars for all the sports shows, so if the network throws in an extra show, you run it.

BARER: Professional football, as you know, is an American obsession and the ratings are absolutely super prime. And yet, the network people that I talk to claim they are just breaking even. Do you guys believe this?

LYONS: They're going to make a buck or lose a buck depending on how they keep their books but they've got remote crews, they've got engineers, they've got cameras and equipment, they've got four or five different remotes to do. I think possibly they are making a buck but guess it's pretty close, the rights costs keep zooming, but advertising rates also have gone up.

MENDELOWITZ: I was wondering if we could discuss program censorship?

RICE: The first *Happy Days* show caused serious problems. It was billed as a great family program. *The Waltons* all over again, nostalgia. It ended up being a pretty suggestive program. There were many parents who were annoyed and perturbed at being bilked into seeing something that they thought was going to be family and seeing what they saw. Based on that prior publicity, we did not screen the program, but we certainly called the network the next day with a very strong statement that either that program shapes up or it's not going to be kept in that early time spot. Our intent would not have been to eliminate the program—it would have been to move it to a later time period. We came very close on *Rosemary's Baby*. We screened the program—and they really butchered it so badly that it became an innocuous film. We did do a disclaimer at the beginning of the program. Not that sex was a problem, but for religious reasons you may not want your children or your family to see this particular program. The licensee, not the network, is responsible for programming. The network has no license. I can't pass the buck any further than myself at our station. I give the final word. I've got to make the decision and the point is that we have a license to preserve. Now, if I felt in all sincerity that a given program was not proper to air, my first policy determination would be not to pre-empt the program but to play it at another time period.

LYONS: I did a preview of the first *Happy Days* program. The network sends down all their prime-time shows on a closed circuit before they air, so you have an opportunity to look at them. I sat in my office and I laughed like gang-busters because I thought that the show was very funny. That evening I watched the show at home with my 7-year old daughter and my 17-year old daughter and I got a different feeling. What you see in the office sometimes does not go into your living room with the same intent. The next day the phones rang off the walls and the letters came into the station. I think the main problem with *Happy Days* was that they promoted it to be a family-type wholesome show. And it didn't turn out that way. Here's a guy trying to get the bra off of a blind date. Well, that's what happened.

CRAWFORD: My question goes into another area. Grand Rapids, Michigan seems to be part of the Bible Belt. I was wondering, how does this affect the problems of local criticism and pressure? And is it comparable to say Peoria?

RICE: The same . . .

LYONS: He's in the Bible Belt, too. We try to get as involved as we can with the religious leaders of the community.

CRAWFORD: What about flak and so on about your programming?

LYONS: We get flak only when we run commercials or shows in kids' time that the mothers don't want their children to see.

MENDELOWITZ: Programs are shuffled around based on the ratings. How do you respond to letters sent to your station about programming?

LYONS: I'll answer that first. Dick Cavett was going to be cancelled by the ABC Television Network. ABC got more mail out of Harvard University than I think they have students up there. Minorities really speak up. They stand up to be counted. There may be only ten of them, but by

God, they make a lot of noise and the rest of the people sit back until you hit them personally. You take off *Star Trek* and that's when you get a real response. We answer all mail. Copies of mail concerning the network programs go to the president of the network. We answer all letters at the station and then send them on to the network.

RICE: We had an interesting situation arise. When we adjusted our schedule in January, we displaced an ABC Network daytime program, *All My Children*. Now, *All My Children* had a pretty good audience and was particularly high in 18-to-49 appeal. So, we decided rather than dropping it, and probably taking a lot of static, we'd delay the program and run it at ten o'clock the following morning. The biggest criticism we received was from the University. Apparently, this was the highest viewed program on the campus. Now, this is not reflected in any rating book, but kids, the University kids, would sit down in clusters of 30 to watch *All My Children* at noon. They liked it, and they said: "Is there any way you could put it on at 3:30 in the afternoon? But don't take it away from us."

BARER: I'm really shocked. I thought that college kids just did not like television in the middle of the day.

GEOFFREY: My students all can tell me what's happening in the different soap operas.

LYONS: In my station in Grand Rapids, my employees will take a late lunch hour to get *All My Children* which comes on at one o'clock. It's a soap opera. You know? Who's sleeping with whom and in what way.

HENABERY: Earlier you said that the government had no right to tell a broadcaster how to program. Would you like to amplify that at all?

LYONS: We're against any intervention by the government into our programming. I hear Whitehead coming out of OTP in the White House saying that I am responsible for the network news. How can I be responsible for that? I'm in Grand Rapids. I can't call on the phone and say "Hey, is that true or is it not true?" The networks are qualified broadcasters. We're all trying to serve the public and at the same time get the money back so that we can re-invest it. I just don't like the government saying: "You're going to have to put a show on now 7:30 to 8:00 some night of the week that deals with public issues, government programming, etc. Where do they stop? They can start with one half-hour a week, ten half-hours a week, two hours . . . and what the hell have you got? You've got the government controlling broadcasting.

RICE: I totally agree with the statement you made. The government has won. They are in it; I see nothing happening but them getting into it deeper. Once you get your toe in the water, and it's not so cold, you know what happens.

GEOFFREY: What kind of flak do you get over the fact that the season is getting shorter and shorter and at Christmas you run re-runs?

LYONS: When I first got into this business, you did 39 originals and 13 repeats. Today, they do about 22 original episodes a season and then they schedule in the pre-emptions and the specials. The biggest dearth that we have today in our industry is writers. Where do we get the writers? We're looking for writers.

MENDELOWITZ: The continous refrain that there aren't enough writers and there isn't enough talent around, seems to indicate that instead of moving toward a proliferation of small, weak stations, in terms of broadcasting range, we should be moving toward reduction of the number of stations and increasing the power.

GEOFFREY: Would the season be extended if you had more writers or are there other economical reasons?

LYONS: Advertisers won't pay the big price that they have to pay in the summertime for a first run show. In other words, you get into the cost of some of these hour shows, *Marcus Welby* has got to cost them a pretty penny; *All In The Family*'s got to cost a pretty penny; they've got to get the money back.

HENABERY: What is your prediction on made-for-television movies?

LYONS: I think they're great. They're an hour and a half and they're doing some beautiful things; they're giving a lot of old actors a new bid on life.

MILICIA: I was looking over some of the things that we said today about programming. The ratings are important to determine audience. The size of the market that you're in; the socio-economic level; the religious tone of the community that you're in, determine the type of program that you'll do. Depending on your place in the market, first, second and third, at different times of the day, determines the type of programming that you'll do and the type of syndicated packages. George said that he programs religious programming at the beginning of the day and at the end of the day. He knows it loses money, but in his community, in the Bible Belt, you have to do this.

HENABERY: God is watching!

MILICIA: That's alright. She'll understand.

TAU GROUP

Discussion Leader: John Kelly (Storer Broadcasting)

Industry Participants: Seymour Horowitz (Program Director, WABC-TV, New York); Alan Perris (Program Director, Post/ Newsweek Stations, Washington, D.C.); William Stiles (Spanish International Network, New York)

Faculty Participants: Susan Cailteux (University of Kentucky); Louis Day (Central Michigan University); William Hanks (University of Pittsburgh); John Kittross (Temple University); Jeffrey Lowenhar (University of Connecticut); Jon Powell (Northern Illinois University); Irving Webber (University of Alabama)

KELLY: The first time that I managed a station someone told me that you'll find everybody from the fellow who selects the paper clips to the banker who holds your mortgage, is a program director. Our problem today is programming. We can't always get the best. We can't always buy it. We don't always have the money at the right time. You may not want to buy it because you think the price is too high and you can't get a fair market return for it.

HANKS: A couple of questions. One, what is the total amount of time that you devote to public affairs? Secondly, what's the percentage of gross revenue you plow back into production of the public affairs programs?

HOROWITZ: The percentage of time on public affairs is about 10%. How much of our revenue is plowed back I don't know. Public affairs does not necessarily have to be a program. It can also be content within a program. In our *AM New York,* which runs two hours in the morning from 7:00 to 9:00, about 50% is public affairs. The *Today Show* on NBC also carries public affairs that touches matters of interest to the general public. We also carry a new program called *People, Places and Things* which just won a New York Emmy Award for the type of programming it's doing.

HANKS: I note that in the rankings by Nicholas Johnson of the 50 network affiliates, WABC-TV with 14% public affairs and other programs ranks as number one on the ratio of money plowed back into program expenses. On the other hand, I hope that you take to the people at WTOP the information that you guys unfortunately have come down substantially.

KELLY: They already know it Bill, believe me.

HANKS: Although you present about 19% public affairs and other programming, one can only conclude that while you present quite a lot of it, it must be very cheaply produced.

PERRIS: Well, no, that was one of the wrong things about Johnson's theory. He didn't say money plowed back into public affairs programs.

KELLY: No, he said plowed back into programming.

PERRIS: The biggest expense a station will have is generally a movie. You buy 300, 600, 1,000 movies and they cost you, in New York for example, $20,000 or $40,000 per movie. If you're in Washington you pay less. If you are in New Orleans you pay less. I would think that if you took that list and generally looked at the stations, money plowed back into programming is going to be less at the smaller station.

KELLY: You're equating program expenses with what is plowed back into public affairs or good programming.

PERRIS: When that study came out, I was working for a station in Buffalo. We came out about 75th in money plowed back into programming. As a joke, but as a joke that maybe had a little more bite in it than necessary, one of the people at the Corporation Club said "How come you ranked so high?" The reason for that is we're still in business and if you can buy something cheap you buy it cheap. Why spend $1,000 if you can spend

$500 for the same show. You can negotiate. I don't think that you put Johnson's report in the correct context.

KELLY: Storer has a station in Atlanta whose budget is almost double its Milwaukee station, which serves approximately the same size market. The Atlanta budget is absolutely just right through the roof. That's because Storer has had trouble against the giant WSB. What I'm getting at is that Johnson reported that our news in Atlanta was the 5th finest-produced news in America. It has the lowest rating of any station in town.

HANKS: Well, I'm sorry not to have brought my data with me, but the fact is I don't think he rated on quality performance. He may have rated it in terms of money.

KELLY: No, it was quality of news. But it was the lowest rated.

CAILTEUX: What kinds of things are you doing to go beyond just public affairs programming? Are you doing entertainment programs which take a serious look at the stereotyping of various kinds of people?

PERRIS: *All In The Family, Mary Tyler Moore,* and *Animal World* are all educational in some respects. I'd rather call them informative or instructional. Educational, when you work with a license, means a show that has been blessed by an educational organization. Otherwise, the show is called instruction. But for the most part, there are instructional/ educational programs that are entertainment. And those are the best. When you have a 40 or 45 share with a show like *All In The Family,* in some markets, that does a better job for you than people sitting down and discussing the same problem on Sunday morning at 11:00.

KITTROSS: I have a friend who makes the point that there may not be any such thing as an informational program because nobody is going to watch it. You can entertain and you can persuade. And sometimes both. When you do that, the information will come along. If you start out just for information, unless you have a compulsory attendance or something like that, believe me, it's not going to go anywhere.

HOROWITZ: The ABC network offers a short program called *Americans All* which follows some evening movies. These shorts cover an individual minority person or a group that has accomplished something in his or her field. We offered a made-for-television movie called *A Certain Summer* which dealt with homosexuality.

CAILTEUX: I didn't mean a specific program. I mean all of your programming and how it relates to daily life.

DAY: I have a question that bears directly on the problem that we're discussing. When you produce a program for a minority group, do you go into the production with the idea of making a profit or do you feel that it's going to be a loss of some kind.

HOROWITZ: No, we don't assume anything. You hope that it will serve its purpose and that you can bring it in on budget. If you can spot it out and sell it, fine.

PERRIS: You can't do public affairs programming with the idea of making a profit on it. Somewhere along the line you make up a budget, you're going to sink some of your profit into that show, you hope to break even on it, you may not. Some of these prime-time specials definitely pay for themselves. Some of the daily shows, however, don't pay for themselves at all. In Washington, D.C. daytime viewing is terribly low. It's a very big working area, 77% of the population works for the government, and there's nobody at home.

KELLY: Bill, you be the NBC program director at 4:00 P.M. and you're running the *Mike Douglas Show*. Seymour, you're running a series of movies at 4:00 P.M. and we're coming into the sweeps. I'd like to get Alan's reaction to what he would program against these two shows and why. Just a brief analysis. You've got Douglas on one station and you have unlimited budget.

PERRIS: Well, I'll start out with a cop out—which is that you really have got to know your market and how many other stations there are. But let's say there are three stations. Most of the time, that third station faced with a top show and a movie, will go to an off-network syndicated property, such as *Mod Squad* or *Bonanza,* depending on where the station is located. In the Southwest it probably would be *Bonanza.* If it's in a metropolitan area it probably would be *Mod Squad.*

KELLY: Would you explain that?

PERRIS: All right. It depends on the market. If it's a market where *Gunsmoke* is a highly rated show, and *Gunsmoke* has been on the air for 18 years, then a *Bonanza* might work very well in that market. But if it's a metropolitan area were *Gunsmoke* doesn't do well at all, because westerns are just out of the phase right now, you probably want a big-city type program. There are more shows coming. *Hawaii 5-0* will soon be in syndication, *The FBI* will be available, *Mission Impossible* is now in the market place. So there is a lot of mystery, action, adventure-type programming available. Those are really the three main staples of late afternoon programming in a three-station market. Common sense would tell you that you've got to do that. Unless you have a specific market where, as in Miami, a talk show does well. There are two talk shows, Douglas and Griffin, facing each other in that market. There are other towns where talk shows won't go at all. For the most part, those are the three major afternoon entertainment vehicles to get an audience.

KELLY: For the purposes of this discussion, Miami is not to be considered a Southern market. Atlanta, for instance, or Memphis, or you name it, Baton Rouge or New Orleans are Southern markets. If you tried to put in Merv Griffin or Mike Douglas, you'd fall right on your face. Am I not correct on that?

PERRIS: Probably.

KELLY: I am going to change it now. You're going to have the movie Alan, and Bill is going to have the Merv Griffin. Seymour, you've got to make a recommendation to your management as to what you would program against these other two stations in the market. This is a 3-station market and there are no other influences other than what the other two stations are doing.

HOROWITZ: Well, the first thing I would think about is audience demographics. Mike Douglas, up until recently, was to the 50 and over. Unless the movies are properly scheduled and chosen, they too can dissipate that audience. Finally, I'd consider the needs of the sales department. I've got to find some properties probably off-net, or there might be some syndicated shows that could compete strongly. I might not get the numbers that Douglas or the movie would but I sure as heck will get women 18-49. *Mod Squad* should attract an audience. I think *Perry Mason* would not. Maybe some of the travel-adventure would have young people appeal.

POWELL: I would like to know why a syndicated show has to be programmed four or five days a week instead of once a week as the networks do. You mentioned playing *Bonanza* five days a week.

PERRIS: Monday through Friday we all think of stripping—that's what it's called. The reason is the audience retention factor. Stripping builds loyalty and habit strength. You can promote it better. It's easier to sell. All the factors that are involved in making money off it and getting a good rating from it, is what tells you to strip.

KELLY: The prime economic reason is the way the programs are made available to the stations. It is economically correct for them to program on a strip basis.

POWELL: It seems to me that this is a formula that has been willingly accepted by a great number of stations, and I think unjustifiably so.

PERRIS: It's been accepted by the audience, you see.

POWELL: But what you've got is a formula that you've been working with because it has been successful. I'm suggesting that you may be working with a formula of success which prohibits you from experimenting with something that might bring you higher rewards.

KELLY: I'd like to answer that if I may. It's been tried. Fifteen years ago the norm was to have a different program vertically every day, Monday through Friday. And it didn't work.

HOROWITZ: At night, ABC-TV, because it could not get anywhere with the *Dick Cavett Show,* started to go into a series of entertainment vehicles. They are pretty much different each night and now we're doing very well.

LOWENHAR: Mr. Perris and Mr. Horowitz have demonstrated to me that to be successful in the business you must be devoid of any philosophy. You must be a pragmatist and react to environment, and that next year or the year after different groups will emerge, different issues, and you will react accordingly. Yet, media are supposed to create environments—new environments—as well as react.

HOROWITZ: A medium is a channel.

LOWENHAR: Is it supposed to create?

KELLY: It comes back to the same old thing. If you're not profitable, or a profit-making operation you don't stay in business. We are still captives of popularity and what the people want.

POWELL: In spite of 10 years of concerted effort, I have not seen any improvement in children's programming. This is especially true of cartoons. It seems to me that we have taken the cartoon medium and perverted it for commercial reasons.

PERRIS: I disagree with you in one respect about Saturday mornings. The trashy cartoons are still on. But there are some other things there too. Infrequent, but they are there. There are the little 3-minute news bits on CBS, and *Multiplication Rock* on ABC.

POWELL: I find there's an inconsistency, Mr. Horowitz and Mr. Perris, in what you've been describing as good programming. It seems to me that if you're talking about good programming and the building of audiences, the idea of holding out that there's a special production every three weeks is hardly a way of achieving consistent quality. For example, in children's programming the only regularly scheduled programs that we have are *Gilligan's Island* types or some other inane nonsense.

HOROWITZ: I have to disagree. Network produced children's programs are scheduled regularly every Saturday or Sunday at specific times every week.

POWELL: I'm talking about afternoons. You get strip programming.

HOROWITZ: Well, you're talking about two different things, local and network.

POWELL: I'm talking about children's hours. Whatever you call it, or however you define it. On Saturday we have regular programs. But in the programs you are describing, there is very little opportunity to know in advance what's going to take place. There is no follow-through after those programs. And there's very little repeat, syndication, or anything else that would put them in a strip programming situation. In other words, children are somehow treated in a different manner than the rest of your audiences.

KELLY: The way this problem is stated there is really only one answer. Alan, Bill and Seymour have given us the answer, and that is try to get as much audience as you possibly can.

HOROWITZ: What I said was that we would want the most effective audience for our sales purposes. I wouldn't want the largest audience. We must concentrate on the creativity of what exists and not try to change it. There's a *Mod Squad* and there's *Naked City*. They're the same show, but one is done in quality.

POWELL: You program for blacks. You program for women, they're a minority, and you do regular strip programming. You program for the people who like soccer, soap operas, or whatever other minority. But when it comes to children that's one minority you do not program for in any regular manner.

PERRIS: You might have misunderstood. We program 9:00 to 10:00 every morning in Miami for children. From 2:00 to 6:00 we have a show called *Arthur and Company,* which has a large budget, a staff of six people, plus educated panelists that help us with this program. There is stripping of children's programs in certain markets on certain stations. But it would be just as dumb to program a show like that against *Sesame Street* as it would be to program Mike Douglas reruns against Mike Douglas' first runs. There is still a competitive factor of trying to reach your audience and get them when you can. It has nothing to do with this. Most major cities now have not only off-network syndicated property for kids that is entertaining—and loaded with commercials—but they have an educational channel that plays three or four hours of this stuff every day.

POWELL: Let me offer this challenge. You know you've got an audience Saturday morning. A children's audience.

PERRIS: That's right.

POWELL: Now, why can't—and I'm not saying there shouldn't be cartoons, and I'm not even saying there shouldn't be the things you're dealing with—but why can't you treat children in terms of quality production as you do in other areas? And in the case of cartoons . . .

KELLY: It's being done, Jon.

PERRIS: We do two hours every Saturday, Jon. There's no rating, but we do it.

KELLY: Three companies have gotten together and they've invested up to, I think at this point it's $80,000 in a new program. It's called *Dipsy-Doodle.* I don't know whether you've heard of it, or not. But it's not a cartoon. It will have live actors—young people, singers, dancers, original music, the whole thing is original.

POWELL: Is it going to have interruptions every two minutes?

KELLY: I really don't care about that. I care about getting the program on the air.

POWELL: Well, this is the kind of thing that I'm talking about. We're presenting information in the most distracting way to our children.

PERRIS: Jon, we put the commercials on our kids' shows front and back with no interruptions in the middle. We do that on all children's programming. There are a lot of things that you're bringing up here that we just don't have the time to tell you. It does bother me when you make a general statement, when we are actually doing what you are saying nobody's doing. And we're not the only company doing it, a lot of them are doing it. We want to make money and we want to serve the public. Also, we want to keep our license. To do that you've got to do two kinds of programming. You've got to do audience programming that gets you gobs of money, and you've got to do non-audience programming, even if it's quality, that won't bring you that return. You know it's necessary and that you should do it. Maybe 4:00 in the afternoon is one of the only places that we can make all that money that supports the other sections of that station. And maybe we don't want to give up 4:00 to 6:00, so we can try to make our money in other areas. But the other areas won't pay for it. The 4:00 to 6:00 pays for it. It's a matter of economics. It's a matter of balancing the balls. Like a guy with 12 plates on the *Ed Sullivan Show*. First plate is a minority group, the second plate is the women, and the third plate is Action for Children's Television and you can go right down the line. Somebody has got to keep their hand on the throttle. We are trying. I'm not using this as a cop-out.

KELLY: Each of you academicians here today can help improve programming. Go back and get to know those people who run the non-commercial station in your market, if you don't already. Discuss programming, creative programming ideas, find money for it if they don't have the budget for it, and please God, create programs that will kick the hell out of commercial broadcasting. The time has to come that, if public broadcasting is to survive—and educational TV *has* to survive—they've got to find a way to program the way commercial television is programmed.

CAILTEUX: Essentially what you're saying is, "Go take care of the job for us because we've got some other things that we can do in that period of time."

STILES: Jack, maybe as a broadcaster who is not so involved directly in this problem, I can say something that I think perhaps you, and Alan, and Seymour are reluctant to say. One of the reasons that children's television is in such hard times at the moment commercially is that the very people who would like to improve it have created situations that have made improvement very difficult. First of all, they've taken all the action out of children's programming because they think it's violent, and kids don't want to watch it now because it's dull. Many of the things that have been put on now are dull, so the audience isn't there. Secondly, they've said "Gee, that's terrible. You shouldn't be selling that cereal to those kids who don't know any better." So, they've taken all the appeal out of the commercials and many advertisers have backed away and said, "We're just not going to get involved in this." Why should they put their money in this medium simply to have the ACT group and the Mother's for Decent Television, or whatever the groups are, come right down their throats. So, advertising money has dried up.

WEBBER: I seems to me, listening to the discussion, that it really boils down to a few points. Alternatives ought to be available. Overall, we're talking about balance horizontally and vertically throughout the day.

I think a good bit of the problem that has been occupying us has to do with whether or not time periods, which are more or less specifically programmed to particular audiences like children, are being utilized properly. Or whether children's programming is being relegated to less desirable time periods in terms of attracting the intended audience.

Sigma Group

Discussion Leader: Philip Spencer (WCSS, Amsterdam, New York)
Industry Participants: George Lyons (Station Manager, WZZM-TV, Grand Rapids); Robert Rice (General Manager, WRAU-TV, Peoria)
Faculty Participants: Albert Book (University of Nebraska); Kent Creswell (Ohio State University, WOSU); Richard Goggin (New York University); David Lange (Duke University); Bruce Powers (Niagara University); Arthur Savage (Ohio University); Ray Steele (University of Pittsburgh)

SPENCER: The subject matter before us is program content. A recent survey found that something like 35% to 40% of the people watching programming on television were watching only because somebody *else* turned that channel on. It raises something I think we could talk about. As opposed to other media, newspaper or radio, television is one on one. In other words one person is reading a paper at a time. You get one copy of the paper but you take turns reading it. With four to five radios in every household everybody can listen to whatever station he wants. Most families can't afford too many television sets so consequently the dominant person in the room gets to watch what he wants and everybody watches that. What are you going to do on your television programs? How would you go about finding what to carry on your television station? How do you go about finding what time to run your newscasts?

BOOK: I come from the Omaha-Lincoln-Sioux City market. Lincoln is a university town and many of the people there would enjoy Shakespeare or Clifford Odets or something equally esoteric, but in Sioux City or in Omaha I surmise they would want *My Mother The Car,* or *The Flying Nun,* or *Peyton Place Fornicates Again.* How can you possibly placate or please such disparate tastes in the audience? Not everybody is going to be satisfied. I can empathize with the broadcaster's problem. I don't think it's your job to elevate the taste of the majority of the people. Your job is to make money. You make money or you go out of business.

LYONS: We are there to make money, yes. But money isn't the all important thing.

BOOK: It's a primary consideration.

LYONS: Nobody is in business to lose money except the government.

GOGGIN: I can appreciate the need to make money but, does broadcasting have to be constantly linked to the concept of mass audience, meaning therefore less diversity and mass commonality? Can we not find reasonable profit and economic viability in a way that radio has done by appealing to specialized audiences?

RICE: Radio is no longer a mass medium with the exception possibly of radio network news. What I'm seeing here is black and white. The *white* is radio's vertical approach and *black* is the way television is doing it today. Now what shade of gray are you looking for? Is television to go to the vertical approach of radio and go that specific? It would be disastrous. It is still a mass medium.

SPENCER: What ways would you suggest that we begin programming, forgetting about having to be number one, or two, or three in the market?

LYONS: You have to go into the market first of all and see what is available. In other words, what programming is available. Then you've got to find out what talent is available. You must determine: Am I going to go after the kids? Am I going to go after the housewife? Am I going to go after feature movies? What segment of what audience do you want? Then you start to put a pencil to it and you may find out that you can't afford the programming the way you think you want it.

SPENCER: The problem is finding out what programs are available for that market and then determining whether or not they will attract large audiences.

RICE: It is expensive to the station to do any kind of local programming. In an 18-hour day you must establish a second shift of people. Because you must recognize that your production people are set to produce the two important news shows per day. Now if you want to do anything in the morning or noon news, you're adding another shift in the course of a day. Well, there are ways you can get around it, and we did. We would physically tape five (non-news, of course) shows. We do one live and tape four shows in one day, and play the taped shows during the week. A good daytime show for us will have the audience.

SAVAGE: When we are talking about television being a mass medium there are diverging opinions. Is it a mass medium, or an advertising medium or a sales promotion medium? I expect all of these fit into the spectrum at some point in time and can be completely compatible with each other. At least that's my approach to it. You are talking about communicating with a mass audience. Yet at the same time, through your ascertainment procedures, you're also talking about supplying a certain amount of public service programming that will address specific issues within the community. How do you program a television station? You find out what is available in the market in the way of programming sources, not only in network but also in syndication.

You can also utilize this same ascertainment procedure to accomplish another whole different array of purposes. Number one, you should turn up new news beats out of it. You should turn up new programming ideas out of it. I think a lot of broadcasters have a tendency to write off public service programming as fulfilling a minority need in the community. All programming that goes on television is not going to draw a mass audience. I think it is completely defensible to write off certain programs as far as ratings are concerned. Put them on simply for their content and whatever appeal they may have to some particular portion of that community. I think television has to take a look at its programming departments and decide to program for specialized audiences. The slack can be picked up with the mass audience kinds of things.

STEELE: That was something that I wanted to ask and I guess you provided a nice lead in. It has to do with leadership in programming. George, you mentioned counter-programming. That's very wise, a very smart move. It's a sales-type notion but it does give you a different kind of saleability. You make some conscious decisions about leadership. Let's just take some gross categories. You will say I can choose three kinds of movies. One is kind of a culture piece. One is kind of an old folks memory-bender which has an awful lot of appeal to young folks, especially the film-oriented young folks today. You make a decision about your responsibility to the community. Do you shoot to what you would consider to be a culture or maybe a good message film? Do you make conscious decisions about things like that? Or do you simply go, "Well the culture costs $35.00 more than *"Beach Blanket Bingo"* and therefore this week it's not worth the risk." Do you want to lead the market or are you better off to make a decision, if you can, that puts you in second place?

LYONS: When it comes to features, you don't buy one or two, you buy a package. Today there are 35, maybe 50 or 60 in a package. Movies are drying up. What have you got to choose from? They have all these X-rated movies that my daughter and all of her friends watch. I'm not a movie goer so I can't answer. I did see a real good movie the other night and I told the network to make it into the series. I wasn't the first one to tell them. I saw *Shaft* and thought it was a fantastic movie. The bad guys took care of the bad guys and none of the good guys got hurt.

It's difficult when you look at the whole package. The most expensive thing you own on film at a station is features. May I take a minute to tell what features cost? Maybe you would like to know? Let's take 50 pictures at $1,000 a title. You run each five times. Now in your head that's $200 a run. Now out of those 50 pictures you haven't got all good ones. You've got a couple of the "mediums" and a couple of "turkeys" and a few little "dogs" in there. But you try to choose the best package from what's available. In those $1,000 titles that you run you try to stretch it out over as many years as you can. You take five runs, or the most runs you can get for the lowest dollar. You bargain. There is no rate card for features or syndication. You bargain for the best deal you can make in the market you're in. People don't realize that everytime you book that feature it costs you $100 for a color print. So your price just went up on five runs an additional $500. And then you've got to ship it in and ship it out and keep a man down in the film room to splice the commercials in and out. So features are damned expensive.

SPENCER: So what you're saying, George, is you buy a big package.

LYONS: You have to. That's all that is available. Occasionally you can buy a small package. I think *Psycho* is one in a short package of two or three titles. But mostly they're 35 titles and up.

SPENCER: So you don't really make a decision whether to show a cowboy film or black film or detective film. You look at all 50 in a package.

LYONS: It depends on what time of the day you're running it.

SPENCER: In other words, would each package of 50 satisfy most any market?

LYONS: No, because some of those films in there I would not run after school, for example. I would run them late at night. Others I would not run late nights. Right now in my market the hottest item is Elvis Presley. So I go for Elvis Presley movies. You look at the time you're running the show and the potential audience. Then you program it.

STEELE: Do all those packages that you talk about, expensive as they are, allow you some latitude for choice?

LYONS: Oh yes, we're in a buyers' market.

STEELE: Maybe what you said answers some of my questions. You do have an Elvis Presley market to some extent and therefore, if you can buy that kind of film and get in on that particular popularity bandwagon you buy that because you know it's going to sell.

LYONS: If you get three Elvis Presleys in your 35 deal, you say that's three I know will play. Length of the film is another determining factor. Our biggest problem is the length of the movie. Is it an hour and a half, is it two hours? What is your time period?

RICE: Let me add to that. I think there has been a big change in the local market based on the fact that the networks have gone in so heavily for movies. You're finding far fewer features being run in local markets than before. We're running two a week now and we used to have 20 features a week, easily, in the past. We would buy packages of 200 as opposed to being able, fortunately, to buy as few as 35. You really had to take an awful lot of junk in that package of 200. We have a Sunday afternoon movie and a Saturday late movie that have two totally different concepts and appeal. One is basically all family or action. *Lolita* would never play on Sunday afternoon on our station. It would play Saturday night. *Lolita* is so calm compared to what we've seen lately that people are playing it anywhere. I'm trying to satisfy many and varied needs, but at the same time I've got to be realistic and maintain the big hitters that have mass appeal, that draw the audience to the station. If you've got enough of these you can begin to knife in or sandwich in the public affairs special in prime-time and feel that you are still going to be strong enough that you can do that kind of blended programming.

LANGE: I was sitting here thinking about something which Al Book said at the beginning of the discussion. He was talking about programs in Lincoln, Nebraska. I suspect what he had to say about the programming there might be said about a lot of other markets in the country. It made me think in terms of something which we used to do a lot of in the late 50's. In most stations, you're either in the same town with or near to a university where there is a theater department or even a school which has television production workshops available. Back in the 50's students used to program two or three hours a week of dramatic productions. Some of them were really rotten but occasionally some of them were fairly good. What I'm wondering is whether it would be possible for the students in the theater department to really mount a production and take it out to a studio at a time, say, when you've got a crew sitting there waiting to do the 11 o'clock news and tape the thing? The economy of this kind of production would depend on your ability to make use of people who are already there. It would essentially cost you the tape, and incidental expenses. You might find it useful to put it in your prime-time access slot or some other place. Perhaps, you could syndicate it. Is any of this feasible?

BOOK: We're doing something along those lines in the area of public service. We recently got a small federal grant for a crime prevention program for the State of Nebraska. I have all my advertising classes involved, newspaper ads, magazine ads, billboards, radio and television. In television there is going to be a half-hour documentary which is going to be done by our own students. Now this may be somewhat akin to what you're talking about.

SPENCER: Dave, were you talking more about drama as opposed to what Mr. Book is talking about?

LANGE: What I was thinking about just happened to be what we used to do in 1957.

SPENCER: Were you talking about the old Studio One and programs like that?

LANGE: Exactly, except when done by students the quality tends to drop. But it may very well be more interesting than the lady who sits up and interviews craft people. It's possible that it might be.

LYONS: No way would I put that kind of show on the air. We don't have any free tape time. We don't have the open studio time. People say, "Oh the guys are there and they're not working." In my station they are working. As a matter of fact my local salesmen who tape commercials have to wait a week-and-a-half to book it in. So everything is taken care of. We work two shifts. We work two 10-hour day shifts.

LANGE: Even that might not be a problem because most journalism schools, I take it these days, that are running a radio/television program have their own broadcast equipment.

LYONS: No, they're either the Sony three-quarter or the one-inch and we use two-inch.

CRESWELL: The idea is terrific and I think it would work on cable systems and may develop to the point where you can get this into commercial operation. But usually, if it's the kind of program content that you can walk into one end of the studio and put it on with the people who are sitting there with free time, it won't sell. And it certainly won't syndicate. But it may some day, Dave. I'm not saying that the idea is completely out.

LANGE: One solution might be Al Book's, which is to get a grant. If there is one thing we are damned good at in the academic game it's getting grants.

RICE: Allow me to just throw in a real barb at that point. I get annoyed at some of the grants educators obtain to try to produce programming. It turns out twice as expensive as we could produce it for them.

SPENCER: That's amateur versus pro though, Bob. I think you would find that in anything. What you're talking about is suggesting that the educational institutions will spend twice as much to produce the same program that you do.

RICE: The thing I'm saying is that the government is not spending my taxes the way I would like to see them spent.

SPENCER: That's something else again.

BOOK: The money that is being spent on this half hour documentary, which possibly is going to do some good in the State of Nebraska, would have been spent in some futile endeavor. Here they're having the practice plus the possibility of doing a worthwhile project which will benefit the citizens of the state. So the money is not being ill spent.

GOGGIN: Audiences are accustomed to seeing a high measure of production quality and they can't help but judge the product coming out of the universities alongside that.

LANGE: Just briefly. I don't mean to beat a dead horse, although I'm not quite sure this one isn't still kicking. Dick Goggin's point, it seems to me, has some merit, assuming that I'm reading you right. The suggestion, for instance, of the analogy between local sports and professional sports and what amounts to local dramatic productions or local documentaries and professionally done documentaries. It seems prefectly clear that you're not going to get the same kind of approach, the same kind of quality. You won't get professional quality in the professional sense that we're accustomed to. But I don't think that has to be the end of it. It seems to me that is a problem in packaging and not a reason necessarily to exclude it. If, for example, you showed a local dramatic production and you led it in right and got it off the air right, you would at least identify it for what it is so that people really could understand that what you were doing was not offering them a Broadway production. You're suggesting that here is something that is being done locally and you can appreciate it accordingly. It doesn't mean that you can't run *Cannon* and *Kojak* back to back on Wednesday night if it means that in some hole you also put some stuff that appeals to a narrower, more specific audience. God knows you do that at the network. Hallmark Cards never worried very much, nor did DuPont, about reaching the mass audience that you're really talking about.

RICE: I would beg to differ with you on those two. They have been very effective in their audience appeal.

LANGE: But it's not a mass audience.

RICE: I can speak to the DuPont thing very intimately because that was my account at BBDO and they did in the beginning do just what you suggested. They did it for several years. They were not reaching the mass audience they wanted and they changed from an hour-and-a-half marvelous *Playhouse 90*-type show to a piece of tripe that went on every week for an hour because they wanted to reach more people. So that was really in the back of their minds.

Cable Television: An Overview

OVER-THE-AIR VHF spectrum space is very limited. Only twelve channels are available and most viewers receive three or four channels. Cable TV has the potential of providing up to 40 channels, and possibly more.

Cable, or as it was first called, Community Antenna Television (CATV), began approximately 25 years ago in such communities as Astoria, Oregon and Lansford, Pennsylvania. At first, Cable involved the installation of master antennas on mountain tops to feed over-the-air TV signals via interference-free coaxial cable to subscribers in the valleys below. Eventually Cable expanded to towns and cities.

The Federal Communications Commission initially disclaimed jurisdiction over the new medium and requested that Congress enact legislation that would empower the Commission to regulate CATV. Congress did not take action and the FCC found it necessary to proceed under the Communications Act of 1934.

In 1962, the FCC denied an application by the Carter Mountain Transmission Corp. for a permit to install a microwave radio relay in order to transmit television signals to community antenna systems. The Commission felt that the TV stations in the area—and thus the public interest—would be injured by the increased competition from additional CATV facilities. The decision was affirmed by the Court of Appeals and the Supreme Court refused to review the case. In 1965, the FCC adopted rules requiring microwave-served CATV systems to carry the programming of local TV stations so that the community would not be cut off from over-the-air broadcasting. In addition, the Commission prohibited microwave CATV systems from duplicating programs already being shown on the local TV stations. A year later, it applied the rules to all CATV systems whether or not they used microwave facilities. The 1966 rules also prohibited CATV systems in the top 100 markets from importing the signals of distant television stations without a hearing. In 1968, the U.S. Supreme Court declared the FCC's Cable rules legal extensions of its powers under the Communications Act.

On February 2, 1972 the FCC issued rules which established national standards for the Cable industry. The rules included a 20-channel minimum capacity; three channels reserved for local use—one each for education, government, and public access; and local program origination—if the system has 3,500 or more subscribers. This last rule, originally issued on October 27, 1969, and challenged by Midwest Video, was upheld by the Supreme Court on June 7, 1972.

The report also finalized the FCC's June 24, 1970 ruling which held that broadcasters may not own Cable systems in localities where they operate broadcast stations, and prohibited the networks from Cable ownership of any kind. On January 17, 1973 the FCC extended the deadline for breaking up the banned cross-ownership to August 10, 1975—two years beyond the original date, and invited individual licensees affected by the ban to seek waivers. The Commission recently indicated that it would modify or rescind the technical requirements.

Today, there are over 3,000 Cable systems operating in the United States reaching about eight million subscribers. In recent years larger and more substantially financed companies have entered the Cable field. Approximately 75% of the Cable systems in the United States are owned or controlled by companies that have other media interests. Over-the-air broadcasters own 34.6%, program producers 19.9%, newspapers and publishers 17.5%, and theatre owners 4.3%. Several large companies have emerged as multiple system operators. Teleprompter is the largest with more than one million subscribers. Warner Cable is expanding rapidly and now ranks second.

Mr. Alfred Stern, Chairman of the Warner Cable Corporation, in his Dinner Address, assesses the present state of Cable and attempts to establish parameters for Cable's future.

Aaron Cohen   Alfred Stern

ALFRED R. STERN

Mr. Stern entered the cable television industry in 1962 after 10 years with NBC as a division manager and vice president. At that time he founded Television Communications Corporation, (TVC). In 1972, TVC became a wholly owned subsidiary of Warner Communications, Inc. Today, under the Warner Cable name, the firm serves over 415,000 subscriber homes throughout the country. Mr. Stern served as Chairman of the National Cable Television Association (NCTA) during 1966-67, and has headed the NCTA's copyright committee since its formation in 1967.

Mr. Stern is a resident of New York City and is an active participant in the community's cultural, philanthropic and civic affairs. He is currently the Chairman of the Board of the Phoenix Theatre; member of the Boards of Directors of Mount Sinai Hospital and School of Medicine, the American Museum of Natural History, the New School for Social Research, and Irvington House.

Address by Alfred R. Stern

I recently read an article by a noted art critic and teacher, who is now involved, from the programming end, with a cable system in one of our larger cities. In writing of his experiences for an industry journal, he offered as his opening statement, the following plea:

"Common decency, one might think, would suspend for at least a while, any more articles on the potential of cable television."

Somehow, the more I continue to address new audiences, the more I begin to feel like the author of that statement. Over the years, my colleagues and I have spent more hours than we care to total on the speaker's circuit enthusiastically talking on behalf of cable. Why do we do it? Why does this industry, founded more than 25 years ago, continue after all this time to require such extensive definition and explanation from podiums and platforms from coast to coast? The answer is simply this. Cable television is so unlike many industries and has inherent capabilities so different from any other technologies that as research and development have continued, this business has undergone incredible change and has been practically born anew every few years.

To illustrate on the simplest level, no system operator in 1955, for example, could have begun to envision the kinds of advanced multi-channel equipment which is now available for his own community, transforming his old 5-channel reception service into a 12-, 18- or 20-channel system with modular capabilities for future add-on services. Step-by-step, as our technology advanced, such new capabilities became realities thereby changing our industry significantly. And so as these changes periodically occur, we took to the speaker's platform to expound and extol these new and frequently wondrous developments. And while we, as speakers, were wending our way to audiences in auditoriums and dinner halls all over the country, our silent counterparts in offices and libraries throughout the nation were penning studies and documents and research reports and magazine articles with the same message for even wider dissemination with emphasis on, for the most part, even greater development yet to come.

At Warner Cable alone, we have a public relations office which features one full wall with floor to ceiling shelving, 70 feet, allowing for an occasional green plant interspersed therein. I'm told that approximately 66 of these 70 feet of shelves are devoted to printed matter about the wonders of cable produced by such authoritative sources as Rand, Arthur D. Little, Mitre Corporation and assorted "think tanks" in universities across the United States. All of these efforts have been undertaken with the best of motives, to be sure. Furthermore, they are the result of an important truth about cable television. This is anything but a black and white, static, easily understood industry or technology. Rather, it is a phenomenon, full of unknowns, a business beset by change and, more important, it is a concept potentially so dramatic in impact that too often, the promise of the future has been allowed to overshadow the realities of the present.

As a result, I'm here tonight with a message somewhat different from that which writers and speakers, myself included, have been promulgating in the past. And I'm here to tell you that unless we heed this new message, this call for a new approach to the realities of our industry as it exists right now, that all of us—entrepreneurs, educators, soft- and hardware "builders" —may unwittingly defeat the grand idea that is cable television.

Allow me to backtrack for a few moments in order to outline the history of our industry so that we may gain some perspective. Just a few months ago, I addressed the National League of Cities Conference of Mayors in Puerto Rico, bringing to them much the same message and background that I'm about to deliver now. I think the historical approach is as valid tonight in Tarrytown as it was in San Juan, so forgive me if I repeat myself in the interest of expediency.

To best understand cable television of the '70s, it's important to recall the days when ours was an industry spreading its earliest roots in small town, reception-poor America where you couldn't string cable fast enough to meet the heavy subscriber demand. So long as we continued to operate in those relatively small communities where our service was a necessity in terms of better reception of off-the-air signals and greater variety for distant signal importation, the atmosphere of euphoria in which we all operated, was justifiable. And so we were spoiled. We had grown up with the luxury of knowing that once you put a subscriber on the cable, he was practically yours for life. It followed, therefore, that getting a franchise was almost the same as having a town full of customers handed over to you lock, stock and monthly payment. As such, what did it really matter how much a cable operator committed to the Town Fathers during franchise negotiations? The worth of the franchise seemed to justify the commitment. Well, so much for history.

Came the dawn of a new era. Our industry set its sights on the big, and as yet unwired, cities and the whole nature of the cable industry began to change, and with that change, came some surprises. First of all, we quickly learned that cable in the larger markets is not an essential service. To the urban residents with a multitude of entertainment and leisure time resources, the cable hook-up is more an optional added luxury than an electronic necessity. He is, therefore, a far more difficult subscriber to secure.

Secondly, we learned that once you do sign the urban resident for your service, you can no longer presume that he's with you to stay. He'll tend to give cable a try. Perhaps decide that it's less needed or less desirable than he expected and then drop it. Thereby creating an expensive turnover problem.

Finally, we learned an important lesson concerning the much-touted added services. During those euphoric stages of our industry's growth, we were anxiously awaiting the day when we would enter the city. We fully believed that those exciting applications which we had all talked about so often in the form of two-way communications, facsimile transmission, utility metering, and such, would surely be available by the time the urban market began to develop. Not only did *we* believe this, so did the research organizations which study and prophesy about our industry and the financial community which helps to fund our efforts. While all of us realized that urban cable systems would be vastly more expensive to construct and much harder to penetrate, we nevertheless faced the future fairly confident that all types of sophisticated new services offering opportunities for added revenues, would be ready and waiting to help finance the higher costs and help lure the urban subscriber.

Well, we were wrong. The hardware isn't there and the software isn't there. At least not at an economically viable cost, nor in a problem-free form. The hard truth is that the development of new services is still in the experimental stage and as chairman of a company which itself is experimenting, for both pay cable and two-way communications, I can tell you with some authority that it could be quite a while before services are ready for delivery on a large scale in a major market.

Prudence dictates that such services be fully perfected before any mass market introduction is undertaken. Now, what has all of this meant for our industry? For one thing, it's been a jolt, an eye-opener. The sudden realization that a rapid, anything goes movement into the cities cannot be economically justified at this particular stage. It has been, I must admit, a bitter pill for all of us in the business to swallow. This is especially so since so much of our recent effort has been aimed towards those urban markets.

But, like it or not, such is the case for whatever reason, our own naiveté or too great a faith in the words of the prophets who had adopted our cause. We had somehow been caught in a rush to the cities with too little understanding of the stringent requirements for success in that unfamiliar terrain. Well then, where do we go from here? Is mine solely a message of gloom and doom, of clouds over cable devoid of silver linings? Quite the contrary. It would hardly be worth the trip to Tarrytown if I didn't believe that there is not only a future worth talking about, but actually an extraordinary future, if we face the facts.

The facts, quite simply, are these. One, the real future of cable lies in the still unwired urban markets where the greatest majority of television viewers reside. Two, these urban markets harbor needs, and desires far different and far more demanding than the rural markets where cable spent its infancy and adolescence, and a concentrated research and development effort must be put into action to help meet these needs and desires. Three, a new cooperative approach between the industry and the cities will be vital in making urban cable a success. An approach whereby the cities no longer make unrealistic technical demands, but rather allow cable operators to build realistic state-of-the-art systems, charge realistic and equitable subscribers' fees, and add the new futuristic services when, and only when, they have been proven economically and technically feasible. And four, the people themselves, whether subscribers or students and observers of our industry, must come to understand cable more fully and must consider not only the exciting future capabilities we may possess, but also the very real present-day limitations which necessarily shape our current service.

Given the problems and considerations I've outlined concerning urban cable, it seems clear that a major re-evaluation by all involved parties is in order. To require, at this time, that big city systems be built with unnecessarily extensive channel capacity and unfeasible technical capabilities is, to my way of thinking, totally out of line. The cable television industry cannot and should not be expected to invest millions of dollars in expensive gear that for several years to come will merely sit on the poles, unused. Such a demand is a waste of everybody's assets and neither the cable industry, nor the public, can benefit from such waste. Furthermore, it is just such demands during recent franchise negotiations which have caused many cable operators, Warner Cable included, to say thanks but no thanks to City Fathers. Tying up millions of hard-to-come-by dollars in equipment that can't be activated for blue sky services that can't yet be delivered is not the way to guarantee successful urban ventures.

It's important, at this time, to make a serious point about our industry. So far as cable television is concerned, there is no energy crisis. This is an industry long noted for what we have been calling its missionary zeal and just as we have prevailed despite years of frustration, in over-regulation, so too shall we overcome the obstacles at the gateways to the urban markets. We have the enthusiasm, the creative talents and the desire to do so. And, one way or another, we are going to find the answer to what makes urban cable tick, but it won't happen overnight. As I emphasized earlier, cable in the '70s is a new business, far different in many respects from the industry as we knew it just a few short years ago. Accordingly, each time our industry is reborn, as the result of advancing technology, we must like any newborn, walk before we run. We must be granted the right to learn through trial and error, to grow through honest experimentation.

At Warner Cable, we take most seriously the importance of creative experimentatation as a potential key to urban cable. So much so, in fact, that we are now embarked on an intensive research and development program aimed at exploring and perfecting new kinds of programming and services for delivery via cable. With each successful break-through, we hopefully build an increasingly impressive subscriber revenue base in a given urban market. These added revenues will then allow us to pursue other programming advances. It's like a domino theory in reverse. I can't emphasize too strongly the importance of an undertaking such as this for our future growth. The very fact that they are underway gives credence to my optimism, and bolsters my confidence in our ability to crack the urban market problem in that long awaited, much heralded, cable report to the President— a document prepared by the Office of Telecommunications Policy (OTP) and representing what is, in essence, the first national policy proposal for cable television. While the OTP Report is far too lengthy and complex for discussion here tonight, suffice to say that its most important value to cable as an industry is its underlying theme that cable will achieve a national penetration figure of 50%, which means in terms of today's television homes, some 35 million subscribers. For an industry currently serving 8 million homes, naturally the question of how to make that quantum leap to 35 is all important and, of course, that's the very problem we're considering here tonight. But, the point is that a rather prestigious document has now been published which believes that we will do it, which acknowledges that it can only be accomplished by urban market penetration and which, to a large extent, offers policy suggestions designed to help achieve that goal.

Well, so much for my views of the problem and promise of cable communication. I've taken a good deal of your time to air these views and I'm sure some of you are now beginning to wonder where you, as educators, fit into all of this. As movers and shakers, in your own colleges and universities, you all have the opportunity, I believe, to play a highly significant role in conveying the plight of urban cable development to the students in your charge. For while we in the cable industry are busily seeking answers from the entrepreneurial end, it is vital that other segments of the community, in this case the academic world, join us in our search by contributing the special resources for exploration which you have available at your particular level. Perhaps the most important contribution that I foresee from the academic world is in the area of content. Let me explain.

The cable television industry is primarily one of technology, construction and management. These are our greatest strengths. We cannot be considered programming experts nor designers and producers of great programs. While we have come a long way in the laboratory, at least, towards the development of the many electronic marvels which someday may find their way into our homes there is still that all-important missing ingredient of specialized entertainment, educational and instructional content for which I am convinced there exists a specialized audience willing to pay. True, Warner Cable, through its research program, is seeking to solve this problem but is our lone effort sufficient? If cable television some day is going to serve one half of all the television homes in this country, then we are surely going to require a far more extensive creative programming effort than any one company, even the size of Warner Cable, can undertake. If you can stimulate your students, and academic colleagues, along these lines—if you can bring to them an understanding of the industry's economic limitations and its needs for creative contributions from the so-called outside world, then our meeting this evening could prove fruitful.

The cable operator at the city's threshold wants to build that urban cable system because he *must* in order to keep his industry alive. The educator on the other hand, wants to see that system built because he envisions the dramatic communications applications which such a system may some day make possible, and the student who represents the creative talent of the near future surely wants to share in the challenge of contributing to and molding a whole new communications outlet. If somehow we can bring these three elements together, then indeed there is hope for a meaningful national communications web reaching all of the people with services never before possible through any other medium.

I hope I have done my job tonight in bringing you a clear picture of the return to reality in cable. If you will now carry this message out of this room and back to your campuses and classrooms, then perhaps, together, we can create a ripple effect which results not only in a greater appreciation for the state of cable as it exists today, but also, and more significantly in a new surge of creativity leading to the urban communications system which could so greatly affect all of our lives tomorrow.

QUESTION AND ANSWER SESSION FOLLOWING STERN ADDRESS

Q. Would you address yourself to the problem of students in the university community who will be wired and unwired, depending upon their tastes, and how your suggestions tonight for reaching the 35 million goal may relate to our assistance in programming and ideas?

Stern: If students have something they want to see, they pay their money and they keep up their payments. We service the University of Arkansas which is a very large campus and we have any number of students on the cable there. I don't think that that's any real problem that we'll have to deal with in Columbus, as to what can be done. In Fayetteville, the University had done an awful lot to create programming which it made available to the students and all subscribers through the cable system. It was a big help to us to have that kind of a relationship.

Q. Student type programming?

Stern: Yes. Well, a student-faculty combination program and it's been well received as far as we can tell. It's been very interesting and very good practical demonstration for the students who are interested in how to get across ideas and concepts and programming to their fellow students. We would hope that you could do the same thing.

Q. I sympathize with the plight of students, but since Temple University is in the heart of the North Philadelphia ghetto, I'm afraid I must ask a similar question. What is going to happen to the residents of North Philadelphia on welfare?

Stern: As far as our experience is concerned, the Teleprompter Corporation operates in Harlem and although I don't know the precise demographics of the Harlem area, I am sure that there are more people on welfare in Harlem than there are with respect to other places in New York.

Q. How can they afford to pay for cable service?

Stern: Well, again, I can't answer that specifically, but I do know that the penetration of the cable system in the Harlem area is as high, if not higher, than it is in other parts of the city. The apparent reason, I think, is this. The cost of $5.00 a month gives them an outlet to information, entertainment, far greater in many respects than they have been able to get. Let me give you one example in Manhattan. It's the only place I know of where a similar situation exists. The professional ice hockey, basketball and other sporting events are brought, as you know, to the cable subscriber at no additional cost. I suspect that won't last too much longer, but at least, that's what's being done now. When you realize that it costs anybody, affluent or on welfare, $7.00 to get into Madison Square Garden to see any sporting event and you realize that in the course of any 30-day period, which is costing our subscriber $5.00, he can see innumerable sporting events. You can see that in terms of even the poorest family, it still is the best entertainment buy and really one of the only entertainment buys that they can afford in addition to television which, of course, is theoretically available to them.

Q. What implications does the split between Teleprompter and NCTA (National Cable Television Association) have for future growth and distribution of cable?

Stern: We have had differences in the cable industry and we are currently having them. Not only is Teleprompter involved in this particular problem, but we have another kind of splinter organization made up of independent cable television operators who are also taking the point of view that Teleprompter is taking. I don't know of how much interest this particular element has to do with the rates we pay for the right to attach our wires to the telephone poles in the country. There are many millions of telephone poles we use and many millions of dollars that we, as an industry, spend with the telephone companies. If you laid all that money end to end, you could buy an awful lot of telephone poles, and we are seeking to adjust this in some reasonable manner on a national basis rather than deal state by state and community by community, to get some national policy with regard to this. There is a rumor that the Bell Telephone Company has some measure of control over their other companies down below. I don't know if that's true or not, but there are some people who think they do. Therefore, we're dealing with them in the hopes that we can get a national rate policy established and one of our fellow cable companies, Teleprompter, the largest company, has taken exception to the tentative—very tentative—negotiations and the tentative conclusions to these negotiations with respect to the payment to the Telephone Company. Simply, they don't want to pay anything more, which is an ideal position to be in. We, as an industry are willing to pay what we consider a modest increase in fees. Now, it goes without saying, that they should never have charged us what they charged us in the 25 years of our industry, but it's happened and we're never going to reverse that law. Teleprompter is in a very precarious financial situation. They just declared yesterday another $2.1 million loss in Newark, N.J. We haven't seen the end, clearly, of the write-offs they are going to have to take in the next 12 months. Teleprompter has about 800,000 poles—our company has about 450,000 poles—and this deal that we have worked out will cause them to pay about 30¢ a pole next year. That's about a quarter of a million dollars. Their disenchantment with the NCTA scheme is understandable.

The Station in a Lagging Market: Does It Need a Band Aid or an Operation?

WHILE THE ECONOMY as a whole is suffering from the effects of inflation and product shortages, the management of station WZZZ is more concerned with their market which is suffering from one of the highest unemployment rates in the country. George A., the General Manager is aware that his opportunity to produce revenue for his station depends to a great degree on the attitude of advertisers and their agencies toward his market. For many years, the station has been successful and returned a profit to its owners.

George A. calls a staff meeting, and outlines the economic problem of the station and the market to the group. "Our market is suffering from growing unemployment, which is leading into a spiral of reduced buying power, a lack of confidence in the economy and tightening of family budgets and borrowing. As a result, many high-priced and, luxury items are gathering dust on the shelf. As our market's economic condition becomes known, fewer and fewer advertisers will allot a 'normal' budget to support their products here. This is heightened by the network situation which seems to be softening and, in effect, is driving down prices and draining away spot dollars. As you know, many of the downtown stores were in financial trouble before the energy crisis hit, and now they are worrying about their suburban stores in the gasoline shortage. Lastly, many of the independent dealers are being bought by the regional and national chains and their advertising funds are being divided into promotions and other marketing devices."

As he looked around the table he knew they were aware of the problems, but could offer no fast solutions. He requested that the Sales

Manager hold another meeting in two days to explore two specific areas. First, what can be done to bolster confidence in their market as a viable economic force? This would include examination of sales and promotion efforts by all segments of the community related to the station. Second, what could be done by Sales to stimulate advertiser interest in their station and the market?

The meeting broke up and George returns to his office to ponder the problem that faces him as a result of his economic difficulties. How can he maintain a profit in view of the basically negative outlook? While he has just left a group that he has depressed with his review of the market, he must now make "adjustments" in his operation, in relation to the projected decline in income. But, there are so many ways to handle the problem, and he hasn't faced the need to economize in years. "Where do I begin?" he asked himself.

Discussion Points:

Can the creation of stimulating short-range spot packages work sufficiently as a finger in the dike until the economy turns around? Should these be made available at the local level only, while you try to maintain a semblance of your national rate card? How do you approach a market presentation that is upbeat at a time like this? How can you use the station facilities to help turn the situation around? What specific recommendations in these areas are you prepared to make to George A.?

How can George undertake a full financial reveiw of station operations and personnel without feeding the morale-depressing rumor mill that is sure to thrive as soon as the smell of budget reviews permeates the station? What cost-cutting procedures are open to him, on a short-range and long-range basis? Is it possible to maintain the look of the station with a reduced news and/or program budget? How much should be cut from budgets? Should he try to match last year's profit level? Should he encourage more barter deals both in programming and advertising? In essence, how should George proceed?

Iota Group

Discussion Leader: Frank Harden (State Broadcasting Company)
Industry Participant: Gary Lewis (General Sales Manager, WMCA, New York)
Faculty Participants: Douglas Boyd (University of Delaware); Peter Clark (University of Michigan); Stanley Donner (University of Texas); Joseph Johnson (San Diego University); Philip Macomber (Kent State University); Peter Pringle (University

of Florida); Carol Reuss, SP (Loyola University); Robert
Schlater (Michigan State University); Charles Steinberg (Hunter
College); Willard Thompson (University of Minnesota)

HARDEN: We have a situation here that is not unusual to a broadcast
operator, where a market may be depressed and things are generally looking very glum. You try to figure out what to do, and you have a lot of
things involved, not only from a stockholder's point of view, in profits
and so forth, but you have staff morale—and there are many, many factors
that enter into it. You've looked at the problem itself. The manager has
called the people together. He's outlined the problem to them; and he asks
the sales manager to hold another meeting in a couple of days to explore
some areas and to come back with recommendations. Meantime, he goes
back and he has a very lonely feeling. I love the way this is worded in
here: "He goes back to ponder his economic difficulties." I can just
picture that now. It's at a time like this that you want to call the
chaplain, or someone, and talk to somebody, and try to find your way out
of it because action is going to have to be taken.

I have a friend who started out in broadcasting, and who has retired
at a very early age; now he's a consultant. He goes for days just totally
relaxed; and then he gets a call from somebody who says, "Gee, I've got
problems galore—come and help me."

He shaves, puts on his suit, picks up his briefcase and hops on a
plane—and spends several days listening and analyzing the problem.
Mainly he listens to the man outline all of his problems, and then he
comes back and writes up his report and sends his bill—which is a hefty
one. And he says that in most instances the people pay no attention to
the recommendations. They just file them in the drawer after they get
the report. What did them more good than anything else was just pouring
out their hearts to somebody they could talk to, confide in. My friend's
made a sizeable amount of money in his retirement simply by listening
to people's problems. And I guess this is what our manager here is about
to do. But he needs more than that—let's kick off with a suggestion for
our station manager?

FACULTY COMMENT: Ignorance begins the debate. I wonder if softening of the economic situation in a market area is always bad for an organization that's involved in advertising? There've been times when it has been
profitable because the retailers increase their advertising. Can he not begin
by devising new techniques to urge his sponsors to do more advertising?

FACULTY COMMENT: It seems to me we need more information—such
as in what category is spot sales down? And which areas of the retail trade
are most hit by the economic downturn?

BOYD: I recall reading an article a number of years ago with respect
to a GM strike in Michigan somewhere, and noted that people tend to

cut down expenditures—those that can easily be cut down, like news-papers. People stopped buying their newspapers because they saw a definite way to save a couple of dollars a week. Well, if people are staying at home more, we might assume that their immediate consump-tion of retail products would tend to increase.

FACULTY COMMENT: (I was there!) The opportunities were incredible because the first thing that happened was a paint shortage. The old lady had the old man painting the house during the strike. What we did was to go around and sell local advertisers what was actually business insurance. I don't know if you can define that; in local radio and television we are many times selling business insurance. And the more we sell them that pays off, the better their business gets. In that year Sears and Montgomery Ward had an incredible home improvements sales record, never equalled. The next year they sent a new manager out and comparable sales are down, so somebody from the home office wants to know what happened to paint sales? It was the strike, of course! Rifles sold that year because it was near the deer hunting season: same question next year—what's wrong? We had furniture stores, meat packers, frozen food outlets, saying "don't pay until 30 days after the strike is settled."

An important point: with radio and TV the local advertiser can get in and out very quickly; with the newspaper it may be three or four days' lead time, and a problem if the strike is settled overnight.

LEWIS: An interesting thing that has happened in New York in the past three or four months is that when management sees an economic situation going a little soft, it cuts the salesmen's commissions! That's the last thing you do—at a time like this you increase the commission. I still can't understand a home office slashing off the most expensive people, so to speak, when these people are the generators of the profit for the organization. Another thing that happens: individual radio and TV sta-tions pull in their own promotions. Yet they're going out and telling the Macys and the Sears that they should increase their budgets. We're quite hypocritical in our own business—maybe some day we're going to realize that we talk out of both sides of our mouths!

DONNER: Anytime you get into a recession you get the psychological matter mentioned earlier of people beginning to cut back: cut back first on things they think in the family are unnecessary and begin to tighten up all the way around. I find we're already doing this in our family, trying to figure out how we can lower this, that or the other. When this becomes endemic the whole community goes that way, and if you had only a slight recession it can move itself to a real depressed circumstance. That's where I think that part of a radio or television station's obligation is to give some clarity of expression to what is happening. What is happening, why it's happening, and to what extent—then possibly you avoid or prevent the panic kind of thing. People are still going to conserve where they can—

and it's probably a good thing—but they're not going to grind to a halt universally.

JOHNSON: There are additional questions (about this problem) that I want to ask, because we're given an economic slowdown in a market and what I don't know is if this is a long-term slowdown or a short one. If there is something unique about this market that makes it look like it is going to be two, three or four years before the market comes out of it, that's a different kind of situation. I think that it might be the kind of thing we're in generally at the present time.

But if the station and if the market begins to act as if there is a recession, that is going to feed the recession syndrome. As that station manager and within my own plant my initial reaction would be to say: "Okay, how lean and how fat are we?" Because if our budget is pretty lean already and we don't have resources to tide us over a tough period, that's one thing. But if on the other hand it means a little bit of cutting back on profit this year, where we're looking to long-term success with this station, then maybe I'd use a different kind of strategy. One area where I would definitely *not* cut back is sales commissions. I would not cut back in programming in any way that you could determine as a potential advertiser or a potential listener or viewer.

Another question: I don't know how competitive the market is. If this is a fairly large market—and maybe if it isn't—a slowdown is not necessarily bad for broadcasting, as has been mentioned, and a slowdown may not be bad for an individual station even if it is bad for all broadcasters in the market. Because if you can get a bigger share of the market you'll have the resources to go full speed ahead and take some advantage of this, make some long-term points; *not* cut back in programming, *not* cut back in some of your services. And if the station can do something; if the program can reflect a concern for the market, can offer constructive helps in moving the market along—then maybe the station will make additional points with its audience.

STEINBERG: Three *don'ts: Don't* cut the rate card; *don't* cut personnel—which has a devastating effect on the morale of the community and in the long run hurts advertising revenues; *don't* cut promotion. As soon as a station or a network runs into trouble, the first department they cut is their own advertising and promotion activity. You can talk yourself deaf, dumb and blind; you can raise this issue over the years and on a philosophical level—and management will agree with you. Top management will say: "Of course. That's the last thing. We're not going to cut promotion." But they *do,* which seems to me to be the most short-sighted thing that can be done. When you run into economic problems and the community gets soft, that's the time to *increase* promotion, and that is precisely what they do not do. If anything comes out of this conference, we ought really to affirm this point. I would push to increase institutional advertising, even if the advertiser didn't have product; I would stay with that rate card come hell or high water, because if you don't the impression that you're running a cheap operation will say even after the upturn comes; and I would never cut personnel.

PRINGLE: I'm listing all of the things George shouldn't do, but I suspect that what he's interested in is what he *should* do. Perhaps intensive selling efforts, with whatever shift in emphasis is required; perhaps programs he should introduce. But sales and programming—particularly sales emphasis—what should he do actively?

CLARK: One of the things we might suggest to George is that he look at other markets that have experienced similar situations, get on the telephone with people and find out what they did to solve the problem, search out ideas and solutions. Solutions possibly much like those we have had suggested, maybe others.

A "do" that he must engage in is a variety of market analysis that is not revealed in the scenario we have here on paper. He ought to know something of the relationship of the medium to the marketplace; also of ad budgets in the market, national spot and cooperative monies and attitudes of major local advertisers. If he hasn't developed that information before, he'd best get cracking at it now. He needs to find out something about trends and types of retail sales that are responsive to conditions in the market; he should have some idea of what kinds of sales areas are most responsive to price or are most price-dependent—because if buyers are in a price-dependent mood that's an area to increase his ad promotion in. He needs to know if national sales are softening. He needs to develop some concept of the prognosis for the local market. Is this a short-run problem? Is it a long-run problem?

In the whole area of programming he should find materials to help his audience to be more economical in consumer behavior. Perhaps the listener participation program: What are you doing to control the family budget? In programming, a number of ideas may emerge: what George needs to do is hold staff meetings that are *idea-generating* rather than gnawing at "where do we cut the budget?" "What about the rate card?" "Who's going to be laid off?" "What about commissions?" All are crisis-ridden and morale-destroying subjects.

FACULTY COMMENT: Along with discussion of cutting things—is it acceptable to consider cutting profits?

SCHLATER: We all know examples, in certain markets, of the growth period of both radio and television where there have been enormous profits. It would seem to me that what George must do is have a plan for the short range. Any broadcast operation must have a contingency plan, if you will, because we want to maintain the rate card, maintain personnel, maintain station promotion. And we do this out of some of those profits.

MACOMBER: The more I work with commercial broadcasters the

more certain I am that profit is the *last* thing that's going to go in the station if the management—a good management—is working for the stockholders to continue the investment. The only way we can talk about solving George's problem in cutting profit is if George happens to have a self-owned station and he might say: "This community has given me a good life for 25 years; I can afford to take a couple of years of beating and go without any profit." But if it's investor money, if it's not George's money, George has to create a profit or George is not going to be in business. It's nice to talk about taking all of these things out of profit—but profit really isn't anything but the right to use somebody else's money, and we've got to protect that or we won't have his money.

FACULTY COMMENT: The average profit in television stations in the country last year was 17.4%; in radio it was 9%, and if you lump all the FM stations together they didn't make any profit. We may have to assume that George is not a fat guy and that he doesn't have a chain of other stations supporting him. So he has to have a contingency plan, maybe a 15% overall cutback. Like it or not.

REUSS: If you don't have good sales work going for you, you're not going to profit anyhow. So what services do you air, or what threats do you give your sales people, to get them to go out after this retail business? When newspapers go on strike, people don't mind getting the ads for large department stores on radio and television because they're hungry to find out what they need and what they can buy. The contingency plan that George should have is to know what this sort of thing means to his community, and to find ways to put his sales personnel on a new route.

HARDEN: Broadcasting is seen—along with its many other attributes—as show business, with creativity and all the rest; yet at a time like this we probably fall short in coming up with creative ideas, how to get ourselves out of a situation with creativity, with a novel approach.

THOMPSON: Most of the emphasis has been on the local market. Can we search out what might be done in respect to the national advertiser? The problem suggests that he's beginning to be wary of this particular market, not wanting to spend his money in it. What is the answer here?

INDUSTRY COMMENT: It may be to try to get your sales representative and your sales manager to get to the right people at the agency level—the planners, the account supervisors, the people who are not the routine buyers—to a favorable decision when the time comes to put your market on the "buy" list or not. That's why it might be a good idea—in concert with your competitors—to do a selling job on the market. You get to the planner and explain to him or her why your market should be on the list—with a good solid market pitch that has a lot of "why" in it. Some sales reps do this; if they don't do it for you, you should do it for yourself.

REUSS: On the national advertising scene, we have some reference to things that we could zero in on a little bit—the things people in your community are doing now that their incomes are cut, the painting of houses and the rest. If the station has the data on what *is* happening, and the sales people can go out and say: "We know that these things are happening, they're doing these things"—you've got to be ahead of the game. And your news team—although they try to stay separated—must enter into this situation. If they get a wire service story that the price of onions is up, and all they do is report that the price of onions is up, it doesn't mean anything to the community. But if they go out to see what this means locally, then they are doing a promotional service for the station even as they offer real news to the audience.

MACOMBER: If it's raining you don't sell golf clubs. You sell umbrellas. And I think that's what the thrust of George's positive approach must be: to analyze his market and sell the umbrellas, if that is what the market can use today. Regardless of what the situation is in the market, there is *something* that the market needs. And the more astute the management can be in analyzing the needs of the market, the more successful it will be. George *can* have more salesmen, doing more business, meeting those needs—and all of the other problems will fall in line.

RHO GROUP

Discussion Leader: Robert Henabery (ABC-AM Radio Stations)
Industry Participants: Donald Dahlman (Vice President, TV Sales, AVCO Broadcasting, Cincinnati); Bill Hartman (General Manager, KDKA, Pittsburgh); Gail Trell (Sales Manager, WCBS-TV, New York)
Faculty Participants: Myles Breen (Northern Illinois University); Gordon Law (Federation of Rocky Mountain States); Allan Mendelowitz (Rutgers College); Maureen Milicia (Marshall University); Wesley Wallace (University of North Carolina)

TRELL: In looking at this question, there is an enormous amount of gnashing and wailing in print and in conversation these days about the lagging economy, the dearth of airline and fuel and automotive advertising, as well as the frightening unknowns yet to be diagnosed from the truckers' strike—in a way this all reminds me of the noises when the cigarette dollars were barred from the air and, therefore, from our coffers. Well, WCBS-TV survived the "cigarette crisis," and thus far we're surviving the gas, car and airline crises. To tell you why, I have to re-title today's case study question: *The Station in a Lagging Market: Does it need a Band Aid, an Operation, or Preventive Medicine?* The WCBS-TV answer has always been the latter. In January, 1971, when the cigarette ban became effective, we were ready with a new sales development—*retail sales development*. We had seen a problem coming, and by the time it came we had isolated potential buyers among non-broadcast advertisers, studied their problems and prepared solutions based on use of our air time. We saw the problem coming and evolved personnel and management policy to deal with it.

Additionally, as usual, the impact was overemphasized. The industry hugely over-reacted to the impending loss; and in today's economy, as in 1971, the fear seems infinitely worse than present reality. Remember, we're discussing oil, cars, airlines as threatened sources of revenue. Well, put together, they total about 12% of total revenue. However, they haven't totally evaporated and I don't expect them to, and we're constantly developing new sources of revenue anyway.

Let's take the threatened groups, one by one, and look at what's actually happening; what problems we really do and don't have, and how to go looking for replacement revenue. First, let's talk about the *big* trouble—oil and gasoline. Indeed they are cut back—substantially, but not altogether. What they're saying is different, and they're saying it less often and less expensively. But oil and gasoline only represent 2% of our total revenue anyway. It's naive on anybody's part to assume that a total section of our economy will go silent. The oil companies are using network television to tell the public that they're looking for new domestic sources of energy; I'm equally sure that when those new sources are located, they will use local spot television to inform the public that they found it—if, in fact, there is a fuel shortage at all.

The absence of oil and gasoline as a category has not caused so much a dollar shortage at our station as an *overage* in quality inventory. Traditionally, gasolines and oils order prestigious prime time, male-oriented prime positions, in sports and news for example. We're bringing in new advertisers, true, but not necessarily the kinds that are rich enough or sophisticated enough to want what's been vacated by the missing oil companies. So we're trading up other advertisers in those spots and bringing in new, smaller ticket advertisers through the development effort. Thus, preventive selling for the loss of gasoline and oil revenue.

Automobile dollars, although presumably directly related to the gasoline problem, have presented an entirely different problem. Car dollars are still here, but *different* car dollars—less, to be sure, saying different things about cars. Who's on the air, saying what? Have you noticed Volvo, Opel, Saab, small Fords, AMC cars, Fiat and Mazda, selling their gasoline efficiencies? And Cadillac and Lincoln advertising heavily about their relative efficiency teamed with their luxury features?

Anyone who has a unique selling position relative to the contemporary concern is on the air exposing it. The ones who are not advertising have not yet evolved a way to position themselves, like mid-to-large size Chevrolets, Fords, Mercurys, Pontiacs and Oldsmobiles. When they do figure out what to say, or solve their efficiency problems, they'll be back. I assure you that General Motors is not going out of business, although they may have to change the way they do business.

To sum up: we diagnosed a problem, dealt with it, and in turn created a climate of confidence in ourselves at the station. Our sales people are not running scared nor should they be; they have the ability, provided by pre-planned stability, to sell television positively rather than defensively. Therefore there's no need for Band Aids, just a thorough, continuing self-examination.

DAHLMAN: Our problem with our five stations is profit. A long time ago we anticipated the variations of the national spot sales dollar and put emphasis on local sales throughcut our Avco group. All of our stations have come up with very big local gains: as a matter of fact, in 1973 our local dollars were greater than our national dollars.

This case study situation actually matches something that happened in our Dayton, Ohio market. Unemployment was rampant; lots of industries were moving out; we were having major problems in the greater Dayton area. The manager of that station had to make certain moves— he had to go in and cut costs in any place he could. He did that in personnel; he did that in programming; he did that in community service as far as he could. He did *not* cut his sales operation because he knew it was vital, but he developed, from the rate card we had, special packages of interest to local advertisers and he made special efforts to sell packages to local retail advertisers, department stores, etc.—efforts which were successful. So he was able to pull himself up by his bootstraps to achieve a profit picture which was comparable to his previous profit picture. He also made great efforts to tie in with community affairs to sell Dayton to Daytonians—a thrust that became an all-community campaign. And by making contributions there with his station, he was able to help the metropolitan area to get back on the track where it is now.

MENDELOWITZ: As far as I can see, when the management of a station responds to change in the local market by becoming a hometown booster, then the financial difficulties of the station cannot be very severe. I have some passing expertise in urban and regional economics, and I can think of no documented case history where the economic fortunes of a town have been relieved or depression has been relieved by hometown boosting—except for psychic depression. I think that you have a critical problem when you have to respond either by cutting your costs or exploring new avenues for revenue. Quite clearly, any station that becomes a hometown booster just does not have a critical problem!

LAW: My reaction (to the case study) is that they'd better fire George A. and hire the sales manager as manager, because it's apparent that *he* has been running the station and George has been living in a never-never world of complacency. Management should have canned him a long time ago!

WALLACE: I'm disturbed by a focus here that I think is inherent: it's in-built in the group; all the experts are *sales people*. Whenever we talk about cutting expenses we're talking about a philosophy that rubs off on programming. Cut expenses at the expense of the product, and the product in the end is programming. It just can't be anywhere else but programming.

So it seems to me there are two ways of looking at it. If you are looking at this market in this case study, *if* this is part of a general recession, then you ride it out and save the money as best you can because it's not a competitive factor—I mean, there is a competitive factor in the market, but it's not competitive with other markets—it's a general recession. *If,* however, this is a peculiarity of this market, I'm going to agree with Mr. Mendelowitz absolutely and say that your media are *not* going to turn this around. We simply *do not have the power* as persuasive media to turn the psychological factors in the market 180 degrees! So then you become competitive in the market. You do the kinds of businesslike things we've been talking about. I don't disagree with many of the things—some have an individual local factor; in your market you can either do it or you can't if it's a union problem.

It seems to me that instead of looking at the situation negatively—"how do we retrench?"—what we really have to address ourselves to is how do we get the station better involved with its community. How do we get a better share of the audience?

DAHLMAN: I don't think there's any argument that if you get bigger numbers you'll get bigger shares of advertising dollars spent in the market. But our real problem in this particular market—we've got a depressed market, and you're getting bigger shares of less total money.

WALLACE: But I'm suggesting that you can't take your medium and all the rest of the media elements in the market and turn that market around. There may well be other factors that are far too complicated for one medium to handle, or even a group effort; some of what I have heard says in effect that we *hope* these factors will work; that there *may* be other factors that are working in the market in a general thrust.

HENABERY: Obviously, I don't think anyone looks to cut costs as a way out. I think we all want to increase sales.

MILICIA: I have a couple of questions for industry people. First: what can be done to bolster confidence in the market as a viable, economic force? And second: what can be done by sales to stimulate advertisers' interest in the station and in the market? We've been talking about cutting costs and about increasing sales. Do you have anything that you can tell us that would help increase sales in this type of market where you can't sell a product to the people, where it seems they just aren't buying? Someone said put another man on and have him beat the bushes. Are there things that you would do if this was your market and you had this problem?

TRELL: When I read this problem I said: I'm a general sales manager, I'm responsible for bottom lines, that's what I do. And I also said to myself: this is not something that I deal with. What I do best is sales, and if your question is in that area, I can apply the answers to any market. If you (as faculty) are sending your graduates out to stations, then you must have particular questions that you want to ask that can apply anywhere, to any market, because good sales people or good management people can start in any market in any place, and bottom lines are always the same. If you're very good at what you do, you'll be successful at what you do, and it can be applied anywhere.

FACULTY COMMENT: There's an old joke among spot sales representatives that goes something like this: "How's business? Don't ask—things are so bad that even the National Safety Council has cancelled." My point is that our case-study friend George has a problem, and he has it *now*. He has, to pick up a word used here several times, a severe case of over-inventory —of unsold spots. We've agreed that rate-cutting is a sure-fire way toward suicide in the long range of business reputation; yet we heard another real-life example of a manager who fought his way out by developing packages for retail advertisers, department stores and shopping malls and what not. Is that rate-cutting, or is it the only way to hike up those bootstraps? And, how much of that time could he well devote to community morale, to "boosterism" if you will?

BREEN: I wonder: "boosterism," especially from the point of view of a station with people oriented, almost trained to listen to it, like WJR Detroit or WGN in Chicago, can be a vital force, because you are actually dealing with psychic depression—the blue collar blues. This is a major problem in the community, and it will be more so in the future.

DAHLMAN: I think that the smaller market has a lot less national spot business coming in. After you get below the top ten you have a lot more local time to sell. You've still got the same time to sell, that same inventory. Now, obviously, an inventory problem is related to costs, how much money, what you charge for a spot to absorb blank dollars. If you can charge double that, you have that much less inventory committed to dollars. So it's possible that even the smallest markets can have inventory problems, but management should never permit that situation to exist. If my sales managers sold me out, I'd fire them. That's because they had to adjust their rate cards to their inventory needs of the moment. We all have, I hope, flexible enough rate cards so that we can anticipate these problems.

HARTMAN: Our friend George not only should have good, creative sales people—we all hope that they are, but we have to be realistic and recognize that some of them aren't—he's also got to be a merchandising guy; he's got to be a creative sales person and sales leader.

INDUSTRY COMMENT: A thought that may come out of all of this— and it's related to the overall broadcast management theme of the seminar— is that George should be many things, wear many hats, to be Renaissance man or the man for all seasons. And that possibly *this* George is not. Somebody suggested that the ownership fire him, and make the sales manager the general manager, because the sales exec was obviously running the station anyway. I think this was said at least partly in jest; I hope so anyway, because we have to admit that—even if the situation is true—it would hardly be a solution to a difficult problem.

George needs help. More importantly, the station needs help but not that drastic a jolt. It goes back to a classic Bill Mauldin cartoon just after World War II, with the German burgher pounding his stein on the table and muttering: "What our country needs is a good strong man to get us out of this mess Hitler got us into." This station needs that sales development and planning process that Gail Trell described so well. It evidently needs that charismatic "image" that several of you implied when you spoke of WJR Detroit or WGN Chicago—and we could all name WCCO in the Twin Cities or WOR New York or a dozen others whose status confounds the program doctors.

It possibly needs that "flexible" rate card mentioned earlier, to entice local merchants—although I wince at some of the cards evidently printed on elastic and stretchable according to need! Community involvement . . . cooperative media involvement . . . hometown "boosterism" . . . we've named quite a number of areas. George may well need a phone booth in his office, where he can rush in, change to his blue jump suit, and fly out the window to go about these many swift duties! All that we may be doing is building our own soap opera, with an enticing teaser something like this: "Can a boy from a small mining town find happiness and success as the manager of a broadcast outlet in a troubled market? Come to next year's IRTS Seminar and find out!"

HENABERY: In terms of relating to this problem—and this is my own editorial opinion—this is *not* a short-term problem. It's long-term, long-range, and I do think that we should explore in some detail—in the second half of the meeting, with the other industry people—what could we do to make a market like George's a better and more attractive place to live. Because, if it *is* a better and more attractive place to live, it will attract people, grow, prosper, and will be a successful market. To me at least this seems very clear.

TAU GROUP

Discussion Leader: John D. Kelly (Storer Broadcasting)
Industry Participants: Ray Barnett (Sales Manager, KNX, Los
     Angeles)
Faculty Participants: Susan Cailteux (University of Kentucky);
     Jon Powell (Northern Illinois University); Irving Webber
     (University of Alabama)

KELLY: Our problem today is to see what we can do to get this
lagging market puffed up. To attack first hand some of the problems that
the manager of the station has. And, the nice part about this is that if
we don't do a good job on solving these problems, none of us is going to
get fired. Those of us in broadcasting have known that if we didn't
do a good job we *were* going to get fired. Today we can let it all hang
out and use all the imagination and all the inventiveness and all the
gifts that whoever it is gave us. What can George do?

BARNETT: First of all, bolster confidence in the market. What are
the things that we can do? You can organize the broadcasters in your
market, possibly, as well as the other major media if you can, with an all-
out drive to accentuate the positive. There have still got to be some
good things about this market. Something's got to be good in there.
People are still living and buying food and eating and that sort of thing.
So, you can do it in editorials. You can do it in promotional announcements on your own air. You can do it in programs—special documentaries.
You can do it in articles in the paper. Accenting positive features of the
market. Now, that's not a panacea, but sometimes these things have a
tendency to feed upon themselves. And, if the media can do one thing,
then maybe it can stop this thing from feeding upon itself, at least to some
degree. Another thing that can be done as far as the market is concerned
is have the representatives of this broadcaster, or this *ad hoc* media committee, work with local government and the local Chambers of Commerce
to go after new industry to locate there.

Those are, to me, a couple of obvious steps. Then, stimulate the
advertisers' interest in the station and the market. You can run promotional spots for an advertiser's use on radio, on WZZZ, on all the radio
stations. For example, if you're not using radio, maybe you ought to
consider this. "The spot that you're listening to right now is reaching
over 100,000 persons. Possibly some of them are your best prospects,"
and so on and so forth. Some time ago, when the car business was down,
you may recall a campaign that said, "You ought to buy now." It was
national, and something like that might be stimulating on the local level.

I think possibly they should build a media war chest for a market promotional campaign. Accenting the positive again. Using business and trade publications. Talking about the market. Once again, there's got to be something good here. It can't be all bad. You could even use promotional contests, hinged around positive sales points and the advantages of the market and directed at client policymakers, account supervisors, planners, and media and research directors.

I'm going to talk about cost cuts. We go under a doctor's care every time we think about that. But we do. So, once again we try to cut. I would say short-range cuts. And if we were going to do it, if George A. is going to cut short-range, probably the first place you're going to look— and I would look if I were George A.—I'd look into the secretarial help. I'd look into everything. Let me back up by saying that the last things I would look into cutting would be anything that would affect the product or the sales effort. You can say that almost anything you do is going to affect that. But I mean directly—secretarial help, possibly accounting, engineers and technicians. Possibly in your traffic department, you might find places where you can economize and cut. Now, a lot of these are going to involve union problems. If you've got a union contract there's nothing you can do in some of these instances. Promotional budgets, though it's hard to cut those, but maybe there's a way you can improve the effectiveness of what you're doing. Possibly the outside program fees, or freelance fees could be cut back to some degree. On long-range cuts, maybe you can delay the purchase of new equipment or new construction or something like that.

Short-range spot packages. The question is "Should George create some short-range spot packages? They're available locally only." I would say possibly, *if* he's going to go after a highly intensified retail effort. It's been my experience that retailers need tons of frequency, by and large. There are exceptions to that rule, but boy, they need it now. Possibly some run of station pre-emptive packages could be created, on a short term basis.

I would much prefer to operate with one rate card if you can possibly do it. In smaller markets that can be very difficult but this is why I would make this available to anybody that wanted to buy it. But it's pre-emptible, and you would not necessarily emphasize this to a lot of your major advertisers and national advertisers.

How do you create an upbeat market presentation? Well, I think you'd find every possible positive aspect of that market. And you might use the 1970 census figures, the latest ones—on income, buying power and retail sales. If this downturn has come in the last couple of years, the 1970 census and all those figures aren't necessarily going to reflect it. You've got to go with what you've got.

You could probably use long-range trends, most of which will probably not reflect this recent downturn. You'd highlight future plans for expansion and growth. Talk about success stories, of advertising efforts in the market. Even as bad as things are, somebody has got to be making some money. Use trading area figures. Certainly radio covers it all. Television covers it all. Don't confine yourself to that area.

Use the station's facilities. How can you use these? We've talked about some of these things. Hard-hitting promotional spots in prime time. Make space available at the station for civic groups to meet. Promote these positive attitudes. Give prominent news coverage to events or meetings that will aid the cause or influence public thinking. Give editorial support. Use local contest promotions built around positive aspects of the community.

INDUSTRY COMMENT: There isn't a major national advertiser that hasn't got Nielsen's Food and Drug Index figures coming out of his ears. One thing that most national advertisers have in common is being able to look at the marketing in this country on a market-to-market basis. On the basis of DMA areas rather than on the basis of how far a salesman can drive in his car to service the territory covered.

So, one of the things that we might suggest in this area is that in order to create the kind of identification that the market needs and the station needs, we actually go out and bring something to the advertiser that we can talk to him about in his terms rather than in our terms. When you get right down to it, the advertiser doing the national advertising doesn't really care about the market area, or the coverage area, or the number of homes; he's got all kinds of figures on that. You can talk to somebody about yourself for maybe two-and-a-half minutes and get away with it. You can talk to somebody about his problems, or his objectives, for a couple of days and he'll listen to you—even if the information that you bring to him is not necessarily on his terms. That's the trick in this kind of thing. When you bring him information about the market you're talking about, that information is not going to match the framework within which he does business. But you've at least started a process where you're talking in his terms rather than in your terms. So, in addition to all positive things that we might look at doing—to identify the market and to create all the positives about the market and the good things that do and must exist in the market—there is that other element that is extremely expensive to do. It means calling upon people one by one and putting together an individual story for each advertiser you call on. But it works. It works. At the very worst, you've created a basis on which you are talking to the people you're doing business with from a standpoint of his opportunity to make money rather than your opportunity to make money.

WEBBER: It seems to me that what's been proposed so far involves work at three levels. The first is the societal level or the community level, and that is to try to turn . . . to make things better by efforts that could be cooperative efforts or not, by industrial development for example. The second kind of thing involves improving the competitive situation of either the station or the medium, or both. And the third involves increasing the efficiency of the operation. And there have been comments on all of these things. Now, one thing that has not been spoken about—and it seems to me that this is interesting—is the product. That is the broadcasts and telecasts we sell. The assumption has been made, I think, that what's going out is good and can't be changed. I may be misreading this, but it seems to me that this is true.

KELLY: We could summarize that by saying, improve the product. Do in-depth studies. Management must keep prodding their creative people, prodding their programming people. To improve their product, a committee should meet daily and assign day segments for monitoring of the station's own air to see where there are goofs being made.

POWELL: There are two things that we're overlooking. One: that we must separate radio and television, if we're going to talk about them, as separate media. Not as the same medium. The second thing that concerns me is the emphasis on feedback or follow-through. We've got to devise methods of feeding back to the advertisers and the potential payers of the program, some kind of data that will satisfy them after the fact as well as before. I think we've got to lay much bigger stress on selling the product after it has been broadcast than we have in the past.

CAILTEUX: One thing I keep noticing in the conversation is that with this problem that we're presented with, we're in that sort of knee-jerk reaction, reacting to an immediate trend. One speaker said he's thinking in his own business of long-term planning. And that's the same thing with the product, it's the long-term plan. And some of these short-term plans seem to be very counterproductive, in the long-term sense. Anything that's going to damage credibility or potentially damage credibility, eventually can turn right around and hurt you more in the future. Because there's been much talk about political pressures, political problems. Well, if you get into a credibility problem ten years from now, the political problems for broadcasters will be more severe, rather than less. And you won't have the support of your audience either at that time if you continue to use 1970 figures and perhaps imply that maybe these might be applicable to 1974 when, in fact, the people will be able to see pretty soon that they aren't applicable to 1974. And I think one of the critical areas that I'm most concerned about is just the slight mention that in your new programming, and in documentaries, you cover certain things that are happening in communities. It's a very fine line that's going to have to be watched. I have some very grave concerns about this crunch that is here, and is coming, and what the reaction is going to be.

FACULTY COMMENT: From what I know about the broadcast industry there is very little knowledge or expertise in the area of real research, real experimentation, survey research, etc. It's very easy to say we'll conduct a survey. It's very easy to get Nielsen to do it for you. And, as you all know, you could have paper a foot high but really what you want is about four pages in summary of what's going on.

KELLY: Let me emphasize that there is need for research in sales terms. If a sales force has a positive attitude about what they're doing . . . if they know to begin with that the medium they represent can move product, and they can develop the marketer's interest . . . develop empathy for the marketer, by pointing out to him that when he successfully advertises he is succeeding in his own business—and, ergo, if that happens in this market, the market tends to grow. If we have better people doing it in this market, with radio, television, newspapers, regional magazines, whatever the medium may be, the market tends to benefit from it. This is a fact.

BARNETT: As George A., I'm going to get this income wherever I think I can get it. In this case, we're going to get it from the newspapers, and we are. Because in the *Los Angeles Times* they spill more than we get. Our approach to them is a very simple one. Let me back up by saying this. On sales staff we have, hopefully, a philosophy that the only way you're going to get somewhere is by helping people. You can't help the guy if you don't understand his problem. Everywhere we go, our guys have a profile sheet. We find everything about the man. We say, "We want to come down and talk to you about your business." And I have yet to have anybody turn me down. So, before we go back we know a lot about his business. What his competition is. What he's trying to develop. What he's trying to do. And as much as he'll tell us. Then we'll come back and make a presentation to him. Later, as we work with him, we talk about ideas.

SIGMA GROUP

Discussion Leader: Philip Spencer (WCSS, Amsterdam, New York)
Industry Participants: Larry Gershman (Sales Manager, WNBC-
    TV, New York); Bob Rice (General Manager, WRAU-TV,
    Peoria)
Faculty Participants: Albert Book (University of Nebraska); Knox
    Hagood (University of Alabama)

SPENCER: Let's talk about economics in a lagging market. Some areas might be what do you do with your rate card in today's market, selling UHF against VHF, local programming versus network, radio's problems versus TV's problems. Let's try to stay in these areas and try to come up with some solutions for problems that stations have in the marketplace today. What do you do? In January and February, when things are very slow, very *very* slow, should you stray from your rate card? If so, how far? Is it a temporary thing? Let's try and address ourselves a little bit in this area.

HAGOOD: Is it a lagging market? Disregarding the beginning of the last half of the first quarter, how do you compare economically this year with last year?

GERSHMAN: I can only respond for New York. Television business in New York is down. Beyond that I'm guessing, but I'm guessing over all the markets. We haven't seen the Arthur Young figures yet. I would guess that New York for the first quarter is probably off anywhere from 10% to 15%—which is a lot of money.

HAGOOD: What do you attribute this to?

GERSHMAN: Well, the supermarkets have pulled out because pricing has gone up and they are trying to keep a low profile. The automotives have pulled out because they have a problem: they're retooling to make smaller cars and it's the wrong time to be selling cars. On the network they are fulfilling commitments which they can't get out of. The gasoline companies have pulled out completely. Some of the airlines have cut back in their expenditures.

Now, *there* is a listing of four categories that represent probably 20% of the pressure in prime time. Prime time is your high cost area. I remember when cigarettes went out. At that same time tobacco, airlines and banks represented easily 60% of the prime time activity. So we have *two* losses there. We lost not only cigarette revenue—I think that's comparable to the energy crisis now because of the allied accounts that pulled back because of that. You lose secondarily because once that pressure is off, then advertisers are coming in saying, "I don't want to give you four thousand for that spot; I'll give you two thousand." *And* you find you're in a competitive position where the other networks are ready to take that offer—do you hold the line and get your head handed to you or do you respond competitively to the marketplace?

SPENCER: Bob Rice, do we have a problem today?

RICE: I would like to put that question in a frame of reference. Let's look at the profit structure. What kinds of profit structures do television stations have? *I* would tend to think that *you* would think that TV stations are very lucrative. But let's compare the New York City 24% profit structure in 1972 to the Peoria, Illinois 7% profit structure for the same year—and agree that there's a lot of difference.

We're talking about lagging markets; fortunately our market is not lagging quite as badly as New York indicates their market is—our first quarter will be up over last year. We don't have the demand for national dollars that New York does; actually 52% of our revenue comes from local sales—and only 13% of our revenue is from network. There are other broad differences. It costs us more money to buy a piece of equipment than it does NBC in New York, because we buy by the unit, not by the dozen lot. A problem is that you're got to be a group operation to stay in the business.

GERSHMAN: Let me add something that I think is very important. While sales are off and the market has softened, costs have gone up enormously. The unions keep coming back; you have to give cost-of-living increases. And it isn't just now. In some markets in this country, stations have not yet recovered from the loss of tobacco business—which happened to come at the same time there was a recession.

SPENCER: Let's get down again to the small markets. Let me give you an example in the northeast. The energy crisis in a little radio station in New York State will mean as much as $2,000 a month lost revenue in terms of *local* automotive advertising, *not* national. The local Ford dealer, the Chevrolet dealer, the Cadillac-Oldsmobile dealer; to local gas stations. Snowmobiles—a big business up that way—might amount to as much as $1,000 a month. *They're out.* What do stations do who lose $2,000 a month when all they ever billed was from $10,000 to $15,000 in the first place? And that's what we're talking about.

GERSHMAN: You obviously have to go out and beat the bushes—we've developed local sales. You develop a retail sales operation, which is where it has to come from. Local has been up in the past year proportionate to national sales, and it's what you have to call "safer" dollars.

BOOK: It's all right to say (a rather good phrase I guess) go out and beat the bushes. Maybe it's more correct to ask: what's the sense in going out to beat a dead horse? Those snowmobile people are not going to advertise no matter how you plead and no matter how much you go out there and tell them your advantages.

INDUSTRY COMMENT: Very true. It's a time to develop new formats, new program concepts, and fit them to new potential advertisers—people who have been content with routine newspaper ads or have given evidence of a little toe-dipping in the sometimes murky waters of short radio spots. *Image-building* for the major local retailer can be a big thing. Maybe he's always had a yearning to be associated with a community-service type program, but thinks it's out of his reach. Maybe he doesn't know that he can buy a saturation spread of spots over a short period, or a close association with news on the hour. The representative you send out to beat those bushes needs a strong machete—in this case it isn't a steel blade but a portfolio of creative advertising vehicles that have the promise of doing something for the retailer. And that *something,* to bring us back to George's case, is the medicine that will produce business!

The Long-Range Economic Outlook for Broadcasting: Or, Have We Topped Out in Revenues and Profitability?

SOME TIME AFTER resolving his station's problems in relation to sales and operations, George A. of Station WZZZ attends a seminar for broadcast executives and finds himself in a group faced with the problem of forecasting the future of the broadcast industry. He views a number of presentations on the growth and current history of the industry and then listens to demographers and sociologists outline the population of the '70s, '80s and '90s. He listens to a team of economists project the effects of inflation on prices and salaries in 1974-2000. He studies the projected growth of competitive media along with projections of new media forms yet to be developed through laser technology, two-way cable, satellite communications and more. With his head spinning, he sits down with his group to ponder the role and future of broadcasting.

DISCUSSION POINTS:

Can the rate card continue to increase? Through the 1950s, and most of the '60s, the percentage of television households market-by-market climbed, and advertising rates went up and up. Radio faltered momentarily; then moved into its own patterns of drive times and weekend and 24-hour-a-day frequency and reach. *But have we reached saturation?*

The other media have sharpened their sales tools, have much to offer. How do we document the unique advantages of the electronic media?

Do the demographics of key buying groups change radically with sophisticated marketing techniques and create a totally different sales approach?

At what point does your increasing rate card turn away advertisers who can no longer see opportunity for growth within the medium and conclude it is uneconomic?

The Long-Range View: The cost of doing business creeps up—salaries, overhead, equipment maintenance and replacement, etc. Despite the short-range problems, what are the *long-range* projections?

IOTA GROUP

Discussion Leader: Frank Harden (State Broadcasting Company)
Industry Participants: Bill Hartman (General Manager, KDKA, Pittsburgh); Robert Rice (General Manager, WRAU-TV, Peoria)
Faculty Participants: Douglas Boyd (University of Delaware); Stanley Donner (University of Texas); Joseph Johnson (San Diego University); John Keshishoglou (Ithaca College); Charles Shipley (Southern Illinois University)

HARTMAN: There are two areas—in dealing with the subject of long range economics—that really bother me and I see broadcast profits shrinking drastically in the next decade and into the next few decades. One is in the area of talent, the other is labor.

The sales situations are easily handled. If you go out and find yourself a good salesman, you don't mind paying well. But when you start dealing with talent in a market like I work in, the salaries range anywhere from $25,000 to $200,000. And that's radio, not television. So we just can't afford to get involved in too many of these high-priced talent people.

We also can't afford to get trapped in the area of our technical unions. We completed a contract just a few months ago after we went through a strike of almost 90 days because we were asking productivity from our unions. When you start dipping into the area of productivity you're going back to contracts unions been negotiating for 30 or 40 years—and the unions will ask specifically for more money and less work. When you talk productivity, they think you want them to do more. Even if you pay more, they're not happy about that. So unless this industry takes hold of that labor problem it's going to destroy us. We do more billing every year, but we make less money. You can track that back for about 15 years. I don't think the problems are any different in television—you'll find that you're doing more business and making less money.

Now I'm not trying to kid anybody. The broadcasting industry has been extremely lucrative since its inception. In the past—and the not too distant past—numerous people have reached in the till and they took everything they could get and they gave very little. Today, for many obvious reasons, you don't do that anymore. You've got to be community minded;

you'd better be interested in what goes on in your community, and you've got to be prepared to spend money to see that you satisfy the demands and needs of your community. Some broadcasters never have, and probably never will, accept that. If they don't, I think the government will be stepping in more often than any of you suspect, and in the very near future. So I project smaller profits, and my primary reason for that deals with the two areas I've just mentioned: talent and labor.

We're also facing the problem of dealing with minorities. There's tremendous pressure today on broadcasters to get minorities involved, and I think that's a good idea. But when you go out and you start to train and you go to the minorities, you will fill those three jobs with four people. So you're increasing payroll all the time. But you do have to do it. This is another instance where you're really touching the profit situation. There is a statement in the case study where George and his friends talk about the long-range view. They say that the cost of doing business creeps up. Well, salaries *are* going to creep up, and overhead *is* going to creep up. He also talks about equipment and maintenance and replacement, etc. I think that's an area where you're going to see broadcasters saving some money with computer-type equipment and modular-type equipment.

However, this does *not* save you anything when you're dealing with people. As a matter of fact, we computerized a major portion of our radio station—traffic, billing, logging, etc.—and we *added* two people! So I think it's a fallacy to assume that if you computerize you can eliminate people. You might see some long-range savings in technical services, with less maintenance needed for this new equipment—but not in the immediate operation. My son wants to be a broadcaster, and my advice to him is that he get into law, specialize in communications law and make a fortune—because that's what we are going to need today, tomorrow and the day after tomorrow.

RICE: There's been too much guessing on the role of the broadcast industry in the '90s and the year 2000, principally because of the potential of the totally dramatic changes that face us. We talk about satellites. I might have to talk about an entirely new concept of how to run a television station. We could end up with nothing but an all-news station, if that era was to come upon us. Cable, if it gets pay-TV, can certainly be extremely detrimental.

Let me use another point of reference—*profits*. The New York market in 1972 had a profit factor (for TV) of about 25%. If you take the three network stations you're going to elongate that profit factor. But when you add in the independents, you come down to about a 25% average. In Peoria the three stations, all network affiliates, averaged a 7% profit factor. For two years we had a profit, but the year before that there was a loss within the market. We're operating at a very narrow profit margin—yet I'm not pessimistic about the future for us in the industry. Projections indicate that total advertising by the '80s should approach the $36 to $45 billion figure.

This is an increase of anywhere from 82 to 128% over 1970. Television is estimated to be about $7 billion. Playing the low end, let's take the $36 billion projection, meaning that TV would be just slightly less than 20% of the total expenditure. Over the last ten years, television has averaged about a 9% growth. The estimate for the next ten years is possibly a 7% growth. It is difficult to predict inflation: that in itself just about blows any projections that you have right through the ceiling. A 7% increase in an average year could mean a standstill. But the point I make is that the industry can afford less profit in the major markets. I think it is an extremely inefficient industry.

The audience will continue to increase. There will be an increase in total homes from 66 to 78 million by 1980, about an 18% increase. I'm particularly aware of how our ABC network has approached the 18- to 49-year-old age group, pin-pointing this age bracket as the essential consumers in America, and projecting that 50% or more of the growth is going to be in that age group. The next significant increase in growth is going to be in the 29- to 35-age group, but not nearly as big as the 18 to 24's. I think all of this will have great bearing on television viewing in the future. Life styles may be changing. We may even now be seeing that, with the energy crisis. And I predict that this will increase television viewing and radio listening.

I see the computer as making us more efficient. I agree that it's not going to save us people, but I see it as providing valuable tools—in the area of lost spot announcements, for example. You'll have the capability on the very next day to know what you lost and to take action to pump it back into the system so that it can be aired. Then you are using the advertising to maximum efficiency, not issuing credit for spots that didn't have to be lost. That situation is an example of the inefficiency I spoke of; I believe we're all a part of it, and maybe more so in smaller stations than in larger ones. We are going to have to find ways, technically, to make the operations more profitable, more efficient.

The *one basic thing* I look to in the future (this is assuming that the pay-cable wires and other technology do not get in the way between now and 1980) is that the responsibility is going to become more awesome for a manager of a television station regardless of market size. There are things that we (Peoria) are doing locally that I don't believe the bigger markets have to do yet. Once they do, they're going to find that it isn't as bad as they feared. They won't have to rely as much on the national advertising dollar; they'll find that they can operate effectively with more and more local advertising dollars. I think this is unknown to many large markets—but it is our life blood in a smaller market.

BOYD: You refer to the labor situation, and I wonder whether this is unique to broadcasting. I realize that you're dealing with unions—talent unions, engineering, maybe news guilds or whatever—and I don't know that the people who make cars are in any better or worse position than the broadcasting industry. I realize that it's a problem but I don't think that it's unique.

RICE: I didn't say it was unique. What I tried to convey was that it was new to broadcasting. We are really neophytes in dealing with the labor unions, and that's our fault. But that's why I'm saying that there is great opportunity in that area for young people, because broadcasting is going to need help. We're going to be in virtually the same position as General Motors or any of the major car or oil people. And I don't think we want to be there. I don't think we can afford to be there.

HARDEN: There has to be some way to pay for these rising costs. Normally you would raise your rates. So the important question is: at what point have you reached the saturation level in raising rates? When do you drive away advertising support to some other medium?

KESHISHOGLOU: That question supposes or assumes that advertising in the future will remain basically the same as it is today, which may or may not be a safe assumption. The advertising on commercial broadcasting may not have the same form ten years from now than it has today. It may have an entirely different form.

RICE: Assuming that the same form will continue I feel that we're inefficient. We have attempted to sell time to advertisers, and that's not what we have to sell. We should be selling the ability of a message to deliver; to sell his service or his commodity. That kind of creativity from the academic world, I think, can allow broadcasting to continue to grow at the pace it has or a similar pace over the next decade or so.

JOHNSON: CATV, Pay TV, and cassettes all point toward fragmentation of the mass audience. All of us watch Walter Cronkite once in a while. All of us have a common frame of reference in that we watch *All in the Family* or the World Series or the Super Bowl, or some kind of national experience. What if we became so specialized that we start reading our own specialized publications and listen to our own specialized radio and television stations. What, in the long run, happens to people who have no common frame of reference and what happens to the concept of "Nation?"

DONNER: I like the idea of a mass means of communication and I think that we are all pretty well satisfied now that broadcasting is the only mass means of communications left in the United States. A country needs the unity and the cohesive force that's given by some kind of mass means of reaching everyone with the same message. We must understand the societal implications of the movement toward fragmentation of audience.

BOYD: As a nation we did all right before 1927 without broadcasting as a mass medium of communication. Now, I realize that conditions today are not the same as 1927, but I don't know if we lost network television if we would be any worse off. Indeed, it's an intriguing idea.

DONNER: One of the purposes of a communication system, whether it's in this country or some other, is to get consensus, isn't it? So television allows that kind of consensus now in this country. But, if television loses that power, then it's got to be picked up somewhere else and I don't really know what the some place else is, but you have to get consensus.

RHO GROUP

Discussion Leader: Robert Henabery (ABC-AM Radio Stations)
Industry Participants: Gary Lewis (General Sales Manager, WMCA, New York); Terry McGuirk (Vice President, WAGA-TV, Atlanta)
Faculty Participants: Kenward Atkin (Michigan State University); Allan Mendelowitz (Rutgers College); Gordon Law (Federation of Rocky Mountain States); Wesley Wallace (University of North Carolina); Keith Mielke (Indiana University)

LEWIS: I think we have to divide the question into two areas: radio and television. I think that television will be facing what radio faced 15 years or so ago. I predict that you're going to see many more problems in the television area than you are in the radio area. With the continued proliferation of cable television and the options that people will have, I think we're going to see all-news television; we're going to see all-country television, and so forth. We went through this in radio a while back, and now we're all top-40 or we're all-news or we're all-country, and fairly successful. Radio is the most underpriced medium available at this point in time in this country. With the paper shortage, and the problems of paper, retailers realize the strength of the broadcast media. The future looks very good. Radio is a personalized medium and probably the only one around where it's a one-to-one relationship and not a mass. The believability is incredible. We're a warm medium, not a cold medium.

HENABERY: Doesn't it seem to you that radio has fragmented now and, assuming that it can stabilize and all these stations find places for themselves in major markets, that the growth will be upward again? All of us in radio have gone through a very difficult period and I think we're coming out of it this year.

LEWIS: We re-grouped and moved further forward by smart programming; by being able to offer to the audience the same thing 24 hours a day. They know what they're going to get when they tune to any radio station, particularly in New York. You know what station it is without hearing the call letters. And this wasn't the case 15, 12, 8, 3 years ago.

MIELKE: Would you define "warm" and "cold" medium for us?

LEWIS: Sure. I think that the greatest persuasion still available to man is word of mouth. I think the human voice is able to do more, and has done more through history, than any other medium. I think the newspaper is a very cold environment; it's a very stiff, black-and-white situation; and not very exciting or stimulating. There's an inflection in the voice that can make a whole big difference in telling a story, but it works.

HENABERY: Do you think that radio is doing a good job promoting itself?

LEWIS: No. I think RAB (Radio Advertising Bureau) is a debacle and everybody should resign tomorrow. I think it's a great place to put cobwebs and it's a history of old things. There's nothing forward about RAB. Their critical problem now is finding storage space—space for the past—and they are forgetting about the future. They haven't really considered it. I think many of these kinds of organizations become political and lethargic and therefore do not achieve anything. It's a retiring place for people who were great in the industry and who can now take it easy.

ATKIN: Radio has been local. In other words, most of your business is coming from retail advertisers and the percentage of the advertising expenditures going into radio has been constant for a long time now. How do you view the long range economics of radio? Are you going to get a larger share out of the local retail advertiser?

LAW: When I was taught to sell I learned that numbers didn't mean a whole lot; performance is what counted. Numbers look nice in the book, but they don't mean that you move a lot of product. I'd just as soon go sell a station that has a 2-rating against a station that has 12 if I know whom I'm selling. If that 2-point station is all Cadillac buyers, and the others are only buying blue jeans, I'm going after the Cadillac buyers.

HENABERY: What about mystique? Isn't this one of the things that radio has to work on in connection with its image in terms of public relations and in terms of reaching people with a less direct assault? It seems to me that this has been one of RAB's problems.

MIELKE: I think we have digressed from the target. We're in the process of sharing conclusions. What is more useful for us is to share the process of reasoning which leads to conclusions. I'm very interested in the topic: How do we look at new technology and how do we untangle the future? We must develop rational projections for the various media of communication. I've yet to hear the first bit of analysis as to, "I think thus and so, thus and so, ergo, conclusion." I'd be very interested if anybody here could get on that target.

MENDELOWITZ: I'm willing to step off into space. I think that for one thing, we're going to always have free broadcasting in this country—radio and television—simply because the income distribution effects are so great that it could never be done away with. But I also think that, for the more affluent members of our society, alternate media will be available—for example, video tape cassettes that will allow you to see what you want to see, when you want to see it. Cable will bring live theatre into your living room when you want and I think that, over the next two or three decades, what you're going to find is that the poorer segment of the population will be the primary audience for the free broadcast media. If you want to ask whether there is a threat to the revenues of the broadcast media, the threat is how many marketers are going to want to spend a lot of money supporting programs when their potential audience of consumers represents the lowest segment of economic distribution.

McGUIRK: I've got to be very honest, my crystal ball is kind of cloudy. I can't see that television will continue to grow at the rate that it grew in the '50s and '60s. We're reaching near saturation on television homes. I think we will show more growth, but I don't think that it is going to continue at the same rate, unquestionably. I think that we're starting to level out and I might add that, as far as I'm concerned TVB (Television Bureau of Advertising), unlike Gary's feeling about RAB, is doing a great job for us.

However, we in television have not started to scratch the surface in selling our own medium. We've had it too easy, really—people come to us. We must reach out and develop new advertisers because the advertisers that we now have on the air weren't with us five years ago; maybe they didn't even have a product on the shelf five years ago—a lot of them. We've got to keep developing new markets and I think this is the future for us. Our retail business has gone up steadily, I mean the specialty shops and the smaller shops. We're approaching them and we're able to get them on television. It's not all that expensive. We'll produce a commercial, that'll do a good job in a half-hour in the studio or maybe an hour, and we can do that for a couple of hundred dollars.

Eventually, we are going to be beset by the problems of channel proliferation. What's an ARB (American Research Bureau) going to look like when somebody in their home has to fill out an ARB diary with 20 channels? You'll have the citizen channels, the movies, pay movies, pay cable; these things are going to hurt us, and we may have to take off on a different tack if we're going to survive. We may have to go into an all-news operation. To me that is a good direction because news is very saleable; it's probably the highest priced item that we have on a cost-per-thousand basis; it's something that can't be assailed by satellite to home, by cable, or by anybody else. I don't see cable to-satellite-to-home putting us out of business. A lot of the smart television operators are in the cable business—my company is. We're not in any major markets but we have something in excess of a 100,000 homes, and if cable is going to be a good business, you'll find a lot of broadcasters in it. But I don't think it's going to eliminate free television or free radio either. I just don't see people paying for these movies or paying for entertainment when they can get it free.

I think we'll continue to sell advertising but we've got to do a better job. We can't sit there and wait for the phone to ring. We've got to get out and develop new markets. We have a sales development team at our station that doesn't do anything else but develop sales. This is a full-time job. Once they've developed a sale, it's turned over to the sales department and then they go on to something else. I'm optimistic over the long-range. I think that we'll be able to survive and be able to continue to make profit.

HENABERY: How do you envision the next 20 years in terms of cable and satellite? What do you think is going to happen?

McGUIRK: I don't think cable can reach saturation within the next 20 years or anywhere near it. Cable people are running into problems, as you know. Tele-Prompter has had some serious problems. Cable is capital— you just don't go ahead and build a cable system that's $4,000 a mile. Cable is an expensive business and it's not nearly as profitable as a lot of people thought it was when it first came down the pipe, and I don't think that cable is going to develop that fast.

WALLACE: You have to be as old as I am and do some remembering. In 1948 and 1949 and 1950, radio was sitting here saying some of the same kinds of things: "Man! That television . . . they are really having a lot of trouble . . . You know? It's going to be a long time before something happens to it, and we in radio have a great big ball going; just don't change anything." What I'm suggesting is that maybe we ought to do a little thinking about television too. Costs of production and operation are increasing while audience size decreases. True, there is still a lot of fat in television so that you can still lose some profits and come out reasonably well. But I'm really looking down the road a little bit. Can you counteract a decreasing con- centration of audience, and increasing costs. Which of those two variables can you counteract? I don't see anything to do but cut costs. You cannot force people to tune in to your channel.

LAW: I'd like to react as I'm the only one here that's in the satellite business. The PBS network pays $8½ million a year to get a signal across the country and they've got a limited income. They must look for a more efficient way to serve 240 stations. The commercial networks have the same problem—as the tariffs go up, it costs more money to inter-connect. If broadcasters and cable systems and translators don't start moving toward satellite technology in a helluva hurry, somebody else is going to own it. It may not be the U.S.; it may be the Japanese, it may be the Dutch or it may be the Indians because it's booming down the road so fast that we're getting behind.

TAU GROUP

Discussion Leader: John Kelly (Storer Broadcasting)
Industry Participants: Larry Gershman (Sales Manager, WNBC-TV, New York); Phil Roberts (President, Greater N.Y. Radio, New York)
Faculty Participants: Philip Gelb (Bronx Community College); William Hanks (University of Pittsburgh); John Kittross (Temple University); Daniel Viamonte, Jr. (University of Hartford); Jon Powell (Northern Illinois University)

ROBERTS: There is a presumption, inherent in the question, that rate cards are increasing and have been increasing and the question is, can they continue to increase? The fact of the matter is that the opposite is true. Rate cards are decreasing. They've been decreasing very rapidly, for two reasons. If you understand what you buy when you buy time on television or when you buy time on radio, what you're buying are numbers of people. And the numbers of people keep increasing, not decreasing. The electronic media and magazines are the only two that I know about that are directly pegged on the number of people reached. If you take a look at newspapers you find that the newspaper rate card has little relationship to readership. Newspaper rates go up because of the cost of paper, because of the cost of printers and that kind of thing. They have no relationship to the amount of value you're getting for your buy. Radio and television are completely different.

Another reason TV and radio rates are decreasing is because of the Rate and Data services. The Standard Rate and Data for television is an absolute fiction. The Standard Rate and Data people will admit that, privately, and they've come out with a new book called "Market Guide on Media" . . . or "Media and Market Guide." What that attempts to do is to give you the realistic estimates of costs from so-called confidential sources on television stations. Radio, unfortunately, is going the way of television to some extent, and now they're going to put out another media market book guide for radio stations. Again, on radio rate cards—the rate card in Standard Rate and Data is a fiction. And it's becoming more and more of a fiction, as our media buying services and advertising agencies play one radio station against another.

Let me give an example, if you're in a major market and there are 10 radio stations, and the traditional buy for that market for radio is four radio stations deep, normally you buy the top four radio stations. Well, radio stations #5, #6, #7, #8 and so on, would like to get a little bit of that money. One of the ways that they can do that is to be efficient. And one of the ways you're efficient is you lower your price, in relation to your audience. And so the #5, #6, and #7 radio stations are very busy lowering their prices. If the top four stations stay firm, it's not going to do #5, #6, #7 any good. But what happens and what is happening increasingly, is the situation where the #3 station and #4 station are getting kind of itchy because #5 and #6 are picking off some of their bucks. So they lower their rates. And then the #2 station becomes a little itchy. So it lowers its rate and the #1 station follows. And that's how rate cards in major markets are being depressed. I'll give you an example that happened two or three weeks ago. Media Buying Service in New York was going to buy 35 weeks of ITT Continental Baking for Wonder Bread and Hostess Cakes. They decided that in some markets they were going to pay $8.00 a rating point and in other markets that they were going to pay $6.50 a rating point, or somewhere in between those parameters. The national representatives of radio stations were asked to submit their costs based upon their rating points. And it turned out that on our Detroit radio station we would have had to sell them time at $11.25.

KELLY: Phil has addressed himself to the problems of rates in the radio business and perhaps from that you can get an overview of what's going to happen to the commercial aspect of the business in the long range. Let me throw out a few questions. You represent, and so do I to much less a degree, a public corporation with stockholders. And that's one of the major problems. There is a basic conflict between stockholder interest and the public interest. Throughout the history of the business we've been looking at the interests of the community with one eye in order to keep our license, and with the other eye, if such a thing is possible, looking back over our shoulder at what the stockholders will say if we do this.

GERSHMAN: I don't find that acting in the public interest, convenience and necessity, and making a profit are mutually exclusive. I think you can make a profit and you have a responsibility to make a profit, I just think that means you have to make every buck count. We do a number of things in the public interest, and I'm sure other stations do as well. We do a show for example called "New York Illustrated," on prime time every week— Sunday night, 10:30-11:00. It's a documentary that almost exclusively deals with problems of the area. And it's an in-depth show. It is not something strung together in a couple of days. Production budget is very high. I would say the average shooting time to pull a show together from script to finish is probably somewhere around seven to eight weeks. We do 28 originals a year. It costs us a ton to do. We never make back in sales what it costs us to produce that show. But we do it because it's an important show.

KELLY: Although all of us would like to see more of those kind of shows, we as broadcasters have a piece of paper that's called a balance sheet. And the big man who sits at the other end of the table says, "Okay,

Kelly, you take in X number of dollars and you're going to spend this much. This is your budget for 1974." And he does that twice a year. And by God, you'd better say the number that he wants you to say. Now, if you don't say it, and you sit there and you fight with him, there's another Larry Gershman or Jack Kelly waiting in the wings. That happens too often, And that's the name of the game—it's corporate profit. But I think really, long-range down the road, even my boss knows that realistically we're going to take smaller profits. It's already happening.

George A.'s problem is an overabundant supply of merchandise. Nobody's coming any more knocking at that door, or flying in over that transom asking for time on his television station. Now what he's going to have to do is to try to figure out where we're going to go economically. What recommendations is he going to make to his people 5, 10, 15, 20 and 25 years down the road?

KITTROSS: Twenty years down the road, I think we're going to see a quite different structure. We're going to see a split. We're going to see on the one side those who make and produce programs—produce the product. It will be syndicated. What we now think of as networks, as syndicators, as local live types, or whatever it may be, they're going to be split off to a great extent from those which are sales and distribution. After all, we talk about spots as our inventory. But our real inventory, of course, is that audience out there. That's what we're really selling. We do it by means of an inventory of spots, but if people aren't listening, nobody's going to buy the spots. That, I think, is pretty clear.

I think we're going to find the local stations as we now see them, and I think we're going to find cable and other means of transmission. If pay cable makes it big, I think that it will have the same economic structure that newspapers have where they get some money back from circulation and some back from advertising. It will spread out the goodies a little. But I think you're going to find the networks aren't going to be distributing programs to be presented at the same time all over the country, again. I think they're going to become syndicators. What we now think of as syndicators. Twenty years down.

FACULTY COMMENT: In Pennsylvania, you have to have cable. It's not a matter of choice. If you're going to watch television you have to have cable in the mountainous areas of Pennsylvania. Which is where it all began. But if you look at New York, where you can get almost everything on-the-air, the reason that they're on the cable now is for the entertainment value of things that aren't presently available over the airwaves.

VIAMONTE: We have to look at the role of the government in broadcasting for the next 25 years. Because, what if 20 years from now the government says, all right industry, you've had a chance to bring cable to the ghetto. You've had an opportunity to bring cable to minority groups and you said it was economically impossible. We will provide every person in the United States with cable; you provide the software.

FACULTY COMMENT: Broadcasting could very easily, in 25 years, replace a lot of the functions of schools, a lot of the functions of libraries, and a lot of the functions of medicine.

GELB: I think what's going to happen is that broadcasting—both radio and television—are going to have to stay, as they are now, competitive to other media. What you're finding is that we're getting more and more sophisticated in finding out who does what. A classic example is that 90% of the flying is done by only 10% of the people. You're wasting all your money if you're reaching 100% of the people when all you want to really reach is that 10%. And that accounts, I think, for the great growth of the special interest magazines. Where they are zeroing in right on target, they hope, by using editorial content to reach certain people who do certain things, who spend certain dollars in certain directions, and areas.

Radio has done that already. You can now decide that you want to reach kids 12 to 17 years of age, if you want to sell them pimple cream. You can buy just those kids and pay only for those kids, and not pay for anybody else because radio is fractionalized. FM helped to do it. And a lot of people don't really understand that yet. If I put a radio or a cassette in the room and said, "What kind of radio station is this?" You would respond "It's a beautiful music radio station." And if I said, "What audience are they looking for?" Invariably you would say, "women," because we've learned that beautiful music is meant for women. Well, that's nonsense. Let's take the country format. There are four separate country formats. There's something called Modern Country. There's something called Blue Grass Country. There's something called Progressive Country, and there's something called Old Country. Now, I'm not equipped to explain to you the differences. But what I'm really saying to you is that the cost of buying specific audiences, the cost of buying specific groups of people that do specific things are coming down. In relation to the notion that you don't have to buy everybody. And I think that's where radio is today. That's where magazines are rapidly getting to, and with your 40 channels, that's where television goes next.

SIGMA GROUP

Discussion Leader: Philip Spencer (WCSS, Amsterdam, New York)
Industry Participants: Ray Barnett (Sales Manager, KNX, Los Angeles); Leroy Strine (Sales Manager, WGAL-TV, Lancaster, Pennsylvania)
Faculty Participants: Richard Goggin (New York University); Joseph Haberer (Purdue University); Knox Hagood (University of Alabama); Kenneth Harwood (Temple University); David Lange (Duke University)

STRINE: The long-range economic outlook depends on a number of factors. First of all, what kind of market are you in, a large market, medium market, small market? What is the competition in the market among the electronic media; especially if you're representing a TV station, what is your TV competition? And at this point at least, radio, in my experience, has not been a great deal of competition directly. The competition for dollars is mostly print. How strong are they? What do they cover? What don't they cover? What do you? What's your potential for increased audience? In our present day that involves population growth. What's that potential? Consider history and what the potential future might be. How is it today versus what it was 5, 10 years ago? Use that in also looking ahead. You would have to talk with your fellow people in industry, as this man has evidently done to get some comparisons. If you are a union operation, you have one set of circumstances and if you are non-union, you are in another. It's well known, I guess, that when you have unions to contend with you are in a much more complicated and costly situation than you would be if you were non-union. So all these different factors have to be considered before you make any decisions about the future. You have to look at the total situation. For example, you have FCC and the FTC and all the other agencies to deal with.

BARNETT: One of the prime things that George should be looking at at this stage of the game more than anything else is the product itself. What is the product? What is he really doing? Of course, I think in terms of radio. Radio in our part of the world is very vertical. You're all album music, or you're all top 40, or you're all news like we are and you can buy it like smorgasbord. You can buy almost any demographics that you want from the standpoint of age and so on. So George A should be looking at what it is going to take to keep him alive in the face of the competition that he's got now and in the face of the new competition—laser beams and satellites and God knows what else is coming.

If whatever George A is doing is of real interest and of real service to his community, then he will be around for a long time. He may have to make some adjustments in some things. But if he is providing a needed service, whether it's a field of information—in our case it happens to be news—whether it's entertainment or whatever, he will attract viewers or listeners. Now it gets down to the point, can he make a profit by where he is going put against his cost to reach them? Well, in the course of what's going on in Los Angeles right now I think there are some stations that are going to get weeded out. As we have just mentioned, it is extremely competitive. I think George A is looking at that farther down the line because it isn't going to get any less competitive, it is only going to get more so. So he is trying to determine what can he do to stay alive. If he's constantly in touch with what the public wants and what their needs are—and of course this is an on-going project—he can attract an audience.

Then to make a profit, he must cut costs. Where can he make it profitable? Possibly he can do this through computerization. More and more stations are going to that to cut costs. How we do this in the news business I'm not really sure, but that is possible. As far as the rate structures are concerned, many of the agencies and services are demanding they buy the same audiences now for less than they bought a year ago. Meanwhile the broadcasters cost have risen and the squeeze is really pretty tight. The fact is that in major markets such as mine we feel that competitive pressure to the point where there are no "must" buys in our area. Maybe *there* are in some areas right now—there are areas where stations have a great deal of dominance. In Los Angeles there isn't one single adult radio station out there that an advertiser can't buy around and come up with a pretty good buy, including us. We like to think that that's not true but it's a fact of life. It's all based on those numbers. I notice one of the questions in here: "At what point does your increasing rate card turn away advertisers?" This is something you're only going to find out, in my opinion, when you get there. I don't know how else you're going to find it. The pending pressure of the marketplace is going to tell you that. I think that is what he is looking at here is a long-range situation where the free enterprise system is really at work, and those who are not providing the service and are not efficient in doing it are going to go out of business.

HAGOOD: I would like to go back to the product and what it may be 20 years from now. Hughes Corporation is going to put up satellites. They are going to package some programs much like magazines are doing now to those specialty markets. It is conceivable that in the future the television networks will go to cable television, producing and preparing what we now see on commercial television. Television will have to change for cable.

SPENCER: We're trying to solve problems for the guy who is operating now, not put him out of business which is what you're talking about. If you want to have one quick comment on it, ok. But you're putting the radio station out of business. What we're here for is to hear from you people with some ideas on how to keep him in business in the future.

BARNETT: I think that is something the free enterprise system itself is going to take care of. When those stations become unprofitable and the licensees can't make money then they're going to go off the air. I personally would be delighted to see about 20 of them go off the air.

GOGGIN: Are they providing overall service that is necessary?

BARNETT: Some of these are small stations. Our FM stations may be serving a limited area geographically. I think when they get to the point where they are no longer providing a service which can be effectively sold they won't be there. They'll be gone.

HARWOOD: The general problem, I think, has been laid out pretty well at least in theory by Max Macomber from Syracuse and North Carolina who has taken the view that the fraction of GNP, the fraction

of our national output going into the total communications media tends
to be pretty near constant in good times and bad. Now if you have a
slowly rising population and if you have a lot of new media coming into
existence, there are only a couple of ways to go. Let's say today you are
a small radio station. One way is to buy into those new media as they
come along. The Steinman stations are a good example of that, they're
getting into cable. The other way is to make sure that your costs are
reduced sufficiently as your slice of the pie gets smaller so that you aren't
incurring red ink.

HAGOOD: Along that line, I think the pattern of the magazines is
the pattern of radio. You spoke to this a little bit ago. I think radio has
handled that very well since television came into being. And perhaps it has
even got to widen that more in the future to continue to exist.

HABERER: What strikes me here is you're talking about creative
aspects of this and it seems to be creative selling. How about tying creative selling to creative programming? We're not talking about a major
New York station—what can a small station do with a very limited budget
to try innovative or imaginative programming and to get advertisers? It
seems to me that aspect of the thing is important. Maybe it is assumed
on the part of the people here, but I have heard nothing about the substance of what goes on in a radio station except in terms of trying to
sell advertising, to sell more goods and services. I'm not against that but
I wonder about the content of programs and how this would tie into what
you gentlemen are trying to do in the case of the radio stations.

SPENCER: Let's stay on programming for a minute, Mr. Haberer.
George A. in the next five to ten years is going to be looking for another
change within the industry. Hagood had mentioned that television is going
to change it. What are some of the ideas you can tell George A. to look
for in the future in programming? What do you think he might be doing
ten years from now that he is not doing today?

LANGE: If we're going to look at programming 10 or 20 years ahead
and we're going to consider the long-term economic forecast, which is the
topic of this conversation, it seems to me that we really can't resist any
longer talking about cable television. We've touched on it in passing
and it may come up again this week, although I really don't think we're
scheduled to deal with it in specific terms.

SPENCER: Can you relate it to the local TV/radio?

LANGE: Sure. One of the problems is we're dealing with things as
they are, which is always a mistake if you're trying to look at things as
they may be 20 years hence. We're looking at them as they are now in a
period which, even were the present administration to remain in office
another eight years, probably wouldn't remain static. That is to say more
shortly, cable television is here. It has been badly mauled by regulations.
It has been badly battered by resistance. My advice to George is, for the

time being, to do everything that has been suggested in creative sales and so on but meanwhile to join an organization like the NAB, for example, and lobby like hell for an abandonment of the present cable television regulations and a change in the entire regulatory structure of television and radio. That's what I'm really suggesting.

HARWOOD: I'd like to ask Roy Strine about George's future with cable TV in a medium-size market?

STRINE: If I were George, and no one else had it, I would certainly try for a franchise. Now it requires some investment and I think the money would be available unless he's in a highly depressed area where everybody has completely lost faith in the future. I don't think that we're talking about that desperate a situation. But I think if the money is available, if he has it or can borrow it, I would think certainly he should invest in a cable franchise.

People: Where Do I Find Them? How Do I Afford to Train Them?

ART B. AND CARL G. are having a quick lunch one day, and the conversation swings around to a topic which has been on their minds more and more of late. People.

Art who is the Sales Manager of station WMMM in Tennessee, and has worked at stations in Oregon, Michigan and Virginia, says, "We've had two jobs open for the past month. I can't find *any* qualified sales people to fill them. It isn't even a question anymore of trying to find the ideal replacement, I looked for a woman. I looked for a black. I'm still looking. Carl, you know what I'm facing. I can't afford the luxury of taking on a person just out of school on the chance that it'll work out, and hope that by some miracle I've hit upon the right person. We are staffed so thin that everyone has to pull his own weight immediately. Maybe its okay for the large stations to take trainees, but I just don't see how I can."

Carl nodded his head sympathetically. "I know what you mean. On our side of the floor in Advertising, Research and Promotion, we've got the same headache. Maybe its a little less troublesome, because we've got one position for a neophyte, but it seems that after six months on the job, they move on to "bigger jobs." I'm getting tired of running a training school for other stations. At the last BPA convention, I heard the same story from a number of station people, so I know it isn't our problem alone. What really gets me is they're not unhappy at the station, in fact most of them weren't looking to move—but were called by another station, and offered a job at a higher salary, because they now were "experienced.""

"What I don't understand is where all the graduates of the Communications schools go?" Art exclaimed. "Lord knows there are dozens of them—with hundreds of students in each. Yet aside for receiving occasional requests for rate information, or data on competitive product expenditures, we never hear from schools or students." "It's true," Carl added, "but you know, I keep having this dream in which the phone rings and it's a professor from the nearby university. He proceeds to offer me the names of three graduating students who have volunteered to work for three months without salary and without obligation. The problem is that it's only a dream."

Laughingly, Art says, "Maybe, *you* should call the school." Carl reacts with a shocked look and whispers to himself, only half amusedly, "Maybe I should, maybe I should."

DISCUSSION POINTS:

Administration in broadcasting has many and diversified opportunities: legal, systems procedures, personnel, actuarial, public relations and advertising, and many other specialties, when intermixed with a basic knowledge of broadcast practice, all make for desirable employment.

A Basic Question:

To what extent are the communications schools geared to produce this kind of graduate?

How can the industry help to spell out requirements to the above end?

How can the industry work to expedite employment for persons with such training and abilities?

What can faculty and schools do to broaden and/or change curriculum design, deemphasize the "creative muse" pursuit in favor of overall broadcasting?

The Television Information Office and the Broadcast Promotion Association recently introduced an awards program for the stations producing the best spots promoting television as a service. The entries, however, were a mixed bag—with most slanted to promotion of the *best news team in town,* the *greatest feature films,* or even the *top ratings.* Very few demonstrated that the *stations* saw themselves in terms other than "greatest-best-tops" in a promotional sense . . . How can the broadcast industry earn a broader image for itself? (And *note* the question uses *earn,* not *promote.*)

IOTA GROUP

Discussion Leader: Frank Harden (State Broadcasting Company)
Industry Participants: Al Grosby (Sales Manager, WAKR-TV,
    Akron); Arthur Hook (Vice President and Station Manager,
    WKBG-TV, Boston); Henry Marcott (Manager-Editorial Service,
    WNBC-TV, New York); Mark Olds (Executive Vice President and
    General Manager, WWRL, New York)
Faculty Participants: Douglas Boyd (University of Delaware); Carol
    Reuss, SP (Loyola University); Robert Schlater (Michigan State
    University); Charles Shipley (Southern Illinois University)

HARDEN: What can faculty or schools do to broaden and/or change curriculum design for students entering the broadcasting field?

GROSBY: We have very good working relationships with Ohio University. It is a relationship that was brought on by a good back-and-forth dialogue between us. I didn't sit back and wait for the university to say we have some graduates, what can you do with them? I went out to the universities in an effort to find good people for our company to hire. I found that, except for sales, there were some good people coming out of the universities. In terms of practical use of the equipment and hardware, there is no problem. Students are getting experience in news, experience in disc jockey work, but they unfortunately are *not* getting any experience from the college in terms of selling time. In terms of what can be done I would suggest more emphasis in the area of broadcast sales.

One suggestion is to have more broadcasters speak at the universities. I sat down with a group of students at Ohio University in a sales marketing class in which there were about five or six women. I suggested that women might look at radio or television time sales. It was a shocker. Not for one moment had any of them even considered it. I came back from a trip to our Dallas station last week. There are seven or eight women selling time on Dallas radio stations now, and two or three selling television time. It is like a shot of adrenalin for the sales departments. There is a crucial problem in the industry today in getting good sales people. You find, moreover, that women are doing a fabulous job, especially in TV.

OLDS: Is there a gap between the colleges, universities and commercial broadcasting? Should there be one? We have had some very interesting comments back and forth and part of the group seemed to feel the need to indicate to us hard-headed businessmen that no, we aren't in an ivory tower and by golly we are practical. A couple of people said, yes, not only is there a gap but there should be a gap because we are different. We're not just "trade" schools teaching people to become plumbers.

I was very taken with that particular comment because it reminds me of some of the things that happen in our own station, or for that matter at any station. You have a meeting with the program director and the sales manager and you don't want one to think in terms of the other's problem. I don't want a sales manager to say this is what we need, but of course I know from a program point of view it won't work. Tell me what you want and need and let somebody else hammer it out. I think that's the way it has to be. There must be a difference between education and current practice so that we can have the innovations that are essential to the broadcast industry. At the same time it seems to me you have to recognize the mission of the student from a practical point of view.

I have been teaching a course at St. John's for the past three years, which has been an eye-opener to me. It is so different from what I think educational communications used to be. I find that there are two classes of students. Some students take the course because they think it's an interesting sort of course to take. It's jolly. We'll do something in broadcasting and learn a little something. There are a few students who are dedicated to the extent of really desiring to get into the industry. Now I think in your own schools of communications you probably get far more of the latter. You have to know precisely what the mission is and part of it probably is general education. It can be explorative and innovative. At the same time I get very upset when I see kids who have no real working knowledge of what it's like out there. They apply for jobs sometimes in very dumb ways. I don't think that all of them necessarily recognize where you have to start or what kind of thing you can do as opposed to what you want to do. You may want to be the short stop or the pitcher but you may be better off as a utility outfielder. You should strive for a suitable mixture of theory and hard practicality so at least the student can get a job in the industry. Otherwise it won't work.

HOOK: Broadcasting is a big industry. Communications is a big industry. There are all kinds of schools. There are all kinds of faculty. There are all kinds of students. One thing I grasped in the conversation is that perhaps we are trying to identify the perfect solution to every problem. I have one man on my staff who, every time we employ somebody new, will come to me within 48 hours and say what are you going to do to guarantee that before this new employee is here too much longer that we really show him or her how things are done around here so that he or she doesn't foul us up?

I found this to be a remarkable approach in perception to what our business is all about, because I happen to have just the opposite view. I think many times we, as broadcasters, should be hiring change agents. We have tremendous egos in the business. Of course you're playing with fire when you send a student out with a kind of comment such as, go in there and shake that industry or shake that station up. But there are

times when I think some of the more astute broadcasters are looking for
that. You have to pick your shots carefully. You have to do your homework and you've got to do your research. I wouldn't want to close the
door on either side of this by saying that we should be training change
agents or we should be training people that have all the skills of the
people in there. I think you've got to do both. And I think that depends
on the student's wishes, intent, skills, where his head is, and then worry
about the marketplace later. On the other hand, the best change agents
in the world get the very fundamental grounding first so that they know
what they're talking about.

MARCOTT: I would like to throw out a little something to the educators. What is really changing right now in your schools to prepare the
people all these gentlemen want in the industry? How do you make the
student well-rounded, somebody who is going to be used perhaps other
than in the newsroom? I would just like to lay that out on the table.

SCHLATER: It would be the best of all worlds if academic people
could lead the industry. Then we would have the lead time to offer these
courses and so forth. I think that probably at every institution represented
at this table we restrict the number of hours, the number of credits students
can take in the major because we don't want to be a trade school. We
give students a broad overview of the industry at the undergraduate level
from the foundations in broadcasting to one course in television directing
to a course in audience research, etc. About a fourth of the students' total
number of credits are in the major. The rest of it is out in the university.
We're giving him a good, broad liberal education and in effect only intro-
ducing him to broadcasting at the undergraduate level. Now there are
ways he can get that necessary experience. He can work in the dorm
radio stations. He can work part-time at the radio stations in the market.
I know at my institution we are doing a better job than we did five years
ago in making damned sure those kids know something about political
science and history.

REUSS: On the point of advising, we've gotten to be more sophisticated too. One of the aids that you people in the industry can give us is
come to our campus and spend some time with the faculty and perhaps
even bring these little books of job descriptions so that we keep up to
date on what's going on. We have students of all varieties coming to us
and we know some are not going to make it in the big-time news operations, but they have great potential for other things and if we know what
you're doing we can better serve them. The other thing is that when
you or your colleagues come to our campus to talk to our classes I hope
that you will be more precise on what exactly you do and also on the
back-up teams that you use for your jobs.

BOYD: I would like to make some observations which stem from
being an undergraduate, graduate, and later a faculty member at several

universities, some big, some small. A student comes in to see you and you say, "What do you want to do." He will say, "Oh, cameraman." I talked to one the other day and said, as an opening comment, what do you want to do? And he said he wanted to be a recording engineer. I find that I spend a considerable amount of time discouraging people in the sense of trying to tell them what it's really like out there. I've noticed that there are a lot of people working in the campus radio and TV stations in production-related jobs, and here I mean writing, announcing, camera work. This is very good. I think they are too ego-involved in the situation and I think, as faculty members, we have an obligation to really tell them what the situation is in the industry, not that it is impossible to get a job but that it is certainly very difficult.

SCHLATER: One of the reasons we get such large numbers in our schools is that this generation now coming to the college level are really turned on by media. They have grown up with television. They're television's children and since they were seven years old one of the things they always thought would be fun was to do a television program. Most of them come into the major as a freshman wanting to make television or radio programs. So we spend four years telling them that there aren't very many jobs in program-making any more, but there are some good jobs in newsrooms and in broadcast journalism and sales. More and more students are coming to the university for job training. Students majoring in English or political science or history or some other non-specific career discipline have come to us because they want some direction in finding a job. English and other liberal arts departments are losing students. People are coming to school to get job training.

GROSBY: It seems that salesmen are also ego-motivated people and I am telling you that we have salesmen who have been with us for 20 and 25 years. I have a thing I just did with Ashland College where I brought a student in for six weeks on an internship program. No broadcaster is going to turn down this deal because I don't have to pay him a nickel. They don't want me to. We assigned the student to one of our salesmen. He took such fantastic pains with this young fellow from Ashland College to teach him, to help him, to work with him you'd think his whole life began again. So it seems to me if you were to go to a Post/Newsweek station, for example, and say you want a student to spend five weeks there and you don't have to pay the student, I would be quite surprised if they turned it down. I think it's conceivable that you can develop a real added dimension to two or three of your students by putting them into one of those stations for four or five weeks on some kind of a program.

SHIPLEY: We will permit a student to take an internship and get nine hours of credit for it. And for this he has to go out and find for himself a full-time position for a period of 10 weeks. Now that means that he comes to you and says I want a job. You look at him and say, yes, I will hire you or, no, I will not hire you. If you hire him then I will give him credit for it. But that doesn't make me responsible for placing him with you.

We have seminars every quarter in our department to which we invite professionals. One time it will be on management and I will have station owners. Another time it will be on news. We quite often have people from the networks in Chicago and also local stations are represented. Another time it will be on sales. A lot of our graduates come to us who are now in management, or news or whatever it may be. They hire a lot of our graduates, incidentally. The Illinois Broadcasters Association had a seminar this fall and came to our campus; it was for students and broadcasters in the area.

We help the students with the preparation of their resumé. We found that has been a very weak part of the students' preparation. Sometimes they simply were unable to express themselves and tell you succinctly what they had done. I bring this up because someone talked about the competition that they have to face in going to you.

We have an internship program. I might just describe it because it's relevant to what you were talking about. We are very concerned when a student goes out into an undefined internship and he winds up sweeping the studio floors. Our faculty get very irate about that and say that they aren't learning anything that way. So we had a great deal of preparation in our internship and it now comes down to a kind of agreement. We describe the intention of the internship to the employer, it may be a station, it may be an agency. We have some students who go to production houses or who go into the news department of a station. They have to pay tuition and at least take five credit hours. We require that they be paid at least the minimum wage because they have to live. But the employer specifies the job that he has for them. Then, we send them students who are qualified. They don't generally go until they finish their junior year. So we only send students who we feel are qualified and they must compete for the job—the employer isn't simply being assigned someone. He auditions them, as it were, and he may not take any of them. The one he takes has to sell himself. We don't send the student until he's qualified and then, at the end, we ask the employer to evaluate the student and also criticize any shortcomings they feel were apparent in our preparation. The student is going for a specific job. Quite often it's a summer replacement. In that respect we find out whether we're training right and the student then has to come back and tell us what he learned, what he got out of it. Some of them serve every summer. One of our graduates, who is a production manager in a production house in Chicago, hires some of our students and they get well-rounded experience.

SCHLATER: At Michigan State University we offer a course in broadcast promotion. We jointly offer it with the advertising department and we get people from broadcast promotion departments in the area. As a matter of fact this past year we have made an association with the national organization, the BPA, to judge their annual awards in the areas of sales promotion, audience promotion, or community involvement.

OLDS: The principal thing to do, and this is what we're talking about, in looking for a job is to try to think in terms of the employer's point of view. That's the only thing he is concerned with. He doesn't care about how badly you want a job. If you can point out to a man that, by golly, you can do something that will enhance his position, sales, or profile in the community he has to at least listen to you and there may be a job coming up sooner or later.

RHO GROUP

Discussion Leader: Robert Henabery (ABC AM Radio Stations)
Industry Participants: Jim Babb (Managing Director, WBTV, Charlotte); William O'Shaughnessy (President and General Manager, WVOX, New Rochell); John Schmulbach (Radio Sales Manager, WRGB, Schenectady); Billy Taylor (President WSOK, Savannah)
Faculty Participants: Bertram Barer (California State University, Northridge); Robert Crawford (Queens College); Gordon Gray (Temple University); Allan Mendelowitz (Rutgers College); Keith Mielke (Indiana University); Maureen Milicia (Marshall University); James Rhea (Oklahoma State University); Wesley Wallace (University of North Carolina)

HENABERY: People, where do I find them? How can I afford to train them? How do I keep them? My own interpretation of this is: What do broadcasters want and what can educators do to supply the needs? With that I would like to ask for an overview from Jim Babb, and his response to this problem.

BABB: I think the problem is a matter of degree. We're very fortunate we're located in the State of North Carolina which enjoys the reputation of having the oldest State University and also one of the oldest communications departments in the country. It's headed by Wes Wallace. The graduates from UNC's communications school virtually staff our entire company from the middle management level up. I know a degree of problems might exist in other markets. Like everyone, we're looking for the real top-notch performer—potential performer, I should say— and we do a very careful screening process. We have a scholarship program that has been in existence for some time both on the university level and for a Radio/TV High School Institute each summer. We have summer interns. So it has kind of been a faucet for us to turn on and off, when we need people, they have been available. We don't limit it to that one resource and one area. We recruit on most college campuses and we have big army bases close by. We have gone out after the people and try to keep them on a list.

HENABERY: There had been a request that we discuss the need for qualified sales people, albeit inexperienced.

BABB: Every session I have been in with UNC we always ask who's interested in sales, and there would be 25 or 30 kids there but no hands would go up. Every time they would get one about chest high they would look around and see everybody was looking and it would go back down. I think to look at the problem from the broadcaster's point of view, we have isolated communications schools from the marketing school, the department of psychology and what have you. We need to do a better job of integrating within the universities in the various departments. We are primarily show biz and then sales types I guess. But we have brought in a lot of people that have come in as production people or creative people, and they have worked into sales once they have gotten into our station.

HENABERY: Wes Wallace, is there a marketing course at UNC?

WALLACE: There are marketing courses. To follow up what Jim Babb is saying, we are not unaware of this problem and our students have a great deal of leeway. I'm not talking about our majors, I'm talking about University of North Carolina students who have a great deal of leeway in what they take. One of the characteristics of students going into broadcasting is that there are as many different kinds of students as there are various sorts of positions. Our majors, when they have a bent for business, are encouraged to take a basic accounting course, a basic marketing course. I think one of the changes that has taken place in the last half a dozen years is that when the question about sales work gets asked now, there *are* some hands that go up. We're trying to say to the student, here's what broadcasting is like. We expose them to meetings, not like this, but we take them to Charlotte, to Atlanta, to the NAB regional. Some of them come to the IRTS College Conference in New York. Some of them will go visit three little radio stations in a small market situation, spend the whole day in that radio station being exposed to varying situations in broadcasting. Then, academically, they can go a whole variety of ways. We resist trying to funnel the students into a specific line. What we're trying to say is here are all the goodies of broadcasting and you decide where you want to go.

HENABERY: Could I ask the academicians to tell the industry people —what is the attitude of the professors in general toward marketing and sales as compared to programming, research and the other broadcast areas? There was a time I can recall that sales was looked down upon. I wonder if that feeling still prevails in some of the schools?

GRAY: I think that depends to a large extent on the type of school and its geographic location. Today, marketing and advertising are still looked down upon in many of the Ivy League schools. If you talk about developing an advertising curriculum you are liable to get your head handed to you. The fact is that they do exist. I think most of the forward-looking schools are doing the kind of thing we do, the kind of thing Wes is talking about, which is to develop specializations within a major, at the same time allowing for the broad kind of preparation so that the student doesn't get straight-jacketed into marketing. For example, in our department, a person who elects a specialization in management or sales or promotion will be expected to take a good deal of work in the school of business in marketing, sales, and personnel administration. He will come back to us for his media specialization courses. We give management and advertising. We don't have a course in sales *per se,* but the student certainly gets exposed to some of the concepts of sales in the media management course.

BARER: We have the same essential outlook as Temple and the University of North Carolina. But we have general areas in which a student can emphasize. We have one area called general studies, another if he is interested in production, management, audience research. Also, we have instructional media. Within management we find a great deal of interest in things like sales and marketing. We find that the field study and internship approach is the most successful and the most easily controlled situation. There are things like professional attitude, and showing up for work. Is the student willing to learn these kinds of behavioral patterns that are part of his success? We also try to offer, outside of management and sales, production outlets as well. Some of the film companies in town have been very much interested. The thing that all of us are pressing toward is professionalism in the true sense of the word. If you're looking to be talent, a performer, you don't belong with us. I'm sure it's true with most of us that in years past if you wanted to be a disk jockey you took a degree in becoming a disk jockey. We find, for example, that even the community colleges that had a trade school concept are beginning to ease off.

MIELKE: I think the picture should be broadened a bit. We have quite a concern at Indiana that the trade school concept should not be taken to mean basket weaving. I think if we're honest we have to say that many of the undergraduate curricula in radio/TV have had that image and, in many cases, richly deserved. We have done grading studies in Production I and Production II that indicated that people got far higher grades there than in their overall curriculum. We now have at Indiana an undergraduate curriculm that is as intellectually challenging as any in the college of arts and sciences. We've accomplished this somewhat at the expense of a trade school emphasis. That is a trade-off that I not only willingly make, but strongly defend. We explained our curriculum, past and present, to the Indiana Broadcasters Association and they said that the days are over when the "broadcasting disciplines" would adequately service the needs of the industry. If they could not find intelligent people with management potential from among the ranks of radio/TV majors they would go to political science, journalism, psychology, history, English and fine arts to find them. In particular they stressed the need for some sensitivity to the real world. Students need to know what "bottom line" means, what a budget looks like, what it meant to live within it, and to have some sense of the business basis of commercial broadcasting. As a result of that we developed a complete minor, in which you can get as many hours through the School of Business as in Radio/Television.

MILICIA: In the six or seven years that I have been at Marshall University we have seen tremendous growth in the field of broadcasting in the same trends that you people are discussing. We now have 97 undergraduate majors and a graduate program. We have four full-time faculty members that teach approximately eight different courses a year. All of us have a background in the industry as well as in public broadcasting and in the academic, book learning areas. We also have an extremely rich field for our young people. We have a public television station at the University and open- and closed-circuit AM and FM stations. We have three television stations in our market, one in Charleston and two in the Huntington area. We bring in broadcasters for seminars. We have internship programs. We place our people not just as disk jockeys at the local station, rather we are trying to train them for sales.

BARER: I think to add another dimension to this, and this is true with many institutions, there are major considerations that all of us are confronted with today. For example, tight budgets, which means that if our program is to grow it has to be justified as being acceptable in terms of the university's policies and objectives and also we must show that the students have somewhere to go outside of becoming talent. The bottom line with us reads that if we start coming up with courses like announcing, they're going to get shot down. If we persist in the unrealistic approach, pretty soon the program will be eroded in campus respectability.

RHEA: I want to make just a couple of comments about our program at Oklahoma. We have a four-year program that all of our radio/TV/film majors take. We have three sequences under the radio/TV/film degree, one in production, one in news, and one in sales. We have about three-and-a-half job offers per graduate. They come out at various times of the year. We have a very heavy industry input. We have many people coming in and we publish the newsletter for the State Broadcasters Association. Generally speaking, we get into some interaction with the state broadcasters.

TAYLOR: There are many reasons why students are relating to this field and want to get in it. They feel it's a field of today. I think when you go to IRTS student gatherings, and you see some of the very bright kids that are station managers of college stations, and you see what they're into and some of the questions that they ask, they really put you on your toes because they know what's happening more than some of us.

HENABERY: I would like to suggest that in my involvement with young people, which was extensive for the last two years, I perceived radio, in particular, to be not only a profession but also a life style. The people live their jobs today. These kids are with it 168 hours a week.

WALLACE: I want some more information, which is why I have been trying to get in here. I can't get enough blacks to come to major with us. We've got a very significant body of majors. I have 167 undergraduate majors, of these 76 are women. I've got about 10 blacks. Now what I want to know is what do we need to do, from your point of view, to make ourselves more attractive to blacks? I want to know how I will be able to serve the needs of every broadcaster who is interested in qualified blacks.

BABB: Part of the problem is right around the room. We have one lady and two blacks. We've got to force-feed the system. We have not done a good job.

WALLACE: How can you help us to get them to come in and major? Or is there any way?

TAYLOR: One way has to start with you in terms of what you're offering. If you are offering them something they think will help them get a job on a station they'll be there tomorrow.

WALLACE: Does it matter to you whether he's a college graduate or not?

TAYLOR: It surely doesn't.

BABB: I think this is a point I want to bring out. Not to disillusion all the faculty members present, but there are an awful lot of very capable people in just about every broadcast organization I know with absolutely zero college degrees. The two top people in our radio division— one has a ninth-grade education and the other one is a high school graduate. I think we can overdo the contributions that the great universities, including yours, can make to the broadcaster. There's just an awful lot of capable people that don't have to have a college education to be a very substantial contributor.

GRAY: To follow up what has been said, Temple is in the center of the north Philadelphia ghetto, but we did not have a large number of black majors in our department, even though we've made efforts to go out to the high schools and try to talk them into the fact that there were jobs waiting for them. We began to get a larger black population when the local stations began to give blacks more visibility. As soon as the black kids up in North Philadelphia could see models on the tube then they began coming to us. Now we have to fight them off. Another problem that we have not solved is the lack of black faculty members.

O'SHAUGHNESSY: It seems to me that today young people are not interested in working on a radio station. We all agree that broadcasting achieves its highest form when it resembles a forum or soapbox or platform for the expression of many different view points. Radio offers this opportunity. I would love college graduates today to try to use some of their ability, some of their genius, some of their talents to get people involved in radio. I don't think they want to do that.

TAYLOR: In a small station we don't have any problem getting people involved. We really try to say, "Look, these are some of the parameters that we want you to at least be conscious of even though you may express if differently." So we don't have any problem getting guys to go out into the community to do things, to participate in that regard.

HENABERY: I would like to ask John Schmulbach if he would care to comment on our discussion in terms of General Electric being an enormous industrial organization with an image as the pioneer in the electrical industry. Perhaps you could tell us what effect that corporate image is having with the three stations in Schnectady.

SCHMULBACH: We have a system of hiring people that includes both hiring and improving from within, and hiring from without. By and large in hiring sales people I have not gone back to journalism schools. I went to the University of Missouri School of Journalism and I thought at first that I could bring all of my old friends into northeastern New York; I found that they didn't want to live in the 45th market. Ours is a market of a million and a half in upstate New York. We try to find people who have experience, if possible. The nature of the industry is such that we are now training people to do jobs that they can do and that they want to do. We don't have people knocking on our doors to do sales jobs. I have often told people when we don't have any openings, "why don't you try to get a job on a small radio station in which you can do a variety of things?" I had more fun when I worked on a 250 watt station in Clarksburg, West Virginia because I got to do everything. That way the individual gets all kinds of experience—writing, announcing, selling, whatever. Once you are involved in a large station you are generally channeled into one facet of the business. Our engineers are NABET. There is little cross-pollinating from announcing to sales or from engineering to sales or vice versa. As a result, for sales people I hire people who exhibit an interest exclusively in selling.

INDUSTRY COMMENT: I've listened to some of these comments and needless to say, my company, because of some of the market sizes we are involved with, doesn't have many of the problems that people in smaller markets have. We can, on a yearly basis, put 30 youngsters into the operation. In our operations we've got a Los Angeles radio station, New York radio station, and stations in San Francisco, Boston, Philadelphia, Baltimore and Pittsburgh. I would say that, perhaps, we turn over on a yearly basis 8% of our people. We truly have them standing in line, not only because of the name of Westinghouse, but because of our market sizes they can trade up. If I had my druthers, insofar as a young person with no practical experience having a college education and one that doesn't, I assure you the one with the college education is going to get that shake, provided that most things are equal. I like the discipline that they get coming out of school, and I also like the exposure that they get with the people they are involved with in the academic community.

BARER: One of the things that I personally have learned through the years of teaching is that if I instill in the best students a professional attitude toward work, I think I've got them on their way to becoming a winner. Discipline is most important. He comes to work in the sense of the word we both understand. What's your feeling?

INDUSTRY COMMENT: Discipline most certainly is important.

BARER: I get the feeling that a lot of kids are graduating with a thoroughly naive view of what it's like to go to work. You're saying these people come in and all they want to do is to be stars. Am I reading you right?

O'SHAUGNESSY: I'm saying they talk about marketing. I've been in radio for 19 years and I don't know what the hell marketing is.

CRAWFORD: At Queens College we don't specialize in radio/television/film, although it's possible for the student to get some exposure. We're very strong on the liberal arts, intellectual approach, and the students take a degree in communications. They may specialize in mass communications and get some contact with radio/television/film so that they come out with as broad a background as they possibly can. We attempt to funnel them into any business or operation that uses communications, which is pretty broad. We feel in the New York market that's the way it ought to be. Let them find their own level through counseling and guidance. One of the things that I wish I could get a little more response on, in which I am personally interested, is after you get your first job what causes you to be fired? In other words, let's say you get a first job. What can you do wrong? What are the things that kind of rub managers and stations the wrong way? I would like to be able to tell these kids what to avoid doing and what has the real currency of coinage.

HENABERY: That's a good question. Would you care to respond Billy Taylor?

TAYLOR: Many of the people who came in to sell for us had no idea, despite our efforts to communicate with them, what we were trying to do in the community and how we were trying to translate our approaches into money. They didn't know what the music was about. They didn't know about the public service, the various things that we were doing. Our best salesman is our general manager. I mean I wish he were three people because we'd be out of trouble. He really can articulate all of the things we are talking about to the guy in the corner store who says, I don't want to spend $100. One reason we have had to get rid of someone is because he went in with the rate card and said, "Look, this is what we want you to do." He couldn't care less. He's trying to do business. He doesn't want to hear my problems. He's got problems of his own.

HENABERY: Can we ask Jim's opinion? What are the things that bug you?

BABB: Breaking it down into two broad categories, one is a bad attitude. I always say we fire or terminate more people that have talent but don't have the attitude to match up with it. That's always very disappointing to see that type of talent slip away. They're going one way and you are going another. You can't operate that way. Then there is a very simple category, those that have insufficient talent to do the job or they are mismatched. We're trying desperately not to let people get too far down the road in those cases.

CRAWFORD: I was wondering about personal habits too.

BABB: Personal habits is included in that too. If a guy is supposed to be to work at 8:30 then basically he's got to be there at 8:30.

INDUSTRY COMMENT: I find that many of the youngsters today who do come to broadcasting come with many personal opinions and feel that through our media they can change the world. They forget that we are a business and as licensed broadcasters are responsible to a community, not to individuals. There is where I have had more problems, not only with young people but with all people. Now if you're a salesman and you've got a budget and all of a sudden you miss that budget by 50% it's pretty easy to decide if the guy is going to be around or not. If you have an on-air talent you take a look at your rating book and have a pretty good appreciation of what the talent is supposed to do. It's pretty simple to make a decision whether that guy is going to be around the following year or not. With some of these people that you are educating for general management or just bringing up in your own business it is not that easy.

MENDELOWITZ: Formal education discourages exactly the kind of attributes the people look for in the business world. You know a good salesman is someone who sticks his foot in the door and doesn't take it out until he has made a sale. This kind of behavior is not encouraged in a university. A student takes an exam. He gets it back. He gets a grade and that's it. If he comes knocking on your door repeatedly trying to get another five or ten points out of that paper he's not going to be very well appreciated. This ties to whether he's going into sales or whether he's selling himself. College students are led to believe that they are it, that because they are in college they know more than anyone else who ever lived or they know more than anyone else who is alive, and when they step through the gates of the university at the end of four years the world is going to be waiting for them because they obviously have more to offer than anyone else who is already out there.

O'SHAUGNESSY: I think Crawford raised a very serious consideration. What kind of guy do you fire after six months? I think that you look for the kind of guy who has some regard for your priorities. Les Brown in his book says that every radio station has to have its own style, its logo, the kind of people you associate with, a certain style. I think you should urge your students to tailor their presentation, tailor their pitch.

BABB: Each university does things differently, in a different style. I think this is true also of broadcasting. As close as we are, there are a lot of differences in the styles of operation from Jefferson Pilot to Group W. What we are saying is find out the style of the particular company you are talking to and maybe you may decide, as a student, I'm not going to fit in that organization. So why knock on that door? There are plenty of other doors to knock on.

TAU GROUP

Discussion Leader: John D. Kelly (Storer Broadcasting)
Industry Participants: Al Grosby (Sales Manager, WAKR-TV, Akron); Arthur Hook (Vice President and Station Manager, WKBG-TV, Boston); Henry Marcott (Manager-Editorial Service, WNBC-TV, New York); Mark Olds (Executive Vice President and General Manager, WWRL, New York)
Faculty Participants: Louis Day (Central Michigan University); Allan Geoffrey (University of Hartford); Richard Goggin (New York University); Philip Gelb (Bronx Community College); William Hawes (University of Houston); Charles Hunter (Northwestern University); John Kittross (Temple University); Lucius New (Texas Southern University); Jon Powell (Northern Illinois University); Irving Webber (University of Alabama); Sherilyn Ziegler (University of Tennessee)

KELLY: As instructors, as teachers, as academicians, we're all salesmen in a sense. And today's subject deals with this bridge. There are two phases to this particular subject. I thought first we'd start on the problem of people. How do we get people into our industry? Where do we go? Would you like to address yourself to this matter of "people" in the industry?

GROSBY: Well, I suppose part of any manager's job is people. I have had a fortunate relationship with one particular school—Ohio University. I don't know what they do there but they come out with super people. We have hired them in sales and in programming. I speak at Ohio University about three times a year to management sales classes. Invariably these 17, 18, 19-year-old students come up to me and say,

"This guy has given us what the business is like." With due respect for the importance of whatever academic things are necessary, during the course of what they teach, they have given the students a very realistic viewpoint on exactly what the business is like. The students I have hired, two girls and two guys, from this school for our station, have turned out to be just outstanding people. On-air people, are very easy to come by. Sales people are much more difficult to come by. In fact, in some of the talks that I've given over the past three or four years, I have tried to influence women to go into sales. We have a station in Dallas, and there must be nine women in Dallas today that are selling for Dallas radio stations. It's nine more than they had six months ago.

DAY: Al brought up the point about not training sales people and he's right. As you well know, most of the colleges have non-commercial licenses so there's really no opportunity for on-the-air selling or commercial selling. But a number of colleges have carrier-current operations which are wired on the campus. We have one at Ohio and we have one at Central Michigan. I know last year at Central Michigan we billed $30,000 in a community of only 20,000. This was just to an audience on campus. A number of colleges are training people this way—not through selling by way of over-the-air stations, but through carrier-current wired on campus.

KELLY: We're going to insist that paid commercials be eliminated from this seminar. There'll be many more thoughts on this, I'm sure.

HOOK: I think it's very difficult to avoid paid commercials on this subject because . . . I guess we're all very proud of our own history and how we got to where we are. Especially if we've had any reasonable degree of success. A lot of people come to us and say, "I want to get into broadcasting. Where do I go to get training?" I think any broadcaster who has been at it for a while tends to have a list in his own mind of the top five. And they all take on certain kinds of characteristics. Surprisingly enough, when I spent time in Ohio I saw more graduates than I have in Boston. I've been in Boston two years and I don't have the relationship with the community educators in Boston that I did in Cleveland. We frequently saw people from Ohio University and Western Reserve. But what I really wanted to contribute was that as a training organization, training people for a career, I think it's extremely important for a university or a college to have a relationship with a commercial station. I miss that in Boston, surprisingly enough. There are broadcast training institutions there but they're kind of at arm's length from the commercial broadcasters.

KELLY: What about this thing of sales that Al talked about?

HOOK: In television sales, I think we're looking more and more at people who have some understanding of marketing. That does not necessarily mean that they have to have done it—that they have to have a record. I think the day of saying, "What was your billing in the last 10 years you've been selling?" as an indicator of what you can do in the future is only one small piece of it. We're going to start very soon in our company giving some form of psychological testing on all levels. In sales management we're going to see what we can uncover in that area. But in sales, as in everything else, I would rather hire a complete broadcaster. By the complete broadcaster, I'm talking about somebody who has had some exposure to broadcast economics, management, philosophy, principles, behavioral science, what motivates other people. I look for interpersonal relationship skills rather than writing ability. I have someone doing writing on my staff right now. It sounds a little weird, but I have a promotion writer whose writing I never looked at before I hired her. I found out that she had the right kind of enthusiasm, understanding and ability to work with other people. This seemed to me at that point to be terribly important.

MARCOTT: My department is very small. I've recently hired a researcher and what we were looking for at the time was possibly somebody with a law degree. Because of the money situation, I settled for the next best thing, and that was a girl who had done a lot of research for a public interest law firm down in Washington. It tends to balance the department because I do have a lawyer who is very conservative and she is a wide-eyed liberal. It works very well. We have an internship program at WNBC-TV with Hunter College. It's a relatively new program, but we recently had a fellow with whom I am very favorably impressed and would like to hire. It is just a great program. We put the students through every department of the station. We give them a chance to find the area that they are most comfortable with and are interested in. These students generally get out of school and have a job waiting for them. It works out well.

KELLY: Thank you, Hank. Mark? What are your thoughts.

OLDS: New York City is a little different in that there are more qualified people always looking for jobs—actors, writers, agency people, broadcasters, talent, and so forth. Consequently, we have access to very qualified people who are just temporarily out of work. It's much harder for people to get started in New York. On the other hand, our company has five stations across the country which are black-oriented. Three of our stations are managed by blacks now. We've been promoting from within but the mere fact that I'm a white managing a black station is an indication of the difficulty of getting people into certain categories. You find the same people leapfrogging from station to station. We have trained, I guess, two-thirds of all the black broadcast newspeople in New York City. They leave us for more money, or a wider scope in which to display talent, or to work at a network or to make it as a general reporter rather than as a special reporter, or the desire not to be pigeon-holed into any particular kind of station. We are delighted when they are successful. I'm a very pragmatic broadcaster. I know what it's like to be in jobs, out of jobs, fired, resigned, to go from city to city—Elephant's Ear, Montana to New York, and six cities in between. I have some idea of what it's like to work as a practical broadcaster. I try to give this general approach to how do you get a job in my classes at St. John's. It's the primary thing I'm concerned with rather than all the theory which sounds fine. I find that kids don't even know how to apply for a job. It's an eye-opener to me to conduct a session where you say, all right, you come in and apply for a job. Ninety percent of the kids—grown people for that matter—don't know what to say.

KELLY: Mark, thank you. I'd like to ask some of the academicians about some of the things that they are doing in their own areas about this problem. What are your contacts with various broadcasters? Let's go right around the room. We'd like to hear from each of you.

GOGGIN: I have a question that keeps buzzing around in my mind: Should we be in the placement business? Should we have some structure that actually operates functionally for the purpose of placing our people in the industry? Is there still a kind of prejudice that existed, at least when I was hiring, about college kids—"these smart college kids?" I used to hate to see them come in. You've got to listen to all this crap before you find out whether they can do a job for you tomorrow. Can you push buttons tomorrow? That's the only thing that you're really interested in. Shouldn't there be some kind of a central pooling mechanism for broadcast jobs? I don't know what the figures are, but I was talking to Phil Spencer, he turns over two people in his small station every year. He said you multiply that by the number of stations in New York State and you've got at least 1,000 new people a year that can be placed *in just one state!* That's incredible. Now, multiply that around the country. The big threat that everybody's concerned with is that we're overproducing for the market. I don't see it. In light of what Phil said, and in light of the fact that we're not only talking about radio and television, but also the cable industry and education, there's no reason why a student shouldn't find employment.

DAY: I've been at the University of Georgia, Ohio, and now Central Michigan. I know when I was at Georgia we felt that we did have a responsibility to place our graduates. We conducted on a credit basis, once a week, a course in how to write a resumé, how to get a job. It was an academic course that lasted the entire quarter. We should go into this kind of thing as part of our instructional program. The outstanding things done at Ohio have already been alluded to. We actually took students to the Ohio Association of Broadcasters. At Central Michigan this year, we are actually bringing broadcasters to campus so that our students can interact with them, get to know them, and hopefully, maybe they are talking to future employers.

ZEIGLER: First of all, I am totally committed to two things in education. The major reason I've stayed in education instead of going into industry is because I want to bridge the gap between industry and the universities. I think we're doing a lousy communication job and it's unforgivable. We are in the business of communication. The second thing is to get away from this terrible trade school notion or image that academic broadcasting has had in the industry for so long. Broadcasting as a discipline is positioned half way between business, marketing, management and economics on one side, and communication, behavioral science, psychology, and sociology on the other. We need to draw the two together. In too many schools it's either one or the other. Almost nowhere do you get this commitment of half and half—bringing the two together.

GELB: I'd like to talk about two courses that I teach. Last year I taught a course called "Mass Media in Contemporary Civilization" at NYU and a course called "Issues in Broadcasting" at Lehman. I only talk for half of the semester and the rest of the time is turned over to the students, and they do something similar to what has just been discussed. They make presentations as if they are presenting something to a station or agency. It has to be something that they haven't done before, that doesn't fall into the ordinary patterns of broadcasting. For example, they come up with 17 different ways of doing a news show that doesn't resemble anything on the air now. I see no sense really of turning out people to do the stuff that you're doing already and doing extremely well.

One of the things I teach them to do is a survey, but not a survey that's competing with Nielsen but, rather a survey that nobody else does. I shouldn't say nobody else because the survey was done about 10 years ago by a truly far-sighted broadcaster. It's a study on violence in the schools which I've duplicated numerous times. I also develop what I call "reasonableness quotient" instead of an IQ. This may sound a bit prejudiced, but black students come out better. Sitting down and just being reasonable, getting down to the problem without telling each other off, and being able to compromise and deal with people as human beings. I don't know how you can test people for this but that's something you fellows said you're looking for in people. I can recommend a fairly good number of black students, and Spanish-speaking students. The point I am getting at here is I would like to think of the concept of fresh ideas rather than our trying to mock and worship the professional field.

POWELL: Our major is called radio/television. Our purpose is really two-fold. One is to ease the transition from the completion of a graduate or an undergraduate degree to the first job, and the second is to give enough of a background to the individual that 10 years from now, in a rapidly changing society, he is able to adapt in a constructive way and help you fellows out there. Now this is not the kind of thing that you can really measure in terms of sales dollars or accounts. That's the general philosophy.

Let's get down to the pragmatics. First of all, I think that you have to be accountable for the kind of faculty you have and the kind of program you have. So the program we have developed rests on the premises that there must be a pragmatic, realistic approach. At the same time your industry is changing. It's including and incorporating ideas and media that have not been incorporated before. I can appreciate the fact that you're looking for quality help and you want people who know what you're talking about.

GEOFFREY: I suppose the whole thing begins with a philosophy and the philosophy is what dictates at the University of Hartford. We are a speech/communication department which includes three areas, communication behavior, theater and mass communications. A student can't major in any one area. Our philosophy has been to concentrate totally on the undergraduate. You've got to learn something here that is useful to somebody besides yourself and myself. If you are here just for yourself you're not going to be any good to anybody else. If you're here just for me it's nice for me, but it's no good for you. If it is good for somebody on the outside, then it's good for both of us. We get a lot of students who are graduates of the Dick Robinson School of Broadcasting. We get a lot of students who are graduates of two-year media programs. The main complaint we get from them is not that they didn't learn the hardware (because they do learn the hardware at these places) but they didn't know *why* they had to learn the hardware. The hardware, because we are a private institution and we have no large endowment, is something that we can't afford to buy.

HAWES: In Houston we have a Department of Communications which includes journalism, radio, film, television, advertising and public relations. We're running about 750 majors right now, half of whom are in broadcasting more or less. I think the main thrust of what we're doing is to develop human beings who may or may not go into broadcasting. We invite a number of faculty from downtown Houston to teach various courses in their specialized expertise on our campus. I am executive producer of a weekly half-hour television program. The show has a magazine format in which our students gain considerable experience. All of this is done at a commercial station in cooperation with that station. Students use it as a practicing laboratory. The students do the producing, directing, act as cameramen, and run the film chains and video tapes. They do everything during the Saturday morning that the station gives us. We have internship programs with the industry for upper classmen. So far the Houston market tends to run a little bit ahead of us. I think we have opportunities for students in the industry that we have not yet solicited and cannot yet fill.

KITTROSS: We do have a lot of kids who want to come in and all they want to do is play with hardware. We try to discourage them. To give you an idea, Frank's management course started out with 15 very worried-looking students, we now put a limit of 70 and stop it there every semester. We search for faculty who have operating background as well as the proper academic credentials. So on our regular full-time faculty we have people, on weekends, who have been station managers and the anchorman for Channel 6 for 18 years. We are seeing more and more of our students becoming interested in management and sales. They're beginning to get the word that if you want to make decisions, management is the place to go. If you want to make money, sales is the place.

NEW: This is the first year that Texas U has offered any kind of degree program in broadcasting. Presently we have 93 majors or minors in broadcasting. In the past there has not been a working relationship with the Houston industry. We expose the student to as much as we are capable of doing but he makes the final decision. Our emphasis to date has been on performance and now it is going to move to production to meet the industry's need for new blood in management and sales. We are now taking a candid look at our capabilities and strengths.

HUNTER: Our advanced course in television directing is taught by the best television director in the city. Our course in advanced film production is taught by a woman who has done the best film production in the area. We are on the periphery of a very large broadcasting entity and I think, even if we wanted to live in an ivory tower, our students wouldn't let us. In our copywriting class the woman who writes the commercial copy for the Hallmark programs visits us. For the past six years we have cooperated with the Chicago chapter of the National Academy of Television Arts and Sciences, and we have given special seminars and special symposia.

KELLY: Irving Webber claims not to know a thing about broadcasting. He says he is only a sociologist. Irving?

WEBBER: I think maybe not being in communications gives me a certain advantage, perhaps keeps me at arm's length from some of the things that are being said. I hope it gives me some insights. I think I would like to look at the whole proposition that has really been at the center of the discussion this morning as analyzable in terms of responsibilities to the student, to the industry and to society. It seems to me that is the way to look at it.

The kind of people you really want are those that can enter at a low-level position and have the possibility of going on and on until finally they are doing something like directing the choice of editorial topics and writing them and so on. In other words, you want people who will move up the line. On the other hand, of course, industry has a very legitimate concern of getting an output from the student who can be put to work without too much additional retraining. The idea, from society's point of view, of producing people who can adapt and who can serve as good citizens is just as fundamental as anything can be. I think there is always going to be dissatisfaction on the part of industry with the output of the schools. And I think that, insofar as this derives from a failure of relationships to be established between the industry and the universities, that's very bad.

DAY: In Central Michigan we have three kinds of broadcast courses basically. One is strictly academic. The second kind would be the skills-oriented course like production. And then we have a third kind somewhere in between as a combination. What do you say to a kid when he says, "Why should I take broadcast history? Will it help me get a job?" I normally give an answer but I'm not sure I'm communicating. Most of them are looking at the real short-range goals, getting a job. How do you communicate the long-range goals of why he should be taking broadcast history or whatever academic type of course when he can't see the long-range value of that particular course?

GROSBY: I think it's very important in order to be a good broadcaster today to know the history of our business, and how things developed in it and also to be knowledgeable of what is going on all over today.

KELLY: I've been a broadcaster since about 1956. I went to the University of Wisconsin Journalism School and, of course, everything has been restructured since then. But at the time I went, all they taught us was writing and how to use the facilities of WHA. I have found that ideally you should have specialists but, for economic reasons you have to be a generalist and boy do I miss a good background in political science, sociology and economics. I was encouraged and gratified to hear the academicians speak of their problems.

SIGMA GROUP

Discussion Leader: Philip Spencer (WCSS, Amsterdam, New York)
Industry Participants: Jim Babb (Managing Director, WBTV, Charlotte); Billy Taylor (President, WSOK, Savannah); William O'Shaughnessy (President and General Manager, WVOX, New Rochelle); Charles White (Director Community Relations, WBNS, Columbus, Ohio); John Schmulbach (Radio Sales Manager, WRGB, Schenectady); M. S. Kellner (Managing Director, Station Representatives Association)
Faculty Participants: James Brown (University of Southern California); Kent Cresswell (Ohio State University, WOSU); Knox Hagood (University of Alabama); Curtis Hamm (Oklahoma State University); Kenneth Harwood (Temple University); Dorothy Johnson (Marshall University); David Lange (Duke University); Arthur Savage (Ohio University); Ray Steele (University of Pittsburgh)

SPENCER: We are going to be talking about people, where to get them, how to train them.

BABB: We are going primarily to the universities and colleges looking for people. The people we're having the most difficulty in finding and encouraging to come into our business are those who are involved in systems-type things. Broadcasting is becoming more computerized as we go along, so we are finding a need for different types of people.

WHITE: We have some problems occasionally with students who are coming out of the broadcasting schools into the profession. I think one of the biggest complaints I've heard from a number of station managers, and this is not just in Columbus but in many areas, is that often students are trained to be advocates rather than having the practical tools with which they can go about their business. I think a problem that we have faced in the industry is that many of these students come into broadcasting without the basic, practical ability to type. There isn't a department in the industry where one is not faced with the need for typing skill. So this is an area that I think I would like to see more emphasis on in all broadcasting schools. There is another area I think station managers sometimes fall into or have a problem with, and that is that they find a lack of communication between themselves and academicians, often because academicians appear to have a preconceived notion about their own propriety. So much so that they can't really communicate with those people who are in the field on a day-to-day basis and who really are faced with the kind of things that they are teaching the students in the classes. I think there needs to be more direct communication between the universities and colleges and the stations themselves to find out a little bit about those practical problems that these people who are working in the industry are facing on a day-to-day basis.

SCHMULBACH: I'm a product of the University of Missouri School of Journalism. So when I got into the business I thought everybody should be a graduate of a journalism school or a communications school. I then began to realize, when I was in a position to hire people, that the schools are not producing people who were sales-oriented. They were production-oriented and news-oriented. I wanted to be a newsman in the beginning, but I found that I could do a little better job in selling because I couldn't speak English too well.

Allow me to talk specifically about how we get people. Many times we get people who have experience from other stations. It's true that many young people right out of college will come to a station like WRGB, which is a 50,000 watt, clear channel station. We have been in business a long time. We have full-range programming. We have live sports. We have a woman's editor. We have news people. There are 140 people working in our combined radio and television operations—AM, FM and TV. So we have access to all of these various people and their backgrounds.

Newswise, we generally hire people who have gone to a journalism school or who have accumulated experience in the news field. On-the-air performers are generally experienced people from other stations. They have worked for a smaller station. We are in the 45th market. It is rare to have somebody come from a major market into our market, although we have acted as a training ground for people who come from our area—Albany, Troy, Schenectady, upstate New York. The anchorman on NBC News in New York is Tony Guida who, we said, was too young to hit the big time but he made it. We hated to lose him at the time. Saleswise, because I had gone to a journalism school, I thought that salesmen should have this kind of background. I found that, in going back to my alma mater, nobody was interested in getting into sales. We go directly through people we know and say, "Hey, we've got a job open, do you know anybody?"

We have been a little more specific now in our hiring during the last few years because of the selection of people based on sex and skin color. We have a high profile of minority groups in our combined operation. Naturally we try to get experience, but we also follow the line that all broadcasters are following at this point with the minority groups. In production we have a number of blacks who are working with people who come into the TV station to make commercials, video tapes and so on. I couldn't get sales people from schools, so I decided to go after people who were sales-oriented no matter what sex, color or background, if they showed an interest. They had to come to us, by and large, and show an interest. We have recruited in the minority groups but I still feel a sales person has to have an inner drive. It isn't something that you can give to somebody.

SPENCER: Where do station representatives get their people from?

KELLNER: I get that question asked me by a number of young people who have come out of college and want to become station representatives. Where do most representatives get their personnel? Originally it was by stealing from some other rep. A guy had a job with your competitors; you go hire him and pay him more money than he was making or make him more promises. But that's been changing. Aside from cannibalizing your competitors, one source of sales personnel was the media departments of agencies. In addition to that, really what you are looking for is someone with sales orientation, somebody with the drive, somebody with the aggressiveness—controlled aggressiveness because you're not selling one person one day and finding another guy the next day. You're going back to the same group, or the same individuals, time after time after time. I don't know of any young person who has come to me who has had real sales training at the university level. Nor do I know whether the colleges should be training people as sales people. I think that is a kind of personality that someone has.

One of the basic things a college should give people is the ability to express themselves in writing. More and more I have found that that is lacking. They just can't compose a decent sentence or get a thought across in writing without blundering all over or abusing the language even worse than I do. There are very few sales people in the national station representation business who have come from local sales at stations. And I think that is too bad. Because I think that experience at a local level is of enormous advantage, not so much in selling to the national advertiser or his agency but in communicating with the station and knowing what the station's problems are.

SPENCER: Thank you. Before we open it up I would like to take a moment to tell you how we find people, because I think you'd better hear from the small market operator to keep everything in perspective. I have three stations. In 1973 I hired six people. Two were graduates of the University of Maryland, one was a journalism major, the other one was a history/political science major who, after graduating from Maryland, went to the Northeast Broadcasting School in Boston which is a one-year wonder course. I hired one graduate of Seton Hall, a radio/TV major, one graduate of Marietta College in Ohio, radio/TV major, and one graduate of Niagara University. The sixth person I hired did not go to college. He is a graduate of the Northeast Broadcast School in Boston.

Because I have three small stations and because I don't pay a hell of a lot of money, I hire, for the most part, beginners. The only people within my company that really have good paying jobs is my morning man in Amsterdam, who is also my chief engineer, and my news director. Those are my two key people from the standpoint of on-the-air. In Ticonderoga and Herkimer we take them fresh out of school. I really don't care whether they're college graduates. I really don't care whether they're graduates of a 14-week wonder school, a one-year wonder school, or if they never went to college, as long as they graduated from high school and they read and are intelligent and have been involved in school activities.

Now how do I get them? Well, two ways. I put an ad in *Broadcasting* and I say "Help wanted, Announcers, has to be intelligent and has to be able to read in a pleasant voice." Then I sit back and listen to 35 or 40 tapes that come in. I will follow it up with a personal interview, bring them into Amsterdam. I do not reimburse them unless I hire them. They know that coming in. I talk to them on the phone. I don't accept collect calls. Now the other way is, I get *Broadcasting* magazine every week and I answer ads from students or prospective employees who put ads in Situations Wanted, Sports Director play-by-play, News Director, Disk Jockey, whatever it is. So I use *Broadcasting* magazine for 80% of my people, both for advertising for help and hiring people who are advertising for help. Another thing I look toward is the colleges that will send out lists every April or May.

CRESWELL: I want to ask the question first of John about the GE stations. Perhaps other people will want to comment on it. In terms of the policy that you are now following in generally promoting from within, do you feel you're fair to yourself in seeing a broad range of available people? Are you fair to the people who are now presently involved in your company and giving them a fair shake in hiring and promoting? The reason I ask this is that I'm working at Ohio State University with broadcast stations where we no longer promote from within. Strictly speaking, we have moved in a new personnel arrangement at the University where we have to release a person and hire him into the new position after opening it for a period of time to anyone. What we have is University personnel postings that go up on the bulletin boards everywhere, and are sent around the city and the state at times to say this position is open now, and do you have a person who would be interested in applying? As you know, it goes to social service agencies. This is related to what we are talking about in terms of community affairs and minorities and personnel in general. Several of us are going to be facing some of this pressure in the future. It's quite cumbersome at first, I guarantee you, because you see a person you would like to move up immediately. Your tradition has been promoting from within and that looks like the easy way to do it. No longer are we able to do this at Ohio State. I'm wondering if you feel that it is still the best way for you to do it?

SCHMULBACH: I think you have to approach it from the job position itself. Men will leave sales positions to go to either a better paying job or a management position. I have lost salesmen because they wanted to become a sales manager and they don't want to wait. Announcers you generally bring in from the outside, because ordinarily there is no one to bring in to an announcer's job from within. Sales people don't become announcers, accountants don't become announcers. Promotion people are satisfied doing what they're doing and they usually don't become announcers. You're getting outside people. So we're really not promoting from within 100% because of the nature of the job. The promotions from within have been into management positions and have been of the minority groups also. That is both intentional and because they qualify. If there is a job at one of the other GE-owned stations then we all know about it at all the locations because if a guy is a skiier and wants to live in Denver that's a golden opportunity.

HARWOOD: Well, if you were to make an employment forecast for total employment for your operation, let's say five since that's a popular number, a five-year employment forecast for January 1, 1979, what would your total employment then be?

WHITE: I think suburban stations and community stations, local stations, will grow to the extent that they deserve to grow. If you have entrepreneurs and guys who are bright and quick they will grow as far as their signals, their fire power and their down position will allow them. I think everybody else is moving to the suburbs and I think that is going to happen in big city radio also.

SAVAGE: Our program at Ohio is to train professional broadcasters. How many of you here, you broadcasters, would be willing to sit down with the colleges and universities in your state-supported institutions that have publicly-financed and publicly-sponsored broadcast education programs and set out a list of specifications that you would like to see people have when coming out of the universities? I mean right down to intense descriptions of skill levels and things of this type. Now we have 575 majors in our program at Ohio University. Obviously, the state of Ohio is not going to take all 575 of our majors over the next 100 years if they all live that long. There is no point in grinding out people—we're fighting our own student credit-hour battle and all of the ancillary problems that go with the process. If we aren't producing people that you guys can use we're really wasting our time. I guess my question would be to you people in the industry, would you be willing to sit down and provide us with a list of job criteria?

SPENCER: By a show of hands how many broadcasters here would be willing to sit down with the universities as Art Savage suggests? All of you.

BABB: I think that we have done this in many forms. We give scholarships to the university in communications. We give scholarships to the high school or radio institute in the summer. We conduct a two-day seminar in Charlotte for the juniors and seniors, a class every year, every spring. They come in Sunday night to meet with all our department heads and go through the whole thing for a couple of days. The type of kids we get now from the University of North Carolina School of Communications that are the most efficient and motivated are production people. But, nobody ever wants to go into sales.

SPENCER: Let me ask you a question now, all of you educators: How do you tell your students to get a job?

CRESWELL: Write. Go personally. Show some initiative. Be an enterpreneur. Also, take a non-broadcast job. I've been listening to the appalling fact that these kids don't want to go into selling because it doesn't have the glamor that they are looking for. If you mention public relations to them they will hit the ceiling, although they don't know what the hell it is. In any event, perhaps my situation is a little bit different because I'm with the advertising sequence and I go through their paces with them in class to show them what selling is all about, how to get out there and do something.

LANGE: I would like to ask you gentlemen, how do you rank your students? I'm asking for information. You send a student out. How does a prospective employer know where he stands in a class? Mr. Babb suggests that if he has done very well that kind of achievement will be recognized. What I'm asking is whether there are any formal ways to reflect that?

O'SHAUGNESSY: When a guy comes in to me I'm the last one to ask how well he has done in class. I will give you a composite of the typical young man in a suburban area of New York today. He drives a brand-new automobile. He stands in front of the mirror and blows his hair for about an hour before he goes on the air. And he is a very introspective guy. He carries home his ear phones with him in a special little case. He'd give you the keys to the station rather than give up those ear phones. All he has been taught in journalism school or radio and television school is how can I entertain, how can I give of myself. It's very difficult to turn these guys into the community. So what I look for is a guy who is interested in the world around him.

BABB: Let me say that we're not just looking for college kids either.

I hate to disillusion you but some of the very best people we have in our company have never seen the inside of a college and are managing some very important divisions in our company.

WHITE: What we are talking about is how to get your graduates jobs and how to place them. You know I think we are overlooking one thing, and I am reminded that guys come in and they are looking for a job. They don't care what kind it is, they just want a job in radio. I dare say that if your graduates would do a little studying and if they decide they want to work for GE go to John and say, "John, you've got it all. You've got the first station." Do a little historical research on the station. He has given his life for 17 years to that radio station. I think if you find out a little bit about his radio station he is going to be friendlier.

SPENCER: Kell, did you want to say something?

KELLNER: I wanted some information from the educators. Art Savage said that he is teaching an area in sales. When you talk about getting into broadcasting there are so many different areas. I think I am not unique in having the impression that the average broadcast journalism school is in the arts rather than in the business division. I hope I am wrong because a good journalist needs such skills as writing, speaking, and typing. With today's emphasis on the technical, the journalist also needs training in computer science and mathematics. Those courses are not in the journalism school, but I should imagine a major in journalism or broadcasting has to be given advice in what courses to take in other areas.

WHITE: May I make an observation? It belongs with what was just said. College conferences have delivered to us an awful lot of students who are excellent. One thing has stood out which has caused us to change our direction—nine out of ten students came to graduation with the expectation of being on the air. They do not understand that there are a great many areas in the broadcasting business besides the actual delivery of words and pictures. An air person is like a fighter pilot. It takes an awful lot of support to keep him in the air or in this case on the air. This is something that has caused us to alter our direction so that we now have at least one full session carefully planned and structured which we call the career clinic for lack of a better name.

TAYLOR: How do you relate the study of broadcast activities to the college community and the surrounding community?

CRESWELL: Many of us have internships and other programs that help.

SPENCER: This has been a good session. I think the broadcasters learned something from you people and maybe you have learned something from us. We do need help, we want help, we want to train. Now what I would like to do is go right around the room and have each individual give one suggestion as to how the broadcaster and the colleges can achieve greater cooperation and mutual benefit. What would you like to see happen?

BROWN: More broadcasters should come to the campus to give guest lectures and participate in class discussions. Also, I think college departments should send out an information sheet on the people that are available for hiring. I urge broadcasters, don't waste your time. When someone comes from an institution, write a note saying give us a paragraph on the person. How do you appraise him or her? He or she spent two, three, four years with us. We know the college kids better than you may know them in three or four months. Why waste three or four months?

FACULTY COMMENT: I would like to suggest that after there are some criteria established, one of the existing national broadcast organizations should serve as a central job pool.

WHITE: I think basically what we have suggested already—getting the broadcasters and the educators together in some meaningful way. I want to emphasize again the importance of typing skills. Typing is a very basic skill that's necessary in this industry. I would like to suggest that the teachers of broadcasting impress upon their students that only a small minority of jobs involve on-the-air performance. Most of the available jobs are for those people who are supporting the on-the-air people.

JOHNSON: I'd like to see the proliferation of internship programs so that students can get exposure to the real world of broadcasting.

HARWOOD: I would like to have a better sense of the month-by-month average employment opportunities according to area and region in the country. I'd know a little better how to store graduates temporarily in places, stick them away in holes until such time as there are openings.

HAGOOD: During the interview don't put too much emphasis on hard commercial experience.

SAVAGE: I would like to see the establishment of and the maintenance of continuous ongoing dialogue between broadcasters and those people who are administering and teaching in broadcast schools.

TAYLOR: I would like to see greater utilization of campus radio facilities. Students should get as much practical experience as possible.

SCHMULBACH: Your comments today have been a great revelation to me of what is available from the schools. This session has broadened my appreciation of what you educators are doing.

STEELE: I think we need to get from the academic institutions and from industry a more practical orientation and career rating earlier in the game as we are advising students.

HAMM: We need more vocational education in the field of broadcasting.

O'SHAUGNESSY: Broadcasting achieves its highest calling when it resembles a platform or a forum or a soap box in the community. I think it would be useful to us all if you would consider encouraging your graduates and students to use the abilities and skills which you have given them, not alone as performers or entertainers, but as people who try to encourage the community to better use of the air waves.

Public Television: An Historical Perspective

ON APRIL 14, 1952, the Federal Communications Commission issued a television allocation plan, known as the "Sixth Report and Order." In addition to channels 2 through 13 in the very high frequency band (VHF), the plan called for the use of channels 14 through 83 in the ultra high frequency band (UHF).

The Commission's Report provided for the establishment of noncommercial television stations—80 channels in the VHF band, and 162 channels in the UHF band. There were no provisions in the Sixth Report and Order, however, for the *funding* of noncommercial television. Only repeated financial transfusions from the Ford Foundation prevented the whole system from collapsing.

Despite the Foundation's efforts, noncommercial TV was virtually invisible to most Americans during the 1950s. In many large cities such as New York, Washington, D.C., and Los Angeles, all the VHF stations were licensed to commercial broadcasters. Most TV sets manufactured prior to 1964 required a converter in order to receive the UHF band, and reception was not clear.

During the early '60s noncommercial television began to receive support. The license of channel 13 in New Jersey, as a result of FCC pressure, was transferred to an educational group. Congress passed the ETV Facilities Act, which sought to encourage the construction of noncommercial TV stations by making available federal funds on a matching basis. Congress also passed a law requiring that all TV sets sold in interstate commerce after April 30, 1964 be equipped to receive all TV channels.

In 1967 a Commission, established by the Carnegie Corporation, urged the establishment of a Corporation for Public Broadcasting, aided by an excise tax on the sale of television sets, which would be empowered to extend and improve programming on public television (a term coined by the Carnegie Commission for noncommercial TV).

The Ford Foundation gave impetus to the Carnegie Report by earmarking $10 million for the establishment of a Public Broadcast Laboratory (PBL). Ford funds provided for the linking of noncommercial stations via AT&T cables. Noncommercial programs on film or videotape had previously been mailed from station to station.

The Public Broadcast Laboratory, under the direction of Fred Friendly, was to explore subjects which were not generally treated in the commercial broadcast system. Friendly met tremendous opposition from noncommercial station managers around the country. Many stations apparently felt that they were being relegated to the status of carriers. PBL's first program, a play by Douglas Ward Turner entitled *Day of Absence,* did not win many supporters, particularly among southern stations. (Turner's play is about a southern town in which all the black residents have suddenly disappeared. The town's people, unable to function, beg the black people to return. What made the play particularly controversial was that the white townspeople were played by blacks in "whiteface." Many stations, apparently informed in advance of the show's content, refused to carry the program.)

On November 7, 1967, two days after PBL's debut, the Public Broadcast Act of 1967 became law. The Act, which was an outgrowth of the Carnegie Commission proposal, created a Corporation for Public Broadcasting (CPB). The CPB is a nonprofit private corporation established to secure financial support for public broadcasting, to distribute Federally appropriated funds, and to contract for national programs.

In 1969 the CPB established the Public Broadcast Service (PBS) as a national distribution arm for television programs. The majority of PBS's board was elected by station managers. PBS began operations in October 1970 and, until recently, exercised authority over program selection, scheduling, promotion, and distribution.

In 1974 the PBS established a "marketplace cooperative" plan, whereby local stations bid on the national programs they wish to have produced and distributed. A catalogue of proposed programs is presented to the 250 noncommercial stations. A station indicates by negative or affirmative vote whether it is willing to pay for a portion of a particular program. If enough money is pledged to cover the production cost of a show or a series, then the project is incorporated into the PBS schedule. Only stations that contribute to the cost of a show are permitted to carry it. The Public Broadcast Service acts as a distribution service with little control over program content.

Since its inception Public Television's most serious problem has been funding. Congress rejected the Carnegie Commission's recommendation for an excise tax and has allocated money to P-TV on an annual basis. Several

proposals for long range funding have been vetoed by the Nixon Administration. The Ford Foundation recently decided to phase out its financial
support of Public Television and alloted a final $40 Million.

The financial picture is not totally bleak. Large corporations such as
Mobil Oil, Exxon and Atlantic Richfield underwrite specific programs for
national distribution. The Senate Commerce Subcommittee on Communications recently approved a five-year financing bill under which the federal
government would contribute $1 for every $2.50 raised from nongovern-
mental sources by noncommercial broadcasters. The bill provides that the
federal government will pay up to $88 million for the 1975 fiscal year,
graduating to $160- million by 1980. Noncommercial stations have initiated
a national fund raising drive.

Few people are more qualified to discuss the problems confronting
public television than Mr. Ralph Rogers, President of the Board of Governors of the Public Broadcast Service.

RALPH B. ROGERS

Mr. Rogers is the Boston-born Chairman of the Board of Texas Industries. Within national public television, he serves as Chairman of the Public Broadcasting Service's Board of Governors, and as a trustee of the Children's Television Workshop.

Mr. Rogers has long been active in public television in Texas, most recently as Chairman and Director of the Public Broadcasting Foundation for North Texas. Mr. Rogers is also the founder of the Arthritis-Rheumatism Foundation, a trustee of Southern Methodist University, and a member of the Corporation of Northeastern University, and the Advisory Committee of the University of Dallas.

Address by Ralph B. Rogers

When the subject concerns Public Television, it is always desirable to begin with some statements which are not too controversial. Here are two:

The first is some advice which I will attribute to my late friend, Gene McDermott, although he would disclaim that it originated with him. Gene always said, when asked about an impending speech, that the audience would never remember what the speaker said, but they would never forget how long it took him to say it.

The second is the result of the courtesies shown to me by Gene Accas. He sent me copies of your programs for the past two years as well as some tapes and speeches from last year's seminar. It struck me suddenly that all of your speakers are professionals! (My simplistic definition of professional is one who gets paid for the activities in which he is engaged.) Lo and behold! Your speaker tonight is not a professional. This is "amateur night"!

This ends the non-controversial statements. Next, let us launch into an "up-date" on that noble experiment called public television.

The days of 1973 were significant, at times even dramatic, for the institution of Public Broadcasting. Since most of you are knowledgeable, I do not plan to take much time to detail all the important developments. In the final analysis, what has been done is never anything more than a prelude to what is to come. It seems more constructive to devote most of our time to recommendations for the future. Nevertheless, there are a few facts which should be summarized before proceeding.

Early in January 1973, certain resolutions of the CPB Board compelled action by many local Board Chairmen throughout the nation. Until that time, most licensees at the national level were represented in some respects by the old PBS or a segment of NAEB. The Chairman's advisory group was, at that time, an informal association primarily concerned with assisting the institution of Public Broadcasting in raising funds.

When the issues came into sharp focus, an attempt was made to form one organization to act for the local licensees at the national level.

On March 30, 1973, that organization came into existence by the vote of all the licensees at a meeting in Washington, D. C. Of those licensees who attended—and most were there, laymen and professionals alike—there was only one dissenting vote to the creation of a new organization to represent all at the national level.

The name chosen was the Public Broadcasting Service (PBS). Policy rests in the lay representatives of the licensees, who elect the Board of Governors. To advise that Board there was created a Board of Managers, elected from the professionals in the system. Both Boards meet together at all duly constituted meetings. Executive committees of both boards are empowered to act between Board meetings.

It should be pointed out that the creation of PBS was not a sudden action. In fact, there had been innumerable suggestions made to create a licensees' organization over the years.

Whether the serious problems facing the system in the light of the veto of the 1972 legislation, or the ferment within the system itself resulted in the conclusion to form PBS is not a matter which needs to be dealt with here.

It is important, however, to state that the birth procedure was long and difficult, for it was necessary for everyone to understand what was proposed, as it is never easy to coalesce 150 independent and autonomous organizations (the local licensees) to agree on acting in concert.

Equally, it is proper to take special note that many members of the CPB Board actively urged the creation of one licensee organization at the national level whom they could recognize as representative of the large majority of the local licensees.

Two months later, on May 31, 1973, an historic partnership agreement was reached between CPB and PBS. A copy of that agreement will be attached to the copies of my remarks, which will be available to any of you who wish to have them.

Legislation

While both CPB and PBS made a fine presentation to the members of Congress and to the Administration, in response to the requests of those bodies to furnish facts and figures, it must be pointed out that, for the first time in the history of Public Broadcasting, the voice of tens of thousands of individuals from every nook and cranny of the nation made known their endorsement and support of the vital need for Public Broadcasting.

It cannot be questioned that the public's interest, as expressed by individuals, was the most significant single factor in obtaining wide bi-partisan support for the legislation.

A two-year authorization bill was passed. It provided $55 million in support funds for CPB for fiscal 1974 and $65 million for fiscal 1975. It provided also for capital funds to assist qualified licensees in the amount of $25 million in fiscal 1974, and $30 million in fiscal 1975.

The authorization bill passed the House by a vote of 363 to 14, the Senate by a vote of 66 to 6, and the bill was signed by the President.

Unfortunately, an authorization bill—despite the trauma associated with cuts, compromises, and controversies—even after passage and signature, is no more than a license to seek an appropriation.

In the appropriation process, Public Broadcasting became a small item in the total HEW appropriations bill. How small can best be illustrated by pointing out that the total HEW appropriations bill, as finally passed, amounted to $32 billion. Our items were cut back to $47,750,000 for CPB funds and $15,675,000 for equipment funds—only for fiscal 1974. This amounts to approximately 2/10 of 1 percent of the bill!

In fiscal 1975 we do not have to go through the authorization process but we do have to start from scratch again in the appropriation process.

Structure

The new PBS was conceived as an institution quite different from the old organization similarly named.

The new PBS is owned by the local licensees, responsive to policies made by them acting through their elected representatives, and is supported by funds supplied by them.

The new PBS does receive compensation, under a contract with CPB, to run the interconnection system, and it may solicit funds for programs and services, as a non-profit organization, to serve the needs of the members.

PBS, its Boards and its Staff, do not have any authority to act for any autonomous licensee at the local level.

Going Forward

All of us recognize that the success or failure of public television is completely dependent upon the programming broadcast to the many audiences we serve.

First we will talk about local programming since this is the sole responsibility of each individual licensee. There is a great deal which PBS can do to help existing licensees with information, ideas, costs, etc., which can be helpful in local programming. There is probably no hotter question in public television than the one which reads "Is the local station fulfilling its primary function, which is to serve its local audiences?" The answer is easy. No public television station is doing the job of serving its local constituency to the degree it would like to be served or to the extent desired by the station.

I suppose the same question could be asked of commercial television stations and the answer would be identical. The difference, however, is that serving the local community is one of the principal aspirations of public television. In fact, there are those who insist that it should be public television's only goal.

At this moment in the public television communities, I suppose I know as many persons, both lay and professional, as does any other single person. I have never found one of them who does not wish to do a better job of serving the needs of his local constituency.

Unfortunately, the funds have never been available to do the job.

Perhaps if we move to the subject of "national programming" it would be easier to illustrate the problem. In public television, national programming is intended primarily to assist all the licensees by providing programs which can be used by a great many of them in conjunction with local schedules.

It is axiomatic that high quality programs, distributed by the interconnection, result in a more economical use of funds. It is equally axiomatic that very few high-quality programs could be financed if their utilization was confined to one local community. The commercial television stations are living proof of the accuracy of those statements. Just what would commercial television programming look like if each local station was compelled to produce its entire program schedule locally.

My best information is that the three major commercial television networks spend in excess of $1 billion per year for national programming alone. Contrast this $1 billion with the $33 million, which is the total amount of money spent last year on all national programming for public television.

Whether you compute the figure of national programming on public television as 3% of what the commercial networks spend, or whether you split the billion dollars into thirds and say that PBS spent 10% as much in national programming as did the average of each commercial network, the fact remains that neither the people of the United States nor any of you are apt to applaud the starvation diet for public television programming.

One last word before we leave this subject. The total Federal funds appropriated by the Congress for the Corporation for Public Broadcasting last year amounted to $35 million. When the cost of financing an interconnection system and the other expenses of the Corporation are subtracted from that $35 million, it is readily apparent that the local stations had to find additional funds for national programming. That's not all! They were compelled to find virtually all the funding to program and to operate, as well as to provide capital equipment for the 250 public television stations now on the air. These 250 stations are, incidentally, more than the number of stations affiliated with any major network.

Probably this is the spot to raise the burning question entitled "Networking." If you have no objections, we will defer it to the question-and-answer period.

We must go back to the subject of programming. This time we will separate it into three major categories: 1. Instructional; 2. Cultural; 3. Public Affairs.

1. *Instructional*

While most of our local stations devote half of their air time to the broadcast of formal, instructional programs, no one is satisfied that television is being sufficiently effective in the field of formal education.

Before the advent of modern technology—television being only one of the many technological advances useful in formal education—a philosophy of education was created in this country. That philosophy substantially continues to this day.

Expressed simply, it has been accepted as axiomatic that each local community and the educational institutions in that community are to decide for themselves how the students are to be taught. The normal structure in public education is the election of a lay Board which in turn engages professional educators.

Similarly, institutions of higher learning, whether public or private, are created and governed in much the same way, although the selection process for Boards usually is not an elective one. No one can quarrel with the right of self-determination which I have just outlined. Unfortunately, this right of self-determination has the result of stifling the opportunity to take advantage of modern technology.

To put this matter in proper perspective, the yearly expenditures (1973-74) for education were . . . . 97.3 billions of dollars

This breaks down into;

  a) Elementary & Secondary schools cost   61.6 billions of dollars
  b) Institutions of higher education cost   35.7 billions of dollars

These costs have been growing at the rate of about $7 billion per year. The question facing the American people is: Can better education—both in quality and quantity—be obtained at the same cost? Or, is it possible to stop the $7 billion increase and perhaps even reduce the cost without lowering either quality or quantity by the use of modern technology?

In the past few years, activities in various sectors have proven that there is more than hope that such accomplishments can be achieved. One need only to refer to programming such as *Sesame Street, Electric Company* and activities by a few local educational institutions working with their local public television stations, as well as consortiums of institutions working together on a few segments of needed curricula.

Where the skilled educators have outlined and then detailed what they want and then turned it over to skilled professionals who know how to use the modern technology, there has been success. Where the educators themselves undertook to become television producers, the results were not encouraging.

In the months and years ahead, there must be a real attempt to convince the public of the potential in the use of modern technology to assist in the formal educational processes.

Perhaps even more important, there must be a real campaign mounted among educators which will lead to their dedication to the use of modern technology rather than just their lip service.

What is the role of public television in this field? Shall public television lead? Shall public television join with other organizations and institutions to bring about the desired results? Or is the role of the public television licensee merely to supply whatever delivery capacity it has to the total effort?

2. *Cultural*

Obviously, it would be desirable if every man, woman and child in the United States could attend performances of great symphonies, operas, plays, etc. Certainly every person would benefit from visiting the great museums or the workshops of painters, sculptors, etc. Visits to motion picture studios, television studios or discussions with writers, poets, and artists would benefit each of us.

The simple truth is that this kind of exposure cannot be brought to every man, woman and child. Even encouragement for such exposure to cultural enrichment is not available to many.

While it cannot be denied that commercial television on occasion brings magnificent cultural programs to its viewers, the number of hours devoted to this type of program in prime-time leaves much to be desired. Public television can and must do an outstanding job in this area. The need exists, the desire and the talent is available. It is only adequate funding which is lacking.

I have indicated that other types of programming are included in this broad cultural category. Who can deny that audiences interested in "how things are done by talented persons" should not be served by public television? There are audiences for chess, cooking and "how to do" an infinite variety of things. We must find the funds to supply the requirements of these audiences. We can never expect commercial television to do the job.

3. *Public Affairs*

The many governments which affect the lives of all of us are not understood by each of us. Despite the magnificent methods of communication which exist, there are very few Americans who understand how our governments—town, city, county, state and federal—really operate. In addition to persons elected to serve in these governmental entities, there exist departments, bureaus and other entities who largely do the job of governing. Our citizens know still less about these entities, how they are created, how they exist and how to cope with them.

There is no likelihood that commercial television will devote its prime time hours to programming which will inform the people about their many governments. Much less will it inform us how we can make those Governments responsive, to the end that our governments may continue to serve us rather than to be our master.

It is obviously impossible for public television to do all the things which need to be done in the area of public affairs. What is not impossible is to interest those who today either lack knowledge or feel frustrated because of their lack of knowledge. To deny the people of the United States an opportunity to be informed about public affairs—their affairs—through public television programming, is unthinkable.

A New Partnership?

In these remarks there have been frequent references to commercial television. It would be no surprise to find some members of the commercial television community who would disagree with some of the things which I have said.

It has always seemed to me that a true partnership between commercial and public television is desirable. Fundamentally, the people of the United States are entitled to have their airwaves utilized in a manner which best will serve them.

As a capitalist and a believer in free enterprise and in the profit system, I have no objection to the continuation of television for profit in the United States. Nevertheless, I must confess to something less than enthusiasm for some commercial broadcasters who talk about commercial television programs being supplied "free" to the American public.

Further, I have no illusions about how many people will choose to watch Bob Hope, *All In The Family* or professional football, even if there may be showing on public television, at the same hour, the best instructional, cultural or public affairs programming available anywhere.

But what's new about that?

In the creation of the Constitution and the Bill of Rights, the one significant and radical departure consisted not in the determination that the majority should rule, but in the flat guarantees that minorities were to be protected.

The majority of the viewers of American television are tuned to the commercial networks and I, for one, do not feel that I have any mission to propose legislation on how those networks should be programmed.

However, the commercial networks and their affiliates, together with the independent commercial licensees, do have responsibilities to all the people in addition to their responsibilities to their stockholders.

The extent to which these responsibilities to all the people are not being met is a subject for another session. I prefer to take a constructive approach. May I propose:

1) That the networks change their policy of denying old programs to public television. Over the years, many magnificent programs have been produced for commercial television. After runs, and sometimes re-runs, they repose in the archives, probably never to be seen again until some distant future archaeologist uncovers them in their search for the ruins of the 20th century.

I propose that each major network allow public television to pick one hour of programming per month from its' archives so that new millions may see and hear them.

2) I propose further, that the archives be opened to scholars selected by public television to put together segments of programs which should be shown in thousands of formal educational institutions. The power of television programs to motivate their viewers to seek more information must not be allowed to remain dormant in videotape and film cans.

3) I propose that leaders from commercial television sit at the side of public television when we, with tin cup in hand, appear before the many governments, institutions, corporations and individuals to plead for the funding which means our very existence.

You must not infer from these proposals the discernment of any plot or even that there is a deliberate decision by the commercial broadcasters to oppose the development of public television. You will recall the statement attributed to Edmund Burke, that, "The only thing necessary for the triumph of evil, is for good men to do nothing". Perhaps we should put it this way: "To prevent the realization of the many accomplishments envisioned by public television, all that is necessary is for those who can bring it about to remain apathetic."

You are not to construe these last remarks as pessimism. Rather are they a call for new and powerful friends to join our ranks.

The simple truth is that the people are beginning to understand that public television is the "people's business"—and I am confident that our ranks will continue to swell to the end that those who have dreamed so long and worked so hard, will see their dreams realized.

QUESTION AND ANSWER SESSION FOLLOWING ROGERS ADDRESS

Q. I wonder what it would take in the way of an argument for adequate funding, say, when *Sesame Street* comes out at a cost effectiveness that has been calculated at the rate of one penny per child per day for the distribution of *Sesame Street?* When those kinds of statistics are possible and that still leads to funding difficulties, what would be a powerful argument, if that is not?

Rogers: There is no question that programs like *Sesame Street* and *The*

Electric Company are, from a cost effective standpoint and from an educational effective standpoint, the greatest bargains that there are. There is only one way to get those programs financed on a continuous basis and that is for the public of the United States to demand that they be financed because the money already exists. Unless the public, and in this case the public should have partners in the educators, get up on their hind legs and demand that it get done, then it will never get done. Some of it could come from federal government, some of it could come from state governments, boards of education, some of it from institutions themselves. And by them getting together in some sort of consortium it would cost each one of them practically nothing. I suppose the only thing that we amateurs can do is arouse the public, which I might say we're in the process of doing. But you can help.

Q. Would you comment for a moment about the political difficulties that arise from using public funds to support public affairs programs?

Rogers: The philosophical argument goes something like this: What right does public television have to take government's money to put public affairs programming on the air? Well, the answer is every right in the world. In the first place, there is no such thing as government money. The money belongs to all the people of the United States. The government doesn't have any money except that which we give them. If we choose to have part of that money used in public affairs programming we have the right to public affairs programming. Now what the people of the United States don't know about the way their governments function and what they don't know about how much power they have to affect the function of their local governments at the local, state and federal levels is nothing short of a crime. And public television can do a great deal to furnish that information without having to be partisan in any way. And for that reason the argument, in my opinion, has no validity at all. And frankly I don't believe that there is anybody today in any high office who thinks that they can make that argument stick.

Q. Back in 1967, I believe it was in the Educational Facilities Bill of '67 which became part of the Public Broadcast Act, non-commercial educational broadcasting stations were prohibited from editorializing in any way. That included stations not funded in any way by CPB or from the government. I wonder if you'd care to comment on that proposition?

Rogers: It's my personal opinion that the American public is grown up and a lot smarter than many politicians give them credit for being. They can listen to editorials and decide for themselves whether they like it or they don't. And I see no reason to have any prohibitions on freedom of speech over the public's own air waves. I think it is important that the stations be fair, be objective, give various points of view. And I don't think that a station will last long or have much credibility if it doesn't. But that's just a personal opinion. And if the law reads contrary to that maybe some day we ought to have that law changed.

Rapporteur Summaries

Moderator: Aaron Cohen (NBC-TV)
Rapporteurs: Peter Pringle (University of Florida; Maureen Milicia (Marshall University); Daniel Viamonte (University of Hartford); James Brown (University of Southern California)
Other Participants: Philip Gelb (Bronx Community College); Charles Shipley (Southern Illinois University); William Hawes (University of Houston); Jeffrey Lowenhar (University of Connecticut); John Kittross (Temple University); Richard Goggin (New York University)

MILICIA: When we sat down to plan this report, we found that we had about 12 hours of notes times four—roughly 48 hours of notes totaling about 50 pages.

VIAMONTE: None of the problems that we talked about resolved themselves. There were no new solutions, most everything that we listed and discussed, had been dealt with by all of us at one time or another. Either we've read or taught or worked with them. So all of us had heard of the ideas and concepts. But I don't think what we had heard were the *attitudes* to each of these concepts. And that is perhaps the most important aspect of what Tau Group did—to air from different points of view common solutions about which people had a variety of opinions.

The first was the problem of a station in a lagging market. Most of us felt that the only approach was a positive one—not an approach that said you simply refuse to accept that there is a problem, there is *no* problem—but one that said despite this problem we will work through it, work around it, by positive constructive means.

Our discussion leader suggested that perhaps any and all of the problems we were dealing with should have been discussed and resolved *yesterday*—meaning before they become problems—and that the things we were dealing with today were the consequences of the fact that they had not been faced yesterday. Hopefully, by discussing them today we would move ahead.

In the first area, the most important factor was just the plain and simple truth that the broadcaster had to know where his market was. If he didn't know, there was no way he was going to be able to plough through this period.

We divided the lagging market and its suggestions, resolutions and solutions into three basic areas: internal, external, and long range. *Internal* included the things that the broadcaster could do in-house from a positive point of view: beef up the air products; create desirability in the staff to think in terms of creative pride—to be happy, to be aware, to be alert, and to try to resolve things by their own input; to encourage things like saving time and money, utilizing facilities and space, and attention to organizational flow charts. Getting rid of deadwood was countered with the recognized need to beef up sales activity and support.

A good suggestion was made that we review all contracts with outside agencies, with the idea that we could perform many of these functions in-house. One example: by buying a printing press.

Maintain morale. If the staff is spending most of its time writing resumés and using the Xerox machine, then you have no chance of creating a positive attitude. But if you kept up the morale and encouraged a positive approach, you might be able to move your staff to consider long range as well as short range suggestions to improve your market and market position.

And then I suppose the ultimate suggestion on the internal side was, if these fail, to *fire the manager!*

There are a lot of things you can do from the *external* side to get the lagging market puffed up. Organize the regional broadcasters to accentuate the positive by editorials, promotional announcements, ads in local papers—all the techniques that all of us know, but for the last 10 or 15 years we have sort of let slide by. Meet with the Chamber of Commerce, meet with community groups, with local organizations in government structure—possibly to stimulate the community into attracting new industry. Work for creative tax-break incentives so that new industry will come to you.

That was pretty much the external idea. For the *long range* goals, for the third year in a row, a common statement by both broadcasters and faculty members was: *More research is needed, specifically qualitative research.*

You should develop a better marketing organization from the jobbers on down so that you can do your job, so that you can get a kind of excitement and enthusiasm going. You should maintain and develop better and more frequent relationships with universities, colleges, two-year institutions and high schools if for no other reason than, as John Chancellor said, to get to know the faculty directory so that you know who's who and who can give you help in your particular problem.

Conduct more coverage studies. Obviously, try to improve the signal. Develop more internship programs. In our group we did hear about several colleges and universities that have developed rather intensive workshops and internship programs with networks and also with local stations.

Study and make sure the community is aware of what the function of your station is to the community. The reason here was obviously to insure its continued position as well as growth in the community.

And, I guess, finally to open your doors—not close your doors to people but to open them to people—I suppose, in similar concept to what several institutions did during the strike period. The idea was that you can utilize more people by attracting them and using your facility for workshops or mini-workshops, for surveys, for all kinds of things, but everybody becomes aware of the fact that your station is there, is viable, it's the best in the market, and they ought to be able to support your station.

PRINGLE: We don't plan this to repeat, although I will say, just for the sake of showing how much insight the Iota Group does have, that we too came to the conclusion rather quickly that the positive approach was the only one that would work in this situation. And that a positive approach should be spread around all members of the staff to allay fears about possible cutbacks in programming, sales staff, and particularly in the promotion department—which is sort of a knee-jerk reaction of most broadcasters once they get into trouble.

The idea of cooperating with the Chamber of Commerce, with business in the area, consulting with state legislatures to try to attract new business to the market, was all discussed at some length.

We zeroed in on what each department in the station might do. Very briefly we came to the conclusion that the sales department would have to get to work. This would involve going out and looking for additional business among merchants whose products, whose services, were still going to be in demand—despite the fact that economic slow-down had come and unemployment had hit the market. Somebody pointed out that a rainy day is bad news for some, but good news for others—particularly good news for the guy who manufactures and sells raincoats and umbrellas. The fact that we do have unemployment in this market, the fact that the man of the house and perhaps the woman of the house, too, are going to be spending time at home rather than at the office or at the factory, means that this is a wonderful opportunity for them to catch up on home improvements. We said, let's make approaches to the hardware stores or the retail merchants who specialize in major services to provide paint and brushes and all these other things for work around the house.

Staff morale: In the sales department what can you do to get the best effort out of your sales staff? We recommended that George should take a close look at the kinds of rewards and incentives he made available to his staff—higher commissions, perhaps a sales contest or bonus. But, just as important, we felt that financial reward at a time like this was not necessarily the most important, and that he shouldn't overlook the opportunity to pass on at every available opportunity his appreciation, commendation, to members of his sales staff who'd done a good job. Give them a feeling that they were part of a team effort if this station was going to get out of trouble.

What about the program department? Obviously at times like this there may be a feeling that we can't afford to put a great deal of money into programming, and yet we were idealistic enough to believe that this station, despite its problems, would want to serve the public interest. How can you do this? A fear expressed in our discussions was that there was nothing worse than for the station itself and the other stations in the market to give the impression to its audience that things were really bad. How do you go about trying to prevent panic? We felt that the program department could set to work trying to explain the causes of the problem and the positive solutions which might be applied. The intention being to try to avoid public panic based on ignorance.

What about the housewife who finds herself with less money than she is accustomed to, having to run the family budget? We felt that a vital service was to have some kind of family budget management/consumer affairs program, with emphasis on how you make those dollars go a little bit further when they are not in plentiful supply.

Despite the fact that unemployment has hit the market, *some* industries, *some* businesses will still be looking for workers. We felt the station might perform a valuable public service by letting the unemployed know where the jobs were and what kinds of skills were required in order to produce those jobs. There was a very strong feeling that the promotion department should not suffer the fate that it apparently does in circumstances like this. There was a common feeling in the group—and I won't be able to say that about many of the observations I'm making now—but there was a common feeling that rather than this being the time to cut back on the promotional effort, it was the time, in fact, to go the opposite direction and to increase it, to increase your promotional effort not only on your own air but, if you could afford it, by taking out ads in the local print media. The idea being to convince, especially the advertisers, but also the members of the audience too that because the market had slowed down and because people were having harder times, the local station was still an indispensable ally in times like this for business and for the community at large.

MILICIA: I think I'm doing Rho Group an injustice by picking little points, because we didn't arrive at these conclusions in a few seconds. Sometimes we had a dichotomy of thought and realized that it depends on the market, the area of the country, the type of solutions that you would suggest.

One thing we decided was that, when you have a lagging market, you should try to establish whether it's a universal recession or if it is just in your own market area. If it's universal, sometimes you just have to ride it out. If it's just in your market area, then you have to retrench and go after your audience and the profits will come.

When you are losing people in a market, you sell your market and not necessarily the station. A lot of the people said, especially the industry people, that profits are a problem. When you are losing money you panic. But there is one thing worse than losing money. If you start neglecting the community then you are in danger of losing your license. And when you start cutting back, probably the last two things that you should tamper with would be your product, which is your programming, and your sales department. You try to cut costs but not to the point where your image is changing and you cause panic.

An interesting statement was that the entire title to this particular question was "The station in a lagging market, *does it need a band-aid or an operation?*"—and that maybe we needed *preventive medicine*. Maybe, when you see this particular problem approaching, you call together management and personnel, and project a philosophy and you go out and you try to ascertain just where in the market are the revenue cuts coming. For instance, in the energy crisis, oil and gasoline, automobiles, airlines, how much of your total profit margin in this particular area bringing in? Say, 12%. All right, look for replacement buyers. Go and try and sell these same people but give them a different sales pitch. Now you're not selling oil, you're trying to tell people how to conserve it. You still need a spot to tell your story. But it's a different story that you're telling. The point is, you try to meet these problems head on; you don't wait until they overcome you and then start worrying about them. It's just a little thing. Maybe the message is, *don't panic*. Sit down and start thinking these things through, and what can *I* do about it?

Personalize your advertising pitch. When you send your salesmen out, let them personalize and tell the little man—go to the little man. It was said that, surprisingly enough in a lagging market, people tend to buy more. The advertisers tend to buy. It is easier to sell a lagging market than it is in times of prosperity. People seem to buy to get their messages across.

Profits are important but your license is also important. Go after the sales. Start grass-rooting. Someone mentioned later on, in another group, that television has been living on its laurels, the days when a buyer would come to you—and have to be put on a card when a spot was open—are over. Now you are going to go out. The money is there if you're going out into the market and you are finding the money. We've become too complacent. It's a different picture.

VIAMONTE: Obviously, it was like looking into the crystal ball and trying to come up with alternative solutions. But there was a statement made by one of the broadcasters in our group that I think bears repeating—maybe that's all that bears repeating because we simply listed the concepts, the future possibilities in cable and cassette and international development of new talent. *U. S. broadcasters can no longer isolate themselves from the rest of the world.* Perhaps that's the biggest input that we got in our group. This particular broadcaster said that for years broadcasters simply sat back and let the stations run by themselves. The reality is, that just doesn't happen any more. Broadcasters need expertise, like anyone else, to sell intelligently, reinvest capital wisely for better programming, research, development, equipment, and become more sensitive to community needs. It is still a very young industry; many of the people in it now were in it just for the bucks only a few years ago. But this has changed. The name of the game is still corporate profit, but profit for a little bit lesser stakes at a higher yield, hopefully, for all of us. So our discussion revolved on ways that higher yield might approach itself.

PRINGLE: I'm afraid when Iota Group looked into the crystal ball we saw a very gray sky, and we saw a broadcaster bracing for a pretty uncertain future—for reasons which those of us who are actively engaged in broadcasting or in communications education are pretty well familiar with. We did see a few bright spots—things like the the fact the experts are predicting something like a 16% increase in homes to be served by 1980, which means more viewing; a change in life-style, perhaps hastened by the energy crisis which means, we think, that people will spend more time listening to radio and watching television. Advances in computerization should, and many people hope, make operations more efficient and result in some kind of savings.

But there was an overriding feeling that there was a lot of gray cloud around, a lot of uncertainty, which seemed to be the common theme. *What if cable?* What if cable is allowed to bid against the networks and to syphon off the very popular and very profitable sports programming and feature film programming? There was another concept raised. This idea that cable, in addition to bringing popular programs into the home, might well be used to serve the special interests of those groups who are very vociferous in society and who claim that their needs aren't being met in over-the-air television. What do you think the impact might be on society if people crawl off into their own corners to spend time watching or listening to programs that suit their particular interests? It was noted that television has served as a mass medium, as a great unifying force, perhaps the last and only unifying force we have. The prospect that the unifying power that television has might be lost was one that terrified some of our participants. Of course this was all based on the assumption that people would be willing to pay for whatever technology would make possible in the future. And in the light of Mr. Stern's dinner address perhaps it's well to re-emphasize the fact that what is possible technologically and what happens in actuality are not one and the same thing, and in fact might be quite different.

Just as we were about to leave the crystal ball we did spot a patch of blue. Perhaps the developments, these pessimistic developments to which we paid so much of our attention, will be good for television. Perhaps they will encourage stations and networks to break out of the rigidity in which they now find themselves and look for new formats to counter the challenge. Radio, when faced with the challenge, showed that it could be done. Now television has a chance to do the same.

MILICIA: We discussed the fact that, in the past, radio has been fairly fragmented because of the force of the idea that we have over 7,000 stations. But they are regrouping now and they have a new direction. We talked about the economy, inflationary prices and the costs. And we said it would probably lead to total automation in television eventually. Then to the idea that TV will not die as a medium, but will change. It will react and adapt just as records did, and radio and movies—television will have to adapt and react to the situation. And, of course, the potential of cable communication satellites. A comment was made that advertisers are not going to leave television, it's just that there will be two other concepts. There will be the satellite and cable people after that same dollar and you are going to have to work harder to get it. Nothing is going to die, but it will change. We didn't project too far into the future but I think we felt that perhaps in the late '70s and the '80s and even beyond that, the way we know communications today, the type of receivers we have in our homes, will change completely. The only thing we could determine was that the people in media for years have been very poor predicters of what was going to happen. But we felt it would be a different picture and perhaps we can look, see, adapt as it comes along and not try to project too far.

BROWN: We listed some major considerations in planning for future growth and survival beyond what you have heard and talked about in your own groups. Appraise ways to cut costs realistically, more use of capital, machinery, less use of labor—in a word, automation. Also, combo persons more and more, at least in small operations—engineering and/or programming plus part-time sales for a person. Possibly diversify into related media. Collaborate with local colleges—they are sometimes cheap but not in the sense of quality research available. Ways to find markets. Ways to find people. Ways to find creative options. How to generate sales and business? In a sentence, do not merely run a station entity living off the market, but become a participant and a catalyst in the total social economic mix which is the community of people who are your audience and are your clients. Try to stimulate the general economy and business in your community. This will rub off on the broadcast business as well.

Maybe you do tamper with programming. The product you sell, in one sense (apart from Les Brown's statement that you sell heads), the product you sell is the station's programming. And people will listen to or view whatever interests them if it serves them on their terms. You've got to find this out through creative research. And perhaps something we will talk about later, the operation that does well in news generally does well over-all in the market, so news is probably the local focus for programming innovation and planning. As for programming in the future, possibly look to other models such as cable or radio because of the great diversity of programming and specialization, even fragmentation of audiences. UHF is doing it. Is there some way, maybe, that even in spite of its mass, VHF commercial television might take a leaf from that book?

GELB: I think I would like to hear some more about what the anxiety or the panic was in your group over losing television as a unifying force. For example, the Inquisition unified the Dark Ages and I think Germany was never more unified than under Hitler. What was the great unifying feeling that your group felt we were losing if we lost free television?

PRINGLE: Well, I wouldn't characterize it as a group feeling. It was one of the possible dangers that was predicted by one member of the group. The idea being that mass, over-the-air television brings people together, not only to view things like Super Bowls but to watch other momentous events in history as they unfold—presidential addresses, state of emergency addresses, political conventions, these kinds of things. The feeling was that as a mass medium television does have that power to make us all think that we're one at such times of national crisis or determination, visits to the moon and all the rest of it. The fear expressed was that if, in the short term or long term future, people's use of media—whatever shape it takes in the home—was to satisfy a personal interest, then people might creep off into a corner, and in one family there might be four or five people off in their own corners of the room doing their own things, perhaps as is the case today with records. Teenagers in the bedroom playing one kind of record and mom and pop in the living room playing another kind of record, this kind of thing. The power of television to bring people together and to give people a common sense of purpose might be lost.

MILICIA: In Rho Group we really didn't take this into consideration, but one of the people made a comment that we will always have free broadcasting for the masses. For the more affluent we will have video cassettes, cable shows, etc. And then the question was asked: If free broadcasting will be for the lowest segment of the population how will we sell advertising time? Other people in the group said that's what we're doing now. We are selling to the masses. So it's not a matter of re-vamping. The mass media will still be there. We're just going to add to the specialization.

COHEN: Anyone else care to comment, add, supplement, contradict?

SHIPLEY: A very minor point perhaps, but in the projections regarding the economic outlook for stations per se I think there was a consensus in IOTA that it would be an increasingly youthful audience having the dominant role and to which we would be playing and selling—18 to 24 instead of 18 to 29.

COHEN: We move on now to Programming.

VIAMONTE: Our group tried to deal with areas like public affairs and a summary of program concepts. We tried to deal with children's programming and we were all very contributive in terms of suggestions and observations. But one member of our group who does not always contribute in quantity does, when he speaks, contribute in quality. Perhaps his statement pretty much wraps up our discussion that lasted for two hours. I suppose it could be called a "Rayism." It's that programming is much like the proverbial catsup bottle. It is duplicated constantly by all manufacturers and yet is one of the worst designed, most unfunctional inventions ever used. But nobody, no one, calls for a better design. So, as we looked at the catsup bottle, we looked at programming and suggested that perhaps we ought to consider seriously the idea of dealing with programs in terms of what they are specifically geared to do. If they look like catsup bottles then we deserve what we get, because no one is clamoring for a different-shaped bottle.

PRINGLE: We took this session's title to get into the age-old debate about what do we mean when we talk about serving the public interest and the many publics that make up the audience. Several observations came forth. Principally, I suppose, they were triggered by the presence of a member of the Spanish International Network. But there was some concern about granting a license to this Spanish International Network to serve the needs and only the needs of the Spanish-speaking and people of Spanish descent in a particular community. First of all, the FCC was operating or causing the broadcasters to operate on some kind of double standard in terms of serving the public interest. And what kind of responsibilities in that circumstance were to be shouldered by the non-Spanish and Spanish stations in a market? We took that, the granting of licenses to the Spanish International Network, as a possible first indication in television growing out of radio licensing practices (the development of specialized formats to appeal to particular segments of the population) that perhaps the FCC, in granting those licenses, doesn't expect television stations to be all things to all people. We concluded that it was never possible to do that anyway. Of course the FCC may be coming around to that point of view.

We took a rather pessimistic approach to program areas. We looked at programming and said what can be done to improve it? We looked at news. News enjoys high viewership, high trust. For many people it is the only source of information about what's going on in the world. Doesn't that very fact impose on television newsmen the obligation to serve the public a little bit better by telling them not only *what* happened but *why?* And we got

into problems of time, the limitations imposed on broadcasting. And at
what stage in the game do you think you've got enough information to be
able to give some kind of significant analysis of the situation?

What about giving viewers a better choice by forbidding head-to-head
programming? Well that sounds not a bad idea. The problem is that once
any regulative body were to get into making decisions like that, it's only a
short step to regulation of scheduling and of program content.

A final observation that might sum up all of our dissatisfactions with
broadcasting: If we accept that television is a mirror of society, isn't it
possible that all of our expressed dissatisfactions with television are, in fact,
nothing more than expressions of dissatisfaction with ourselves and the
society in which we live?

MILICIA: We said that a program that may fulfill one function in one
market may perform another type of function in another market. So you
must ascertain your audience and the market you're in. We all know how
to go out and find what the people are thinking in the market. The idea
was that the prime source of programming input, that is for a network
affiliate, is from the network. Then the very next thing in local programming, practically the only thing, is *news programming*. We made a statement
that if you have *good news* then you have a good station. Your station gets
its image from the news programming. One other statement—we felt that
programming has (idealistically) this kind of priority: 1.) It is the intent of
any station in its programming to first serve the public; 2.) to gather an
audience; 3.) to make a profit. That is, *idealistically.*

BROWN: Practically, make a profit, then do what you can. And that
leads to the problem of *half*-ascertainment, which isn't so good.

Is television a mass advertising medium, a mass sales medium, a mass
emotion medium, a mass cultural medium? Of course it is. Probably all of
these. Caution: trying to do everything for everybody is doing nothing for
nobody. That establishes the caution well, I think. Probably the most
important programming the local station has is news. What is good? Good
is what the people in the market want. How do you know what they want?
You start with the ratings, what the numbers tell us, and then move back
into qualitative analysis (or forward) into that.

COHEN: In this hour we want to open up the summary, to try to hit
some highlights, partial patterns, to give some sense to three days. Questions?

HAWES: One of the main differences here is that we are accepting the
programming in a depressed economic picture this year. So, in effect, the
educators are not asking for great and imaginative improvements in children's programming, and more extensive news coverage and the greater
glorification of the public interest, because this year we are taking a look at
the economic problems and the business uncertainties of the industry. That,
I think, is the main difference.

PRINGLE: There is another significant difference. Last year we were a group of academicians dreaming about the world we'd like to see. This year we were brought down to earth a bit. We had broadcasters sitting at the four corners of the table saying: That sounds very nice, but have you stopped to consider this . . . ?

COHEN: Let's turn to comment on the restrictive area of regulation.

VIAMONTE: On the issue of equal time the public has been denied an important facet of the American way of life. Instead of equal time it has given us *no* time. It should be abolished. As it now stands, it applies only to candidates. News is exempt. Endorsement of candidates by broadcasters creates an unreal equal-time problem.

Media in general have a high belief-factor in the presentation of news, candidates and issues. But the question of need is still very controversial. Broadcasters as a whole have been very fair in dealing with major, viable candidates. The problem comes with fringe candidates. Historically, third party candidates have not been given fair treatment in the media. What about the role of women as portrayed by programs or news as stereotypes? Is this an issue of the Fairness Doctrine?

In license renewal, the role in which the broadcaster has been placed makes the subject a time-consuming, economically unsound and energy-draining repetitive period. The concept that more paper work creates better community service is a bureaucratic concept not worthy of itself. It's nonsense. The procedural system for license renewal is not viable. The bureaucracy should be reduced and the responsibility of meeting local needs placed squarely on a confrontation, daily confrontation, basis between the community, the challenger and the station personnel. The television license, in terms of the consensus of the group, should be good for at least five years.

Some of the suggestions: Let the broadcaster and the interested challenger negotiate in good faith. In most instances these problems can be worked out the same day as the complaint. Perpetual licenses? That's not the answer. The assumption that people never change only creates a greater access problem as new and viable persons arrive on the scene. No need to force all stations to spend the time, the money and the energy and the resources if all parties can agree that the community interest, convenience and necessity factors are satisfied.

How can we help to avoid wrong-doing and circumvent the perpetuating bureaucracy that always puts the broadcaster on the defensive? One of our broadcast guests said, vividly: "Get off my back! I'm trying the hardest I can." The assumption that the broadcaster is always guilty until proven innocent must be resolved. There should be a collection of qualitative data, performance data, to develop the validity of these challenges.

PRINGLE: Iota Group spent most of its time discussing license renewal. It took note of the terrible man-hour and man-dollar drain; the expense involved in putting all the information together, particularly through the ascertainment of community needs process; putting all of that together and

Xeroxing the many copies for the use of the FCC and its staff. At the risk of oversimplifying, but in the interest of saving time, what about solutions? In our group we had something which came to be known as the Donner plan. It's a plan for license renewal that would work like this: broadcasters would have an equivalent of the IRS Form 1040A—a short form. The FCC would act much as the IRS acts in doing spot checks on submissions. If the Commission had questions about a licensee's promise versus performance, or the way he was serving the public interest, *then* it would call for all the documentation the broadcaster had developed and compiled to substantiate his case. This would, hopefully and from his point of view, result in his license being renewed.

The advantages? It wouldn't relieve the broadcaster from the obligation to continue ascertaining the community's needs—this should be a continuing process, and the Donner plan would demand that. But it would free station personnel from all the time and effort in assembling, every three years, all this welter of material—which probably swamps the FCC staff anyway.

We also felt that, even going through an ascertainment of community needs, no matter what the process, a broadcaster still doesn't really know what he has to do to make certain that his license will be renewed. *Now* might be the time for the Commission to issue some guidelines to bring satellite-age execution to a radio-age concept known as the public interest, convenience and necessity.

MILICIA: In our group it was suggested that Justice Burger, when he was talking about pornography, really had the right idea that you can't set national standards on pornography any more than you can rule on what is substantial in every market. A conclusion on license renewal is that we need guidelines and standards—but flexible enough to reflect different markets and the problems in those markets.

Regarding Section 315, we felt that no change would be coming soon—although many bills are in the hopper right now. Nothing will happen in this Congress because Congress has a vested interest in this particular ruling, and the broadcasters felt they could live with it. We made a statement that there is no such thing as equal time because there is no such thing as equal impact.

BROWN: I was surprised—and I think some of my colleagues were surprised, at least interested, certainly receptive to the broadcasters' general attitude in our group—that regulation isn't all that bad. Predictions by them were that we won't be getting rid of the problems that regulations have brought to broadcasters. "There will perhaps be more, but in the process they may make us better broadcasters."

The pressure, one broadcaster said, is not so much from government initiative as from the public. Perhaps non-representative and sometimes irresponsible members or groups in the public, but it's the public out there that's bringing the pressure.

Summation: The comfort afforded by regulation—*comfort* in the relative stability of some kind of inchoate guideline establishing some standards of accountability, some support for longevity—this comfort must be taken along with the duodenal pains and ulcers it might create. You can't have it both ways. Regulation being so complex and with so many factors involved may seem more directionless than it truly is.

LOWENHAR: Government doesn't generally step in to regulate within the various segments of the economy unless there are things that are very much in the extreme. I think it's incumbent on the industry, if it wants to minimize federal regulation of broadcasting, to go after those extreme violations that would prompt federal action—and remove them. It was the consensus of our group that one of the major, if not *the* major, problems dealing with fairness and right and wrong, this and that, whatever the legal definitions are, was the question of *untruthful advertising*. There is so much of it on the air today as to invite federal intervention.

KITROSS: Two items of emphasis I sensed from Tau Group: one: everyone deplored the paperwork, the sheer tonnage. We all love trees; why cut them down for this? *But* that broadcasters generally were pleased with the end results of input from the ascertainment process.

Second, was Fairness versus Access. I'm not sure that we achieved any consensus that Access might be a way out. But one of the things to watch out for is that Access can lead to the common carrier approach, and I don't think there are many broadcasters who subscribe to that idea.

GOGGIN: We all recognized in Sigma Group that broadcasting is broadcasting, but within broadcasting there are two different media—radio and television—and solutions are not necessarily uniform. We learned that ascertainment and license renewal procedures differ greatly between the two. Is it not possible in future discussions to identify distinctions as we go forward in radio and in television?

PRINGLE: A question we addressed was why would a commercial broadcaster who is interested in increasing the profitability of his station get himself involved in an activity like news? It costs him money! The easy, cynical answer might be that without news and some kind of public affairs activity he might have some awkward moments before the FCC at license renewal time.

But there's more to it than that (the Post-Newsweek influence was strong in our group). *People want news.* They want to know what's going on, what happened while they slept. They want to know whether to take a raincoat or an overcoat to work. They want to know which route to drive to avoid traffic snarls. And because of all of this, advertisers are *willing to buy news.*

MILICIA: We talked about news as an image projector for the station. It helps gain numbers. It helps in sales, promotion; it's a vehicle for all kinds of sales. We discussed consulting firms' researching and packaging of news for a local station, and expressed concern. Some of our group felt that stations can get too worried about the cosmetics, and sacrifice content for numbers, and that, if broadcasters did more to work on *news content,* the numbers would follow.

We had a unique experience in our group. We had a man from Danville, Virginia who has a very unusual radio news operation. They do 48 newscasts a day, 12 from the Mutual network and the other 36 are local. Of the 36, 12 are five-minute newscasts and the others are one-minute newscasts. His prime source for news, from the community, is from telephone tips—50% he says. It isn't that the news in the area is necessarily biased or lacks credibility. The biggest problem, he finds, is that the newsman either walks in a minute before he goes on the air or that he is on the telephone taking down a news story, and when he gets on the air he can't read his own handwritten notes!

This is a bit different from what we are talking about here, but I wanted to report that it exists. This is the number one station in that market, with a fleet of five cars and two trucks, an extremely lucrative business and a large promotional budget!

BROWN: Just for the record, broadcasters in our group predicted an increasing role for consultants in outside critiquing, of not just the station or the programming, but specifically news.

VIAMONTE: In the area of seeking qualified personnel, it was an eye opener to some of the broadcasters in Tau Group to discover that educational institutions—the stereotyped ivory tower faculty—were indeed trying to cover areas which most broadcasters felt we weren't covering. One very pragmatic attitude by broadcasters said, in effect: We are looking for students who can do the simple thing of going through a job interview and doing it right; prepare some kind of resume or audition tape or portfolio materials of things they *can* do. They've got to be willing to apply for jobs that may not be as attractive as they would like. They have to have a realistic approach to the job market.

PRINGLE: Dan Viamonte summarized the areas which inevitably come up when broadcasters and broadcast educators get together. In general or specifically: How much practical training? How much liberal arts? Let us do the training, or whatever. One idea we did toss around for a while was how to strike that balance between putting the student in touch with reality—the broadcast world as it really is, without going too far—so that we end up producing imitation copies of the people who are making the decisions and doing the work in broadcasting today.

It was felt that nothing could do the industry greater harm than to try to turn out every broadcast newsperson to be like Walter Cronkite or Barbara Walters. The future of the industry depends not only on new blood but on new ideas of how to meet the changing challenges that broadcasters and broadcasting are going to have to face in the future. This is not as easy as it may sound. One of our problems is that we would like to be able to look into that crystal ball and assist broadcasters in predicting where the future is going to lie. Unfortunately, we are not able to do that. So we find ourselves in the miserable position of having to follow the industry rather than lead it. Academic administration is remarkably slow, as you know, and what may seem to be a good idea for a course this year may not seem so good one year from now.

All of this—the student, the curriculum, the needs of industry—we're going to have to give more and more thought to in the future. We've just gone through an accreditation procedure, and one of the comments was that really, as an academic institution, we ought to be raising our sights a little bit. Rather than concentrating on turning out producers and directors and broadcast newspeople we should be trying to turn out a "people product" that might fit into the structure just a little bit higher up the ladder. Is it possible? Is it desirable? Will the broadcaster accept it? Will the student accept it? I think we should give a good deal more thought to that.

MILICIA: We noted that many colleges and universities are losing enrollment. But it seems that interest in our particular communications discipline is growing. We tried to find some reasons for this growth—that these youngsters were raised with radio and television, and maybe they find it the medium that they can best express themselves in, so they want to come into our field. I am really very proud of our group and our leader. I'm going to editorialize for a minute, because we found that the schools represented—like the University of North Carolina and Temple and even our little Marshall University—seem to try to give the broadcasters what they want. It seems we also are in accord with them, and we're trying to do that type of thing. We understood their problems, and they understood our problems and why we are doing what we are doing.

We talked about the different criteria students should have when they go into the marketplace, and to give them a liberal outlook and a better education. Interesting questions were asked, like: Why do you *fire* someone? *Not* why do you *hire* someone. These broadcasters told us the types of things that disturb them and why people either make it or don't make it in a particular market. Someone said that you don't have to have a college-educated person to do a job if we train them properly. As academicians and as industry representatives, we do indeed have more roads to explore.

BROWN: Some of the things needed: A balance in training, not merely of advocates but of people who can handle the tools of the business. Sales orientation seems to be lacking, according to the broadcasters' appraisals of academe and their product. There's a serious need to turn out people with controlled aggressiveness, initiative, yet knowing how to keep the business and the client for the call-back and all the rest of it. A very practical point, besides the fact that not all graduates are of equal quality (that's why we have grades, possibly!).

There is also the need to somehow instill in them enough experience to get the job. That's what the business is going to ask of them. What kind of jobs are there? Just a quick count of how many fulltime employees in all categories—January 1, 1973 versus January 1974 projections at the same station. The various broadcasters gave us these numbers: 25 now, 25 next year; 11 now, 12 next year; 6 now, 6 next year. In other words, not much change in numbers, but 15% or so hiring from the outside because of attrition, turnover, better judgments, whatever.

So it's not a big labor force, but there are jobs continually coming. And there are few on-the-air spots generally, except in small radio. And if by small radio they mean a little cinder block station on Sunset Boulevard and the Hollywood Freeway—that's a problem!

A final comment then, that through the IRTS April College Conferences in New York, and through participation in the BEA (formerly the APBE) in association with NAB, and by reading the *Journal of Broadcasting,* there are ways to keep this collaboration. *I* feel kind of uncomfortable with much of what I have been saying because I'm very concerned, not about job placement, but about the role of liberal arts and humanities as serving human beings who can also be broadcasters—but *not necessarily*—and that's my own bracketed comment.

MILICIA: Many, many thanks to IRTS, and to our co-chairmen Gene Accas and Aaron Cohen, for what has been—and I have to use the vernacular of my students—a truly *mind-blowing* experience!

Appendix A: Participants

SᴇᴍɪɴᴀR CᴏᴍᴍɪTTEE

Co-Chairmen: Gene Accas (Leo Burnett, USA); Aaron Cohen (NBC-TV)

Faculty Recruitment: William Behanna (A.C. Nielsen Co.); Daniel McGrath (D'Arcy, MacManus, Massius); Neil Walden (WCBS-TV)

Field Trips: Gene Jankowski (CBS Television Stations)

Industry Recruitment:
   Participants: Sam Vitt, Jonne Murphy, Richard Olsen (Vitt Media International)
   Guests: John Fernandez (ABC-TV); Craig Oscarsson (Sheridan & Elson Communications)

Logistics: Marti Stein (NBC-TV)

Problem Development: Howard Coleman (Lutheran Church of America); Daniel McGrath (D'Arcy, MacManus, Massius); Robert H. Stanley (Hunter College, CUNY)

Research: Charles B. Schneider (NBC-TV)

Special Fund-Raising: Charles Tower (Corinthian Broadcasting)

Special Technical Advisors: Peter Willett, William Wilson (United Press International)

Acknowledgements:
Art: Courtesy Andrew Ross Studios
Photography: Courtesy CBS-TV and NBC-TV

Publicity: Courtesy The Softness Group
Tapes: Courtesy NBC Radio Network
Transportation: Courtesy ABC-TV, CBS Press Relations, and
    Oldsmobile Division of General Motors
Technical Equipment: Courtesy United Press International

INDUSTRY PROBLEM PRESENTORS

Richard Adams (News Director, Post/Newsweek Stations,
    Washington, D.C.)
Ed Allgood (VP & General Manager, WDVA, Danville, Virginia)
Jim Babb (Managing Director, WBTV, Charlotte)
Ray Barnett (Sales Manager, KNX, Los Angeles)
Russell Barry (VP & General Manager, KNXT, Los Angeles)
George Carpenter (Sales Manager, WHO, Des Moines)
Joel Chaseman (President, Post/Newsweek Stations,
    Washington, D.C.)
Suzan Couch (Sales Manager, WXLO, New York)
Donald Dahlman (Vice President, TV Sales, Avco Broadcasting,
    Cincinnati)
Wallace Dunlap (Vice President, Group W, Washington, D.C.)
Larry Gershman (Sales Manager, WNBC-TV, New York)
Al Grosby (Sales Manager, WAKR-TV, Akron)
Charles Harrison (Manager-News, WGN-TV, Chicago)
Bill Hartman (General Manager, KDKA, Pittsburgh)
Arthur Hook (Vice President and Station Manager, WKBG-TV,
    Boston)
Seymour Horowitz (Program Director, WABC-TV, New York)
M.S. Kellner (Managing Director, Station Representatives Association)
Gary Lewis (General Sales Manager, WMCA, New York)
George Lyons (Station Manager, WZZM-TV, Grand Rapids)
Henry Marcott (Manager-Editorial Service, WNBC-TV, New York)
Terry McGuirk (Vice President, WAGA-TV, Atlanta)
Lee Morris (General Sales Manager, WSB, Atlanta)
Mark Olds (Executive Vice President and General Manager, WWRL,
    New York)
William O'Shaughnessy (President and General Manager, WVOX,
    New Rochelle)
Alan Perris (Program Director, Post/Newsweek Stations,
    Washington, D.C.)

Robert Rice (General Manager, WRAU-TV, Peoria)
Phil Roberts (President, Greater N.Y. Radio, New York)
Herb Saltzman (Vice President and General Manager, WOR, New York)
John Schmulbach (Radio Sales Manager, WRGB, Schenectady, New York)
Stanley Spero (Vice President and General Manager, KMPC, Los Angeles)
George Spring (Station Manager, WRGB, Schenectady, New York)
William Stiles (Spanish International Network, New York)
Leroy Strine (Sales Manager, WGAL-TV, Lancaster)
Billy Taylor (President, WSOK, Savannah)
Jack Tipton (Station Manager, WMGH-TV, Denver)
Gail Trell (Sales Manager, WCBS-TV, New York)
Charles White (Director Community Relations, WBNS, Columbus, Ohio)

Iota Group

Discussion Leader: W. Frank Harden (State Broadcasting Company)
Rapporteur: Peter Pringle (University of Florida)
Boyd, Douglas (University of Delaware)
Clark, Peter (University of Michigan)
Donner, Stanley (University of Texas)
Haccoun, Robert (Ohio State University)
Johnson, Joseph (San Diego University)
Keshishoglou, John (Ithaca College)
Macomber, Philip (Kent State University)
Reuss, Carol, SP (Loyola University)
Schlater, Robert (Michigan State University)
Shipley, Charles (Southern Illinois University)
Steinberg, Charles (Hunter College, CUNY)
Thompson, Willard (University of Minnesota)

Rho Group

Discussion Leader: Robert Henabery (ABC Radio Stations)
Rapporteur: Maureen Milicia (Marshall University)
Atkin, Kenward (Michigan State University)
Barer, Bert (California State University at Northridge)

Breen, Myles (Northern Illinois University)
Crawford, Robert (Queens College)
Geoffrey, Allan (University of Hartford)
Gray, Gordon (Temple University)
Kearns, Frank (West Virginia University)
Law, Gordon (Federation of Rocky Mountain States)
Mendelowitz, Allan (Rutgers College)
Mielke, Keith (Indiana University)
Rhea, James (Oklahoma State University)
Wallace, Wesley (University of North Carolina)

TAU GROUP

Discussion Leader: John D. Kelly (Storer Broadcasting)
Rapporteur: Daniel Viamonte (University of Hartford)
Barnhill, Richard (Syracuse University)
Cailteux, Sue (University of Kentucky)
Day, Louis (Central Michigan University)
Gelb, Philip (Bronx Community College)
Habiby, Raymond (Oklahoma State University)
Hanks, William (University of Pittsburgh)
Hawes, William (University of Houston)
Hunter, Charles (Northwestern University)
Kittross, John (Temple University)
Lowenhar, Jeffrey (University of Connecticut)
New, Lucius (Texas Southern University)
Powell, Jon (Northern Illinois University)
Webber, Irving (University of Alabama)
Ziegler, Sherilyn (University of Tennessee)

SIGMA GROUP

Discussion Leader: Philip Spencer (WCSS-Radio)
Rapporteur: James Brown (University of Southern California)
Book, Albert (University of Nebraska)
Creswell, Kent (WOSU, Ohio State University)
Goggin, Richard (New York University)
Haberer, Joseph (Purdue University)
Hagood, Knox (University of Alabama)
Hamm, Curtis (Oklahoma State University)

Harwood, Ken (Temple University)
Johnson, Dorothy (Marshall University)
Lange, David (Duke University)
Powers, Bruce (Niagara University)
Savage, Arthur (Ohio University)
Steele, Ray (University of Pittsburgh)
Treble, James (Ithaca College)

BIOGRAPHIES

KENWARD L. ATKIN

Dr. Atkin holds B.A. and M.B.A. degrees from the University of Michigan and a Ph.D. degree in Communication from Michigan State University. He is currently Professor and Chairman of the Department of Advertising at Michigan State University.

BERTRAM BARER

Dr. Barer received his B.S. in Broadcasting from Syracuse University and his M.A. and Ph.D. in Speech-Theatre Arts from the University of Minnesota. He is currently Chairman of the Department of Radio-Television-Film at California State University at Northridge.

RICHARD B. BARNHILL

Mr. Barnhill received his M.S. from Syracuse University. He is currently a Lecturer of Television Production, Programming and Management at Syracuse University.

ALBERT C. BOOK

Mr. Book received his B.S. in English and Journalism and his M.B.A. in Marketing and Advertising from New York University. He is currently a Professor in Journalism at the University of Nebraska.

DOUGLAS A. BOYD

Dr. Boyd received his B.F.A. in Journalism from the University of Texas, his M.A. in Speech Communication from the University of Maryland and his Ph.D. in Speech Communication from the University of Minnesota. He is currently an Assistant Professor of Speech Communication at the University of Delaware.

MYLES P. BREEN

Dr. Breen received his M.S. in Radio-Television from Syracuse University and his Ph.D. in Mass Communication from Wayne State University. He is currently Associate Professor at Northern Illinois University.

JAMES A. BROWN

Dr. Brown received his B.A. in Latin, his Ph.L. in Philosophy and his M.A. in English from Loyola University. He received his S.T.L. in theology from Bellarmine School of Theology and his Ph.D. in Communications from the University of Southern California, L.A. He is currently Professor and Chairman of the Department of Telecommunications at the University of Southern California.

K. SUE CAILTEUX

Dr. Cailteux received her Ph.D. from Ohio State University. She is currently Assistant Professor in Telecommunications at the University of Kentucky.

PETER CLARK

Dr. Clark received his B.A. from the University of Washington and his M.A. and Ph.D. from the University of Minnesota. He is currently a Professor and Chairman of the Department of Journalism at the University of Michigan.

ROBERT P. CRAWFORD

Dr. Crawford received his Ph.D. from the University of Utah. He is currently Professor of Communication at Queens College, City University of New York.

KENT W. CRESWELL

Dr. Creswell holds a Ph.D. from Ohio State University. He is currently the General Manager of Broadcast Services at Ohio State University in Columbus, Ohio.

LOUIS A. DAY

Dr. Day received his B.A. and M.A. from the University of Georgia and his Ph.D. from Ohio University. He is currently on the faculty at Central Michigan .University in the Broadcast and Cinematic Arts Area.

STANLEY T. DONNER

Dr. Donner received his B.A. from the University of Michigan and his M.A. and Ph.D. from Northwestern University. He is currently Professor of Communication and Education at the University of Texas at Austin.

PHILLIP S. GELB

Prof. Gelb is currently an Associate Professor of Communication Arts and Sciences at Bronx Community College, City University of New York.

ALAN F. GEOFFREY

Mr. Geoffrey received his B.A. in Economics from Duke University and his M.B.A. in Marketing from the Wharton School of the University of Pennsylvania. He is currently an Instructor of Marketing at the University of Hartford.

RICHARD J. GOGGIN, SR.

Professor Goggin received his B.A. from Manhattan College and his M.A. from University of California, Los Angeles. He is currently Professor of Film and Television at New York University.

GORDON L. GRAY

Dr. Gray received his B.A. from Cornell College and his M.A. and Ph.D. from Northwestern University. Hs is currently Professor and Chairman of the Department of Radio-Televison-Film at Temple University.

JOSEPH HABERER

Dr. Haberer received his B.A. from San Francisco State College, his M.A. from Columbia University and his Ph.D. from the University of California, Berkeley. He is currently Associate Professor and Director, Program in Science, Technology and Pubilc Policy, Department of Political Science at Purdue University.

RAYMOND N. HABIBY

Dr. Habiby received his B.A. in political science from the American University in Beirut and his M.A. and Ph.D. from the University of Minnesota. Dr. Habiby is currently teaching in the Political Science Department of Oklahoma State University.

ROBERT R. HACCOUN

Dr. Haccoun received his B.A. in Psychology from McGill University and his M.A. and Ph.D. in Industrial and Organizational Psychology from Ohio State. He is currently Assistant Director of the Organizational Research Service of Ohio State University and a Visiting Assistant Professor of Psychology.

W. KNOX HAGOOD

Mr. Hagood received his B.A. from the University of Alabama and his M.A. from Northwestern University. He is currently Professor and Chairman of the Department of Broadcast and Film Communication at the University of Alabama.

B. CURTIS HAMM

Dr. Hamm received his B.S. and M.B.A. from Oklahoma State University and his Ph.D. from the University of Texas. He is currently Professor of Marketing at Oklahoma State University.

WILLIAM E. HANKS

Dr. Hanks received his B.A. in Theatre from the University of Denver, his M.A. in Theatre from the University of Miami and his Ph.D. from the University of Pittsburgh. Hs is currently Visiting Assistant Professor at the University of Pittsburgh.

KENNETH HARWOOD

Dr. Harwood received his B.A. in Zoology and his M.A. and Ph.D. in Speech from the University of Southern California. He is currently Professor of Communications and Theatre at Temple University.

WILLIAM HAWES

Dr. Hawes holds M.A. and Ph.D. degrees from the University of Michigan. He is currently Associate Professor in the Department of Communications at the University of Houston.

CHARLES F. HUNTER

Dr. Hunter received his Ph.D. from Cornell University. He is currently Professor and Chairman of the Department of Radio, Television, Film at Northwestern University.

DOROTHY R. JOHNSON

Dr. Johnson received her B.A. from Wheaton College, her two M.A. degrees from the University of Pennsylvania and Northwestern University and her Ph.D. from Ohio State University. She is presently Associate Professor in the Department of Speech at Marshall University in Huntington, West Virginia.

JOSEPH S. JOHNSON

Dr. Johnson received his B.A. from the University of Utah and his Ph.D. from Michigan State University. He is currently Associate Professor in the Department of Telecommunications and Film at San Diego State University.

FRANK M. KEARNS

Professor Kearns is currently the Benedum Professor of Journalism at West Virginia University in Morgantown, West Virginia.

JOHN E. KESHISHOGLOU

Dr. Keshishoglou graduated from Anatolia College in Thessaloniki, Greece and from Morningside College in Sioux City, Iowa. He received his M.A. in Broadcasting and Film from the University of Iowa and his Ph.D. in Educational Communications from Syracuse University. He is currently the Dean of the School of Communications at Ithaca College.

JOHN M. KITTROSS

Dr. Kittross received his B.A. from Antioch College, his M.S. from Boston University and his Ph.D. in Communications from the University of Illinois. He is currently Professor of Communications and Associate Dean in the School of Communications and Theatre at Temple University.

DAVID LANGE

Mr. Lange is a graduate of the University of Illinois College of Law. He is currently Associate Professor of Law and Adjunct Associate Professor of Communications Policy and Public Affairs at Duke University.

GORDON LAW

Dr. Law received his B.A. from Denver University, his M.A. from Syracuse University and his Ed.D. from Washington State University. He is currently Project Director, Satellite Technology Demonstration, Federation of Rocky Mountain States, Denver, Colorado.

JEFFREY A. LOWENHAR

Dr. Lowenhar received his B.S. from Fairleigh Dickenson University, his M.B.A. from New York University's Graduate School of Business and his Ph.D. from the Graduate School of Management, Syracuse University. He is currently on the faculty of Temple University Business School.

ALLAN I. MENDELOWITZ

Dr. Mendelowitz received his B.A. in Economics from Columbia University and his M.A. and Ph.D. in Economics from Northwestern University. He is currently Assistant Professor at Rutgers College, Rutgers University.

KEITH W. MIELKE

Dr. Mielke received his B.M.E. from Phillips University, his M.S. in Television-Radio from Syracuse University and his Ph.D. in Communications from Michigan State University. He is currently Professor of Radio-Television and Mass Communication at Indiana University.

MAUREEN B. MILICIA

Ms. Milicia is currently working on her Ph.D. in Education Communications at Kent State University. She is presently Assistant Professor of Speech at Marshall University.

JON T. POWELL

Dr. Powell received his Ph.D. from the University of Oregon. He is currently Associate Professor, Coordinator Radio-Television-Film, Department of Speech Communication at Northern Illinois University.

BRUCE R. POWERS

Dr. Powers attended Brown University for both undergraduate and graduate degrees. He is currently Assistant Professor of Literature and Film Studies, Media Studies Coordinator and Director of the Flm Repertory Center at Niagara University.

PETER K. PRINGLE

Dr. Pringle graduated from the University of London, he received his M.A. from the University of Florida and his Ph.D. in Mass Communication from Ohio University. He is currently leading seminars in broadcast problems and the mass media at the University of Florida at Gainsville.

CAROL REUSS, S.P.

Dr. Reuss received her B.A. from Saint Mary-of-the-Woods College and her M.A. and Ph.D. from the University of Iowa. She is currently Associate Professor at Loyola University, New Orleans.

JAMES W. RHEA

Dr. Rhea received his B.A. from the University of Nebraska, his M.A. in Radio-TV-Film from the University of Kansas and his Ph.D. in Mass Communication from Ohio University. He is currently Chairman of the Radio-TV-Film Department at Oklahoma State University.

ARTHUR L. SAVAGE

Dr. Savage received his B.A. in Radio Arts from the University of Alabama and his M.A. and Ph.D. from Michigan State University. He is currently Associate Professor of Radio-Television at Ohio University.

ROBERT SCHLATER

Dr. Schlater received his B.A. from the University of Nebraska, his M.A. in Journalism from Columbia University and his Ph.D. in Communications from Michigan State University. He is currently on the faculty of Michigan State University in the Department of Television and Radio.

CHARLES W. SHIPLEY

Dr. Shipley received his B.F.A. from the University of Kansas, his M.A. from Northwestern University and his Ph.D. from Florida State University. He is presently Chairman of the Department of Radio-Television and Director of SIU Broadcasting Service at Southern Illinois University.

RAYFORD L. STEELE

Mr. Steele received his B.A. from DePaul University and his M.A. in Communications from Northern Illinois University. He has also attended law school. He is currently Assistant to the Provost at University of Pittsburgh.

CHARLES S. STEINBERG

Dr. Steinberg received his B.A., M.A. and Ph.D. degrees from New York University. Dr. Steinberg is the former Vice President of Public Information at the CBS Television Network. He is currently a Professor of Communications at Hunter College, City University of New York.

WILLARD L. THOMPSON

Dr. Thompson received his B.S. in Journalism from the University of Illinois and his M.A. and Ph.D. in Mass Communications from the same University. He is presently Professor of Journalism at the University of Minnesota.

JAMES R. TREBLE

Dr. Treble received his B.S. from State University College at Fredonia, New York and his M.A. and Ph.D. from Syracuse University. He is currently Chairman of the Television-Radio Department at Ithaca College.

DANIEL VIAMONTE

Dr. Viamonte received his B.A. in Speech from Hofstra University, his M.A. in Radio and Television from Syracuse University and his Ph.D. in Mass Communication from Wayne State University.

He is currently the Chairman of the Department of Communication and Theatre at the University of Hartford in Connecticut.

WESLEY H. WALLACE

Dr. Wallace received his B.S. from North Carolina State, his M.A. from the University of North Carolina and his Ph.D. from Duke University. He is currently the Chairman of the Department of Radio, Television and Motion Pictures at University of North Carolina at Chapel Hill.

IRVING L. WEBBER

Dr. Webber received his B.A. and M.A. in Sociology from the University of Florida and his Ph.D. also in Sociology from Louisiana State University. He is currently Professor and Chairman of the Department of Sociology at the University of Alabama.

SHERILYN K. ZIEGLER

Dr. Ziegler received her B.A., M.A. and Ph.D. in Communications from Michigan State University. She is Currently Associate Professor at the University of Tennessee teaching Mass Communications.

Appendix B: Public and Broadcasting
FCC PROCEDURAL MANUAL

The following information is taken from the Federal Communications Commission's revised procedural manual entitled "Public and Broadcasting" issued on September 5, 1974.

The Federal Communications Commission is an independent Government agency responsible for regulating interstate and foreign communication by radio and wire. One of its responsibilities is to determine who is to operate the limited number of broadcast stations, to regulate the manner in which they are operated, and to generally supervise their operation, to the end that such operation may serve the interests of the public. This booklet deals only with this one aspect of the Commission's responsibilities.

The FCC is composed of seven members, who are appointed by the President subject to confirmation by the Senate. Normally, one Commissioner is appointed or reappointed each year, for a term of seven years. One of the Commissioners is designated by the President to serve as Chairman, or chief executive officer, of the Commission.

The Commissioners, functioning as a unit, supervise all activities of the Commission. They are assisted by a staff of approximately 1,500 persons. Note that the term "Commission" refers both to the seven Commissioners as a unit and to the entire agency, including the staff.

INTRODUCTION

Establishing and maintaining quality broadcasting services in a community is the responsibility of broadcast station licensees and the Federal Communications Commission. It is also, however, a matter in which members of the community have a vital concern and in which they can and should play a prominent role.

Licensees of radio and television stations are required to make a diligent, positive, and continuing effort to discover and fulfill the problems, needs, and interests of the communities they serve. The Commission encourages a continuing dialog between stations and community members as a means of ascertaining the community's problems, needs, and interests and of devising ways to meet and fulfill them. Members of the community can help a station to provide better broadcast service and more responsive programing by making their needs, interests, and problems known to the station and by commenting, whether favorably or unfavorably, on the programing and practices of the station. Complaints concerning a station's operation should be communicated promptly to the station, and every effort should be made, by both the complainant and the licensee, to resolve any differences through discussion at the local level.

The Commission is responsible for seeing that stations do in fact meet their obligations to the community. It considers complaints by members, of the community against a station and before issuing or renewing a broadcast station license, must find that its action will serve the public interest, convenience, and necessity. However, to effectively invoke the Commission's processes, the citizen must not only concern himself with the quality of broadcasting but must know when, how, and to whom, to express his concern. On the one hand, the Commission is in large measure dependent on community members to bring up matters which warrant its attention. On the other, if resolute efforts are not first made to clear up problems at the local level, the Commission's processes become clogged by the sheer bulk of the matters brought before it.

If direct contact with a station does not produce satisfactory results, there are a number of formal and informal ways for members of the community to convey their grievances to the Commission and to participate in proceedings in which the performance of a station is judged and legitimate grievances are redressed. The purpose of this manual is to outline procedures available to the concerned citizen and to provide information and practical advice concerning their use. It is not a substitute for the rules of practice and procedure (47 CFR Part 1). We are hopeful, however, that it will help community members to participate effectively and in a manner which is helpful to the Commission.

PROCEEDINGS INVOLVING PARTICULAR APPLICANTS AND LICENSEES

INITIATING A PROCEEDING

Complaints generally. A complaint against a broadcast station can be filed with the Commission by any person at any time. You can go about it any way you wish; there are no particular procedural requirements, except as noted below. You should, however, bear the following facts in mind:

(a) During fiscal year 1973, the Commission received 84,525 complaints, comments, and inquiries concerning broadcast stations. Of this total, 61,322 were complaints.

(b) Almost all of these communications are initially considered and dealt with by approximately five Commission employees who are specially assigned this function. Additional personnel are assigned to a matter only if, on the initial examination, the complaint appears to raise novel or difficult legal questions or appears to warrant extensive inquiry, investigation, or formal proceedings. In light of this situation, there are a number of practical steps you can take which will be helpful to the Commission and will increase your effectiveness in making a complaint. These are set out below:

(1) Limit your complaint to matters on which the Commission can act. With

minor exceptions (the provision of "equal time" for candidates for public office, for example), we cannot direct that a particular program be put on or taken off the air. Nor are we arbiters of taste. Our concern, moreover, is with matters which affect the community generally (the public interest) rather than with the personal preferences or grievances of individuals. Another publication, "The FCC and Broadcasting," contains more detailed information (in areas in which numerous complaints are received) regarding what the Commission can and cannot do. Copies will be furnished by the Complaints and Compliance Division of the Commission's Broadcast Bureau upon request.

(2) Submit your complaint first to the station involved. The station may well recognize the merit of your complaint and take corrective action, or may explain the matter to your satisfaction. If you are not satisfied with the station's response, it will aid and expedite action on your complaint to the Commission to enclose a copy of your complaint to the station and all subsequent correspondence between you and the station. (Though this way of proceeding is generally far preferable to complaining initially to the Commission, this is not always the case. If, for example, the complainant has reason for not disclosing his identity to the station, he may complain directly to the Commission, requesting that his identity not be disclosed.)

(3) Submit your complaint promptly after the event to which it relates.

(4) Include at least the following information in your letter of complaint:

a. The full name and address of the complainant.

b. The call letters and location of the station.

c. The name of any program to which the complaint relates and the date and time of its broadcast.

d. A statement of what the station has done or failed to do which causes you to file a complaint. Be as specific as possible: Furnish names, dates, places, and other details.

e. A statement setting forth what you want the station and/or the Commission to do.

f. A copy of any previous correspondence between you and the station concerning the subject of the complaint.

(5) Try to appreciate that the person reviewing your complaint must make rapid judgments regarding the gravity of the matters related and the action to be taken. There are a number of simple things you can do to make his job easier and to aid your own cause: State the facts fully and at the beginning. Subject to fully stating the facts, be as brief as possible. If the facts are self-explanatory, avoid argument; let the facts speak for themselves. Avoid repetition or exaggeration. If you think a specific law or regulation has been violated, tell us what it is. If possible, use a typewriter, but if you do write by hand, take special pains to write legibly.

A complaint received by the Commission is dealt with as follows:

(1) If the complaint does not allege a substantial violation of statute or of Commission rule or policy, if inadequate information is submitted, or if the factual statement is not sufficiently specific, a letter (which is often a form letter) explaining these matters is directed to the complainant.

(2) If the complaint does allege specific facts sufficient to indicate a substantial violation, it is investigated, either by correspondence with the station (which may produce a satisfactory explanation or remedial action) or, in rare instances, by field inquiry. (Since the Commission's investigatory staff is small, the number of complaints which can be investigated by field inquiry is limited.) If further information from the complainant is needed, he is asked to furnish it. If the staff concludes that there has been a violation, it may recommend to the Commission that sanctions be imposed on the station; it may direct remedial action (such as equal opportunities for a candidate for public office); or, where extenuating circumstances are present (as where the violation follows from an honest mistake or misjudgment or where the station otherwise has a good record), it may note the violation but not recommend a sanction. Possible Commission actions range from the imposition of monetary forfeitures not exceeding $10,000 and short-term renewal of license to revocation of license or denial of an application for renewal

of license. The imposition of sanctions involves formal proceedings (which may include a hearing) and, in connection with such proceedings, the complainant may be asked to submit a sworn statement or to appear and give testimony at a hearing before an administrative law judge. In some circumstances, the complainant is entitled, and may choose, to participate as a party to the proceeding. A hearing is ordered in a renewal or revocation proceeding only if substantial questions have been raised concerning the licensee's qualifications.

Four types of complaint require compliance with specific procedures and submission of specific information. These complaints involve compliance with the requirement of equal time for political candidates, the fairness doctrine, the personal attack rule, and the rule governing political editorials. Generally, these matters should be taken up with the station before a complaint is filed with the Commission. However, where time is an important factor, you may find it advisable to complain simultaneously to the station and the Commission. In such circumstances, complaints are often submitted and answered by telegraph and, where the matter is most urgent, by telephone.

Political broadcasting. Section 315 of the Communications Act, 47 U.S.C. 315, provides that if any Commission licensee shall permit any person "who is a legally qualified candidate for any public office" to use a broadcast station, he shall afford to all other candidates for that office equal opportunities to use the station's facilities. Appearances by candidates on the following types of programs are exempt from the equal opportunities requirement:

1. Bona fide newscast;
2. Bona fide news interview;
3. Bona fide news documentary (if the appearance of the candidate is incidental to the presentation of the subject or subjects covered by the news documentary); or
4. On-the-spot coverage of bona fide news events (including but not limited to political conventions and activities incidental thereto).

However, where candidates appear on programs exempt from the equal opportunities requirement, broadcasters must nevertheless meet the obligation imposed upon them under the Communications Act (to operate in the public interest) and the fairness doctrine (to afford reasonable opportunity for the discussion of conflicting views on controversial issues of public importance). The equal opportunities and fairness doctrine requirements are applied to networks as well as to stations.

A request for equal opportunities must be made directly to the station or network and must be submitted within 1 week after the first broadcast giving rise to your right of equal opportunities. This is most important, as your right is lost by failure to make a timely request. To make it as clear as possible, we offer the following example:

A, B, and C are legally qualified candidates for the same public office. A makes an appearance on April 5 on a program not exempted by the statute. On April 12, B asks for an equal opportunity to appear on the station and does, in fact, appear on April 15. On April 16, C asks for an equal opportunity to appear. However, he is not entitled to do so, as he has failed to make his request within 1 week after A's appearance.

There is an exception to this requirement where the person requesting equal opportunities was not a candidate at the time of the first broadcast giving rise to the right of equal opportunities. See 47 CFR 73.120(e).

If you are a candidate or his designated agent and think that the candidate has been denied equal opportunities, you may complain to the Commission. A copy of this complaint should be sent to the station. Your letter of complaint should state (1) the name of the station or network involved; (2) the name of the candidate for the same office and the date of his appearance on the station's facilities; (3) whether the candidate who appeared was a legally qualified candidate for the office at the time of his appearance (this is determined by reference to the law of the State in which the election is being held); (4) whether the candidate seeking equal time is a legally qualified candidate for the same office; and (5) whether you or your candidate made a request for equal opportunities to the licensee within 1 week of the day on which the first broadcast giving rise to the right to equal opportunities occurred.

A political broadcasting primer ("Use of Broadcast Facilities by Candidates for Public Office"), containing a summary of rulings interpreting the equal opportunities requirement, has been published in the FEDERAL REGISTER and in the FCC Reports (35 F.R. 13048, 24 F.C.C. 2d 832) and is available from the Commission upon request, as is a question and answer pamphlet ("Use of Broadcast and Cablecast Facilities by Candidates for Public Office") (37 F.R. 5796, 34 F.C.C. 2d 510). See also 47 U.S.C. 315 and 47 CFR 73.120.

Fairness doctrine. Under the fairness doctrine, if there is a presentation of a point of view on a controversial issue of public importance over a station (or network), it is the duty of the station (or network), in its overall programming, to afford a reasonable opportunity for the presentation of contrasting views as to that issue. This duty applies to all station programming and not merely to editorials stating the station's position. The station may make offers of time to spokesmen for contrasting views or may present its own programming on the issue. It must present suitable contrasting views without charge if it is unable to secure payment from, or a sponsor for, the spokesman for such views. The broadcaster has considerable discretion as to the format of programs, the different shades of opinion to be presented, the spokesman for each point of view, and the time allowed. He is not required to provide equal time or equal opportunities; this requirement applies only to broadcasts by candidates for public office. The doctrine is based on the right of the public to be informed and not on the proposition that any particular person or group is entitled to be heard.

If you believe that a broadcaster (station or network) is not meeting its obligation to the public under the fairness doctrine, you should complain first to the broadcaster. If you believe that a point of view is not being presented and wish to act as spokesman for that point of view, you should first notify the broadcaster. Barring unusual circum-

stances, complaints should not be made to the Commission without affording the broadcaster an opportunity to rectify the situation, comply with your request, or explain its position.

If you do file a fairness doctrine complaint with the Commission, a copy should be sent to the station. The complaint should contain specific information concerning the following matters: (1) The name of the station or network involved; (2) the controversial issue of public importance on which a view was presented; (3) the date and time of its broadcast; (4) the basis for your claim that the issue is controversial and of public importance; (5) an accurate summary of the view or views broadcast; (6) the basis for your claim that the station or network has not broadcast contrasting views on the issue or issues in its overall programming; and (7) whether the station or network has afforded, or has expressed the intention to afford, a reasonable opportunity for the presentation of contrasting viewpoints on that issue. The requirement that you state the basis for your claim that the station or network has not broadcast contrasting views on the issue or issues in its overall programming does not mean that you must constantly monitor the station. As the Commission stated in its *Fairness Report:*

While the Complainant must state the basis for this claim that the station has not presented contrasting views, that claim might be based on an assertion that the complainant is a regular listener or viewer; that is, a person who consistently or as a matter of routine listens to the news, public affairs and other non-entertainment carried by the station involved. This does not require that the complainant listen to or view the station 24 hours a day, seven days a week . . . Complainants should specify the nature and should indicate the period of time during which they have been regular members of the station's audience. Further, a basis for your claim that the station has failed to present contrasting views might be provided by correspondence between you and the station or network involved. Thus if the station's or network's response to your correspondence states that no other programming has been presented on the subject and none is planned, such response would also provide a basis for your claim.

Following the Commission's broad-ranging inquiry into the efficacy of the fairness doctrine and related public interest policies, the Commission issued its *Fairness Report,* 39 FR 26372 (1974). Copies of this and an earlier fairness primer containing a summary of rulings interpreting the fairness doctrine. "Applicability of the Fairness Doctrine in the Handling of Controversial Issues of Public Importance," 29 FR 10416, 40 FCC 598 (1964) are available from the Commission upon request.

Personal attacks. The personal attack rule requires that when, during the presentation of views on a controversial issue of public importance, an attack is made upon the honesty, character, integrity, or like personal qualities of an identified person or group, the broadcaster must, within 1 week after the attack, transmit to the person or groups attacked (1) notification of the date, time and identification of the broadcast; (2) a script or tape (or an accurate summary if a script or tape is not available) of the attack; and (3) an offer of a reasonable opportunity to respond over the station's facilities free of charge. See 47 CFR 73.123(a). The personal attack rule does not apply to attacks made in the course of a bona fide newscast, a bona fide news interview, or on-the-spot coverage of a bona fide news event (including commentary or analysis by newsmen offered as part of such programs). Though the specific requirements of notice and an offer of an opportunity to respond do not apply to such programs, the other requirements of the fairness doctrine do apply. For other circumstances in which the personal attack rule does not apply, see 47 CFR 73.123(b).

If you believe that you or your group has been personally attacked during presentation of a controversial issue, and if you are not offered an opportunity to respond, you should complain first to the station or network involved. If you are not satisfied with the response, you may then complain to the Commission.

If you file a complaint with the Commission, a copy should be sent to the station. The complaint should contain specific information concerning the following matters: (1) The name of the station or network involved; (2) the words or statements broadcast; (3) the date and time the broadcast was made; (4) the basis for your view that the words broadcast constitute an attack upon the honesty, character, integrity, or like personal qualities of you or your group; (5) the basis for your view that the personal attack was broadcast during the presentation of views on a controversial issue of public importance; (6) the basis for your view that the matter discussed was a controversial issue of public importance, either nationally or in the station's local area, at the time of the broadcast; and (7) whether the station within 1 week of the alleged attack; (i) notified you or your group of the broadcast; (ii) transmitted a script, tape, or accurate summary of the broadcast if a script or tape was not available; and (iii) offered a reasonable opportunity to respond over the station's facilities.

Political editorials. When a broadcast station, in an editorial, endorses a legally qualified candidate for public office, it is required to transmit to other qualified candidates for the same office (1) notice as to the date and time of the editorial, (2) a script or tape of the editorial, and (3) an offer of a reasonable opportunity for the other candidates or their spokesmen to respond to the editorial over the licensee's facilities free of charge. Where a broadcast station, in an editorial, opposes a legally qualified candidate for public office, it is required to send the notice and offer to the candidate opposed. The notice and offer must be sent within 24 hours after the editoiral is broadcast. If the editorial is to be broadcast within 72 hours of election day, the station must transmit the notice and offer "sufficiently far in advance of the broadcast to enable the candidate or candidates to have a reasonable opportunity to prepare a response and to present it in timely fashion." See 47 CFR 73.123(c). See also, the fairness primer described above.

If you are a candidate or his authorized spokesman and believe that the station, in an editorial has opposed the candidate or supported his opponent and has not complied fully with these requirements, you should complain to the station or network involved. If, in response to your complaint, the station does not offer what you consider to be a reasonable opportunity to respond to the editorial, you may complain to the Commission. Send a copy of your complaint to the station.

RULE MAKING

A rule is similar to a law. It is a statement of policy to be applied generally in the future. A rule making proceeding is the process, required by law, through which the Commission seeks information and ideas from interested persons, concerning a particular rule or rule amendment, which will aid it in making a sound policy judgment. There are other ways, when a rule is not under consideration, in which the Commission seeks information needed to meet its regulatory responsibilities. It may issue a Notice of Inquiry, in which interested persons are asked to furnish information on a given matter and their views as to whether and how the Commission should deal with it. If needed information cannot be obtained in proceedings on a Notice of Inquiry, the Commission can order an investigatory hearing, in which witnesses and records can be subpenaed. If the information obtained indicates that rules should be adopted, the Commission then initiates a rule making proceeding.

PETITION FOR RULE MAKING

The principal rules relating to broadcast matters are set out in the rules and regulations of the Commission as Subpart D of Part 1, Part 73 and Part 74. Other provisions relating to broadcasting will be found in Parts 0 and 1. If you think that any of these rules should be changed or that new rules relating to broadcasting should be adopted by the Commission, you are entitled to file a petition for rule making. 5 U.S.C. 553(e); 47 CFR 1.401-1.407. No specific form is required for such a petition, but it should be captioned "Petition for Rule Making" to make it clear that you regard your proposal as more than a casual suggestion. An original and 14 copies of the petition and all other pleadings in rule making matters should be filed.

The petition "shall set forth the text or substance of the proposed rule . . . together with views, arguments and data deemed to support the action requested . . ." 47 CFR 1.401(c). This is important, for unless statements supporting or opposing your proposal are filed, you are afforded no further opportunity, prior to Commission action on the petition, to explain or justify your proposal.

When a petition for rule making is received, it is given a file number (such as RM-1000) and public notice of its filing is given. The public notice briefly describes the proposal and invites interested persons to file statements supporting or opposing it. Statements must be filed within 30 days after the notice is issued and must be served on the petitioner, who may reply to such a statement within 15 days after it is filed. The reply must be served on the person who filed the statement to which the reply is directed.

If a petition for rule making is repetitive or moot or for other reasons plainly does not warrant consideration by the Commission, it can be dismissed or denied by the Chief of the Broadcast Bureau. See 47 CFR 0.280(bb). In that event, petitioner may file an application for review of the Bureau Chief's action by the Commission. See 47 CFR 1.115. In most cases, however, the petition for rule making is acted on by the Commission. Action is ordinarily deferred pending passage of the time for filing statements and replies. Where the changes proposed obviously have (or lack) merit, however, action may be taken without waiting for the submission of statements or replies. In acting on a petition for rule making, the Commission will issue (1) an order amending the rules, as proposed or modified, or (2) a notice of rule making proposing amendment of the rules, as proposed or modified, or (3) an order denying the petition. In the event of adverse action by the Commission, you may petition for reconsideration (47 CFR 1.106).

RULE MAKING WITHOUT PRIOR NOTICE AND PUBLIC PROCEDURE

Rule making proceedings are conducted under section 4 of the Administrative Procedure Act, 5 U.S.C. 553. See also, 47 CFR 1.411-1.427, section 4 provides that an agency may make rules without prior notice and public procedure in any of the following circumstances:

(a) Where the subject matter involves a military or foreign affairs function of the United States.

(b) Where the subject matter relates to agency management or personnel or to public property, loans, grants, benefits, or contracts.

(c) Where the rules made are interpretative rules, general statements of policy, or rules of agency organization, procedure or practice.

(d) Where the agency for good cause finds (and incorporates the finding and a brief statement of reasons therefore in the rules issued) that notice and public procedure are impracticable, unnecessary, or contrary, to the public interest.

The rules of organization practice and procedure (47 CFR Parts 0 and 1) are rather frequently amended, often without prior notice and public procedure. However, prior public comment is requested if the matters involved are particularly significant or there is doubt or controversy concerning the wisdom, precise effect, or details of the rule. Where notice is omitted pursuant to (d) above, it is in circumstances where the effect of the rule could be undermined by actions taken during the period allowed for comment, where the rule merely repeats the provisions of a statute, where the provisions of the rule are beneficial to all and there is no reason to expect unfavorable public comment, or in other similar circumstances constituting good cause under the statute. The other exceptions to the requirement of prior notice are of lesser importance.

If you are dissatisfied with a rule made by the Commission without prior notice, you may file a petition for reconsideration. You may also request that the effect of the rule be stayed pending action on your petition. All orders changing the Commission's rules are published in the FEDERAL REGISTER, and the 30-day period for filing the petition for reconsideration runs from the date of publication.

RULE MAKING WITH PRIOR NOTICE AND PUBLIC PROCEDURE

Except in the circumstances listed above, the Commission is required to give prior notice and to afford an opportunity for public comment before making or changing a rule. If you have something to say concerning the proposed rule, you are entitled to file comments. Notice is given by issuance of a notice of proposed rule making, and by publishing that notice in the FEDERAL REGISTER. The text of the proposed rule is usually set out in the notice. On occasion, however, the notice will instead indicate the subject involved and the result intended, leaving the precise method for obtaining that result to a later stage of the proceeding following consideration of public comment. Whether or not the text is set out, the notice contains an explanation of the proposed rule and a statement both as to the Commission's reasons for proposing the rule and its authority to adopt it. The notice also lists the dates by which comments and reply comments should be submitted and states whether there are limitations on Commission consideration of nonrecord communications concerning the proceeding. Requests for extension of the time allowed for filing comments and reply comments may be filed.

Rule making proceedings are relatively informal. When a notice of proposed rule making is issued, the proceeding is given a docket number (such as Docket No. 15000). Papers relating to the proceeding are placed in a docket file bearing this number. This file is available for inspection in the Commission's Public Reference Room in Washington, D.C. Because comments and reply comments are sometimes filed by hundreds of persons, the Commission does not require that copies be served on others. To find out what others have said in their comments, you may inspect the docket file or arrange with a private firm (for a fee) to furnish copies of comments filed in the proceeding. See 47 CFR 0.465. Often, those who have filed comments will furnish copies as a courtesy upon request. All papers placed in the docket file are considered by the Commission before taking final action in the proceeding. To assure that your views are placed in the docket file and considered by the Commission, all comments, pleadings, and correspondence relating to the proceeding should (in the caption or otherwise) show the docket number.

The rules require that an original and 14 copies of comments be filed, that they be typed, doubled-spaced, timely filed, and so forth. See, e.g., 47 CFR 1.419. As a practical matter, it is important for you to meet these requirements. The 14 copies are needed for distribution to Commissioners and members of the staff involved in making a decision. If you submit only an original, it will be placed in or associated with the docket file and considered by the staff member assigned to write a decision but probably will not be seen by other Commission officials. Handwritten communications are also placed in the docket file and so considered. You should appreciate, however, that you are more likely to get your point of view across to the persons making the decision if your presentation is typewritten. In making a rule, the Commission is interested in getting as much information and the best thinking possible from the public before making a decision and does not reject comments on narrow technical grounds. However, failure to comply with the filing requirements adversely affects your right to have the comments considered and to complain if they do not receive what you consider to be full consideration.

The comments should explain who you are and what your interest is. They should recite the facts and authority which support your position. They should not ignore facts and authorities which tend to support a different position, but should deal with them and demonstrate that the public interest requires that the matter be resolved as you propose. They should be carefully worded and well organized and free of exaggeration or vituperative comment. They should be explicit. If the details of the proposed rule or one of several provisions only are objectionable, this should be made clear. Counterproposals may be submitted. If the rule would be acceptable only with certain safeguards, these should be spelled out, with the reasons why they are needed.

In rule making proceedings, the Commission's responsibility is to make a policy judgment and, in making that judgment, to obtain and consider comments filed in the proceeding. It may tap other sources of information. Unless otherwise expressly stated in the notice, staff members working on the proceeding are generally prepared to meet with and discuss the proposed rule with anyone who is sufficiently interested. They may initiate correspondence or organize meetings to further develop pertinent information and ideas. They will utilize information available in the Commission's files and draw upon the knowledge and experience of other Commission personnel or of other Government agencies. Generally, the Commission hears oral argument only in rule making proceedings involving policy decisions of the greatest importance. However, you may request the Commission to hear argument in any proceeding, and that request will be considered and ruled upon. When argument is heard, interested persons appear before the Commissioners, orally present their views, and are questioned by the Commissioners. Other devices, such as panel discussions, have, on occasion, been used to further develop the information and ideas presented. An evidentiary hearing is not usual in rule making proceedings. Nevertheless, if you think the circumstances require an evidentiary hearing, you are entitled to ask that one be held.

After comments and reply comments and the record of oral argument (if any) have been reviewed, a policy judgment is made and a document announcing and explaining it is issued. There are a number of possibilities. The proposed rules may be adopted, with or without changes. They may be adopted in part and, in that event, further comment may be requested on portions of the proceeding which remain. The Commission may decide that no rules should be adopted or that inadequate information has been obtained and, thus, either terminate the proceeding or issue a further notice of proposed rule making requesting additional comment on particular matters. If final action as to all or any part of the proceeding is taken, the final action taken is subject to reconsideration (47 U.S.C. 405).

PETITION FOR WAIVER OF A RULE

Except as they implement mandatory statutory provisions, all of the Commission's rules are subject to waiver. 47

CFR 1.3. If there is something the rules prohibit which you wish to do, or if there is something the rules require which you do not wish to do, you may petition for waiver of the rules in question. The petition must contain a showing sufficient to convince the Commission that waiver is justified on public interest grounds (that is, the public interest would be served by not applying the rule in a particular situation) or, in some instances, on grounds of hardship or undue burden.

PUBLIC INSPECTION OF STATION DOCUMENTS

Local public inspection file. All radio and television stations maintain a local public inspection file which contains materials specified in 47 CFR 1.526. The file, which is available for public inspection at any time during regular business hours, is usually maintained at the main studio of the station, but the rules permit it to be located at any other publicly accessible place, such as a public registry for documents or an attorney's office. A prior appointment to examine the file is not required, but may prove of mutual benefit to the station and the inspecting party.

The local public inspection files of all radio and television stations include recent renewal applications (FCC-Form 303), ownership reports (FCC-Form 323), various reports regarding broadcasts by candidates for public office, annual employment reports (FCC-Form 395), letters received from members of the public concerning operation of the station (see 47 CFR 73.1202(f)), and a copy of this Manual. In addition, the local public inspection files of commercial television stations also include annual programming reports (FCC-Form 303-A) and annual listings of what the licensee believes to have been some of the significant problems and needs of the area served by the station during the preceding twelve months. All television licensees are required to make the materials in their local public inspection files available for machine reproduction, providing the requesting party pays any reasonable costs incurred in producing machine copies.

Public inspection of television station program logs. In response to formal requests from various citizen groups, the Commission's rules were amended in March 1974 to require television stations to make their program logs available for public inspection under certain circumstances. The contents of these logs are specified. See 47 CFR 73.112. It should be emphasized that because the logs are intended primarily to serve Commission needs, the information they contain is limited and is essentially statistical in nature. Although, for example, the logs include the title and type (that is, the program category such as news, entertainment, etc.) of the various programs carried by the station, and the times these programs were broadcast, the logging rules do not require descriptions of the actual content of individual programs nor a listing of program participants or issues discussed. Despite their limitations, however, the logs do contain relevant information concerning station programming, including commercial practices.

Television station program logs are available upon request of public inspection and reproduction at a location convenient and accessible for the residents of the community to which the station is licensed. All such requests for inspection are subject to the following procedural requirements set forth in 47 CFR 73.674:

(1) Parties wishing to inspect the logs shall make a prior appointment with the licensee and, at that time, identify themselves by name and address; identify the organization they represent, if any; and state the general purpose of the examination.

(2) Inspection of the logs shall take place at the station or at such other convenient and accessible location as may be specified by the licensee. The licensee, at its option, may make an exact copy available in lieu of the original program logs.

(3) Machine copies of the logs shall be made available upon request, provided the party making the request shall pay the reasonable costs of machine reproduction.

(4) An inspecting party shall have a reasonable time to examine the program logs. If examination is requested beyond a reasonable time, the licensee may condition such further inspection upon the inspecting party's willingness either to assume the expense of machine duplication of the logs or to reimburse the licensee for any reasonable expense incurred if supervision of continued examination of the original logs is deemed necessary.

(5) No log need be made available for public inspection until 45 days have elapsed from the day covered by the log in question.

47 CFR 73.674 provides that the licensee may refuse to permit public inspection of the program logs where good cause exists. When it included this provision in its 1974 amendments to 47 CFR 73.674, the Commission indicated that lacking experience with the operation of public inspection of program logs, it was in no position to describe all situations in which there would be good cause for refusing to permit access. Two illustrations which it did offer, however, were (1) a request from a financial competitor of the station or of the station's advertisers which was based solely on competitive considerations and (2) a situation in which the request represented an attempt at harassment. Harassment would exist if the primary goal of requesting examination of the logs was the disruption of station operation or the creation of an annoyance. If, for example, an inspecting party or parties situated themselves in the inspection location hour after hour, day after day, refusing to indicate which, if any, logs it wished to have duplicated, and refusing to engage in dialogue with the licensee regarding further inspection, it would not be inappropriate to characterize that inspection as an attempt at harassment.

While the probability of misuse and abuse of requests to inspect program logs and the danger of harassment was not sufficient to cause the Commission to refrain from making the logs generally available, the provision regarding refusal of access for good cause was inserted in amended 47 CFR 73.674 as a recognition of legitimate concerns of broadcasters. In the rare case where an unresolved dispute arises between members of the public and a station regarding whether good cause exists for not making the logs available, the dispute can, of course, be brought to the Commission for resolution.

Index